Beyond Communities of Practice

The concept of "communities of practice" has become an influential one in education, management and social sciences in recent years. This book consists of a series of studies by linguists and educational researchers, examining and developing aspects of the concept which have remained relatively unexplored. Framings provided by theories of language-in-use, literacy practices and discourse extend the concept, bringing to light issues around conflict, power and the significance of the broader social context which have been overlooked. Chapters assess the relationship between communities of practice and other theories, including literacy studies, critical language studies, the ethnography of communication, sociocultural activity theory and sociological theories of risk. Domains of empirical research reported include schools, police stations, adult basic education, higher education and multilingual settings. The book highlights the need to incorporate thinking around language-in-use, power and conflict and social context into communities of practice.

David Barton is Professor of Language and Literacy in the Department of Linguistics at Lancaster University. He is Director of the Lancaster Literacy Research Centre. His main work has been concerned with carrying out detailed studies of literacy practices in different domains of life and with rethinking the nature of literacy in contemporary society.

Karin Tusting is a Research Associate at the Literacy Research Centre at Lancaster University. She has recently worked on the Adult Learners' Lives project, an ethnographic study of the relationship between learning and other aspects of people's lives, working with adult literacy, numeracy and ESOL learners.

D1533078

LEARNING IN DOING:
Social, Cognitive and Computational Perspectives

Series Editor *Emeritus*
John Seely Brown, Xerox Palo Alto Research Center

General Editors
Roy Pea, Professor of Education and the Learning Sciences and Director, Stanford Center for Innovations in Learning, Stanford University
Christian Heath, The Management Centre, King's College, London
Lucy A. Suchman, Centre for Science Studies and Department of Sociology, Lancaster University

Plans and Situated Actions: The Problem of Human–Machine Communication
Lucy A. Suchman

The Construction Zone: Working for Cognitive Change in Schools
Denis Newman, Peg Griffin and Michael Cole

Situated Learning: Legitimate Peripheral Participation
Jean Lave and Etienne Wenger

Street Mathematics and School Mathematics
Terezinha Nunes, David William Carraher and Analucia Dias Schliemann

Understanding Practice: Perspectives on Activity and Context
Seth Chaiklin and Jean Lave

Distributed Cognitions: Psychological and Educational Considerations
Gavriel Salomon

The Computer as Medium
Peter Bogh Andersen, Berit Holmqvist and Jens F. Jensen

Sociocultural Studies of Mind
James V. Wertsch, Pablo Del Rio and Amelia Alvarez

Sociocultural Psychology: Theory and Practice of Doing and Knowing
Laura M. W. Martin, Katherine Nelson and Ethel Tobach

Mind and Social Practice: Selected Writings of Sylvia Scribner
Ethel Tobach, Rachel Joffee Falmagne, Mary Brown Parlee, Laura M. W. Martin and Aggie Scribner Kapelman

(Series list continued after Index)

Beyond Communities of Practice

Language, Power and Social Context

Edited by

DAVID BARTON
Lancaster University

KARIN TUSTING
Lancaster University

CAMBRIDGE
UNIVERSITY PRESS

CAMBRIDGE UNIVERSITY PRESS
Cambridge, New York, Melbourne, Madrid, Cape Town, Singapore, São Paulo

Cambridge University Press
40 West 20th Street, New York, NY 10011-4211, USA

www.cambridge.org
Information on this title: www.cambridge.org/9780521836432

First published 2005

Printed in the United States of America

A catalog record for this publication is available from the British Library.

Library of Congress Cataloging in Publication Data

Beyond communities of practice / edited by David Barton, Karin Tusting.
    p.   cm. – (Learning in doing)
Includes bibliographical references and index.
ISBN 0-521-83643-3 (hardcover) – ISBN 0-521-54492-0 (pbk.)
1. Organizational learning.   2. Language and education.   3. Social learning.
I. Barton, David, 1949–   II. Tusting, Karin, 1973–   III. Title.   IV. Series.
HD58.82.B49   2006
302 – dc22   2004030653

ISBN-13   978-0-521-83643-2 hardback
ISBN-10   0-521-83643-3 hardback

ISBN-13   978-0-521-54492-4 paperback
ISBN-10   0-521-54492-0 paperback

Contents

List of Contributors

David Barton is Professor of Language and Literacy in the Department of Linguistics at Lancaster University and Director of the Lancaster Literacy Research Centre.

Angela Creese is Lecturer in Education at the School of Education, University of Birmingham.

James Paul Gee is the Tashia Morgridge Professor of Reading at the University of Wisconsin at Madison.

Mary Hamilton is Professor of Adult Learning and Literacy in the Department of Educational Research at Lancaster University.

Steven Robert Harris is a Researcher at the University of Glamorgan Centre for Astronomy and Science Education, School of Applied Sciences, and the Hypermedia Research Unit, School of Computing.

Maria Clara Keating is Lecturer in the Department of Linguistics at Coimbra University, Portugal.

Mary R. Lea is Lecturer in Teaching and Learning in the Institute of Educational Technology, Open University.

Deirdre Martin is Lecturer in the School of Education, University of Birmingham.

Greg Myers is Senior Lecturer in the Department of Linguistics, Lancaster University.

Frances Rock is Lecturer in English Language and Linguistics at the University of Surrey Roehampton.

Nicola Shelswell is Head of School for Adult Basic Education and English for Speakers of Other Languages at Coleg Morgannwg, South Wales.

Karin Tusting is a Research Associate at the Literacy Research Centre, Lancaster University.

Series Foreword

This series for Cambridge University Press is becoming widely known as an international forum for studies of situated learning and cognition.

Innovative contributions are being made by anthropology; by cognitive, developmental and cultural psychology; by computer science; by education and by social theory. These contributions are providing the basis for new ways of understanding the social, historical and contextual nature of learning, thinking and practice that emerges from human activity. The empirical settings of these research enquiries range from the classroom to the workplace, to the high-technology office and to learning in the streets and in other communities of practice. The situated nature of learning and remembering through activity is a central fact. It may appear obvious that human minds develop in social situations and extend their sphere of activity and communicative competencies. But cognitive theories of knowledge representation and learning alone have not provided sufficient insight into these relationships. This series was born of the conviction that new and exciting interdisciplinary syntheses are under way as scholars and practitioners from diverse fields seek to develop theory and empirical investigations adequate for characterising the complex relations of social and mental life, and for understanding successful learning wherever it occurs. The series invites contributions that advance our understanding of these seminal issues.

Roy Pea
Christian Heath
Lucy Suchman

Introduction

David Barton and Karin Tusting

The concept of *communities of practice,* developed by Jean Lave and Etienne Wenger (Lave and Wenger 1991, Wenger 1998) as a central idea in situated approaches to learning has been taken up across social, educational and management sciences. It has been used, applied, criticised, adapted and developed by a wide range of researchers in these fields. It is currently one of the most articulated and developed concepts within broad social theories of learning.

This book consists of ten specially commissioned chapters, brought together as a coherent volume. Each chapter examines a specific aspect of the concept of *community of practice,* examining it in depth and developing it in some way. The title *Beyond Communities of Practice* is to be taken in two senses. Firstly, the book takes Wenger's 1998 *Communities of Practice* book as its main reference point, and it examines learning situations which are broader than the very specific notion described in the 1998 book. Secondly, this book goes beyond the notion of communities of practice in developing the concept in several ways. The key contributions are framings provided by theories of language, literacy, discourse and power and understandings of the broader social context in which communities of practice are located.

THE CONCEPT OF COMMUNITY OF PRACTICE

The starting point for the idea of a community of practice is that people typically come together in groupings to carry out activities in everyday life, in the workplace and in education. Such groupings can be seen as distinct from the formal structures of these domains. These groups are characterised by three aspects. Firstly, members interact with each other in many ways, which Wenger refers to as *mutual engagement*. Secondly, they will have a common endeavour, which is referred to as *joint enterprise*. Thirdly, they develop a *shared repertoire* of common resources of language, styles and routines by means of which they express their identities as members of the group. *Situated learning* then means engagement in a community of practice, and *participation* in communities of practice becomes the fundamental process of learning. These ideas are developed in Wenger's book by means of a theory of interlinked concepts concerned with practice, meaning and identity. We return to these concepts as the various chapters of this book amplify different parts of this theory.

The concept of community of practice has been taken up and used by people working in many different areas. It has had an immediate appeal and perceived usefulness across a range of situations. Like any useful concept, people have used it in a variety of ways. Some have kept close to the original formulation, and some have developed it. Some have found it to be exactly what they want, and others have criticised it and identified its limitations, proposing alternatives. Some have taken the whole theoretical apparatus of situated learning. Others have taken just the phrase and adapted it to their own uses, combining it with concepts from other fields and incorporating it into other theories. For some, it has become a central concept which a whole theory revolves around; for others, it has been more peripheral and has been incorporated into other theories. This is probably the fate of any useful concept.

Examination of current journal publications and simple web searches shows the range of fields where notions of communities of practice are drawn upon. Whilst we will not provide an overall review here, individual chapters draw upon this literature. The concept has been taken up particularly in management, in education and in understanding virtual worlds. It has been most developed practically in business management but has also proved useful to the radical educator and to the political activist. The range of interests in the concept is broad – from religious missionaries using it to draw up the management frameworks for overseas evangelising (Goh, Thaxter and Simpson 2003) to social scientists using it to understand contemporary witches (Merriam, Courtenay and Baumgartner 2003).

There are many reasons why the concept has been taken up so widely. It appears to resolve some pervasive concerns of social sciences about learning. It presents a theory of learning which acknowledges networks and groups which are informal and not the same as formal structures. It allows for groups which are distributed in some way and not in face-to-face contact. The overall apparatus of situated learning is a significant rethink of learning theory of value to anyone wanting to take learning beyond the individual. It is attractive as a middle-level theory between structure and agency which is applicable to and close to actual life and which resonates with detailed ethnographic accounts of how learning happens. It has proved useful as a theory and has been of value in practice.

Part of its appeal is that a seemingly natural formation which enhances learning can be consciously developed, which is important for those implementing change. This can be seen within management sciences, where the concepts fit in easily with work in management learning, with ideas of there being a New Work Order characterised by a shift from traditional hierarchical structures to people working in small, creative and relatively autonomous teams (Gee, Hull and Lankshear 1996). This implicit linkage between the workplace and education has been criticised by Gee (2000) analysing how it draws schools and the new workplace together into a common endeavour.

In education, it takes learning out of the classroom and addresses the variety of groups and locations where learning takes place, including adults learning, learning in the workplace and learning in everyday life. It helps identify commonalities across these settings and contributes to understanding differences between formal and informal education.

In understanding new technologies, it provides ways of talking about learning in groups formed at a distance and the many varieties of virtual groups. Understanding the strengths and limitations of this concept and its similarities to and distinctiveness from other groupings, such as speech communities (as in Holmes and

Meyerhoff 1999; Eckert 2000) and, more crucially, discourse communities (Swales 1998, Prior 2003), is important here and is pursued in some of the chapters of this book.

DEVELOPMENT OF THE CONCEPT

A brief historical background shows how the concept has developed. Contemporary work on communities of practice has its roots in Scribner and Cole's original work, where they found a cognitive framework inadequate in accounting for their data on Vai literacy and, drawing on anthropology, they begin to sketch out 'a practice account' (1981, pp. 234–238). This work has developed over the past two decades, particularly in the research associated with Jean Lave and Etienne Wenger. In all of this, one can trace a progression, with a psychological model with the social as a context developing into a model which is essentially social. This development can be clearly seen in books which have been published in this period: Rogoff and Lave (1984); Lave (1988); Lave and Wenger (1991); Chaiklin and Lave (1996); Wenger (1998); and Wenger, McDermott and Snyder (2002).

Rogoff and Lave's 1984 edited book – *Everyday Cognition: Its Development in Social Context* – like Scribner and Cole's work, was a psychological account rooted in the Vygotskian tradition. Although the set of papers in Rogoff and Lave is interdisciplinary, the overall framing is essentially cognitive. The research covers a range of contexts, mixing the educational with the everyday (including grocery shopping, workplaces and skiing) and emphasising the importance of context in thinking: "thinking is a practical activity which is adjusted to meet the demands of the situation" (1984, p. 7). Lave's 1988 book, *Cognition in Practice: Mind, Mathematics and Culture in Everyday Life,* develops ideas of cognition and practice; and here cognition is viewed as being distributed across people. Practice has become more central as a concept, and there is a definite shift from a cognitive psychological framing to one which is more in tune with social anthropology. The co-authored work by Lave and Wenger in 1991, *Situated Learning: Legitimate Peripheral Participation,* explicitly talks of communities of practice: concepts of learning are shifted from apprenticeship, through notions of situated learning to communities of practice. In particular, the notion of communities of practice provides a set of concepts which view learning as a form of participation in activities. A later collection by Chaiklin and Lave in 1996, *Understanding Practice: Perspectives on Activity and Context,* develops notions of practice by focussing on issues of context and, again, provides rich portraits of everyday practices, including navigation, psychotherapy, artificial intelligence and being a blacksmith. These books provide some historical roots for Wenger's 1998 book, *Communities of Practice: Learning, Meaning and Identity,* an elaboration of these earlier ideas, which moves away from Vygotskian roots and draws on a broader background, including anthropology and aspects of social theory. The book identifies communities of practice as the central concept in a theory of learning. Wenger's 1998 book is the main focus for our current book, but reference will also be made to Lave and Wenger (1991) and to Wenger, McDermott and Snyder (2002), a later work which applies communities of practice to business management. This book takes for granted the neo-liberal narrative of the way that the world is developing, addressing organisations directly and offering advice on the fostering of communities of practice in ways which improve economic competitiveness.

Meanwhile Lave's work has developed some of the issues raised in Chaiklin and Lave (1996), notably in Holland and Lave (2001), which focuses more on subjective experience and identity in relation to participation in practice. They engage with issues of individual and collective identity and struggles for social change, drawing on the work of Bakhtin and Bourdieu as well as Vygotsky. The work associated with Rogoff since the 1984 co-edited book remains more psychological and provides a complementary strand of development. Rogoff (1990) examines the process of guided participation, particularly between children and adults. Rogoff, Turkanis and Bartlett (2001) examine how such learning worked in a particular school and pursue the idea of this particular community as a learning community. Rogoff (2003) develops this into a more general theory of human development where guided participation in communities is central.

This overview provides important background for some of the chapters of this book. Several other parallel fields – such as the developments in activity theory, sociolinguistic work on context and the contribution of the journal *Mind, Culture and Activity* – would also need to be included in a full account of these developments.

Our own interest as linguists is that framings provided by theories of language, literacy, discourse and power are central to understandings of the dynamics of communities of practice, but they are not brought out in Wenger's formulations. We set out to be critical of the concept of *communities of practice* as described by Wenger. On initial close reading of the book, we were frustrated that we could not pin down the components of the theory, and we found concepts slippery and elusive. More broadly, we were concerned that the critical edge of earlier work had been lost, that the contribution of Jean Lave had been eclipsed and that the ideas were being taken over by the certainty and oversimplifications of management training. We aimed to deconstruct the concept in the book in a straightforward academic way and to propose an alternative vision. There were various ideas we wanted to develop, coming from social linguistics, discourse studies, literacy theory and social theory more generally.

In doing this, we remain respectful of the book. It has a richness of vision and a clarity of expression. There are wonderful turns of phrase and incisive observations throughout. It ranges over theories of learning and theories of meaning and contributes to social theory. It is at ease in the space between the social and the psychological. It does understand its limitations and does point to the areas which need development. Many of the ideas we want to develop are to be found already sketched out in subsections and footnotes of the book. Space remains for us to explore, critique and develop the concepts, and we do this, mindful of the strengths of the work.

OUTLINE OF THE BOOK

The ten chapters of this book address a variety of areas which tend to be overlooked within the theory of communities of practice as it is often currently taken up, including theories of language, literacy and discourse; issues around power, resistance and inequality; micro-interactional and sociolinguistic takes on negotiation of meaning, tension and conflict; multilingual and other hybrid situations and theories of risk and stigma. Some of the chapters draw on empirical research in a variety of settings, and others explore the ideas on a theoretical level.

In the first chapter, David Barton and Mary Hamilton develop the notion of reification from the perspective of literacy studies. They demonstrate the centrality of literacy to Wenger's data, drawing out from the descriptive vignettes in Wenger (1998) those elements which are relevant to key concepts in literacy studies. This reveals the textually mediated nature of the social worlds described and shows the potential contribution of literacy studies to developing communities of practice theory. They go on to engage with a range of social theory which examines the role of stable but portable entities which cross contexts in social life, suggesting that the work of thinkers such as Ron Scollon, Bruno Latour, Dorothy Holland and Dorothy Smith can fruitfully be drawn on to develop both literacy studies and communities of practice theory and that a focus on reification is one key way of linking macro-level and mid-level social theory.

Karin Tusting develops a related point in the second chapter, drawing out the implicit significance of language within communities of practice theory, particularly in relation to the concept of negotiation of meaning. She suggests that any theory which places participation and reification at its heart needs to conceptualise how language is part of these processes, since it is one of the key means by which we communicate. By re-examining some of the examples used in Wenger (1998), she demonstrates the centrality of language in the practices described. She argues that research in communities of practice needs a theoretical model of language, and one which enables the researcher to analyse language as part of social practice. She outlines a model from critical social linguistics which offers this capability. This is a theory which draws out the links between language and other elements of the social world, enabling us to look at the way power relationships are played out and maintained through language use in communities of practice.

Angela Creese's chapter continues the focus on language. She draws on data from an ethnographic study of a high school, comparing the insights that can be gained from looking at the school as a "community of practice" to those which come from seeing it as a "speech community", and drawing attention to the lack of a theory of language-in-use in the theory of communities of practice. Creese shows how the ethnography of communication, with its focus on the interpersonal function of language as well as its referential one, is more powerful in enabling the researcher to describe the complexity of positions taken up around social events. She examines texts produced as part of a protest organised by some students in a multilingual school setting, describing a struggle over the legitimacy of the girls' protests, which centres on whether they are positioned within or outside the boundaries of the school community, defined in terms of an "equal opportunities discourse" which the protesting girls are perceived not to be using. Seeing the school as a "speech community" enabled her to examine which discourses were privileged and which silenced in the school, contributing to an understanding of how power relations and conflict were created and sustained – an understanding which would be difficult to reach using communities of practice theory alone.

Frances Rock presents more sociolinguistic evidence, from a study of the statement and explanation of the right to silence for people under police arrest in the UK, to show further ways in which a focus on language can enrich the communities of practice approach. She demonstrates how membership of communities of practice is accomplished and ratified through talk, and how looking at language processes in this detailed way reveals the diversity and multiple patterns of officers' community memberships. She draws on interviews with officers and recordings of actual practice, examining the way processes of negotiating joint enterprise and mutual engagement are played out through language and describing the role of language in learning the community's shared repertoire. She analyses one detailed example to show the different ways these resources are used and transformed in practice. She then examines what this sociolinguistic data can bring to the concept of the 'community of practice', showing the influence of broader police-level initiatives on local communities, and the multiplicity of communities which exist within the police as a whole and to which any given officer may belong. This bringing to light of diversity, in both Creese's and Rock's accounts, shows how a focus on language use can challenge assumptions about homogeneity which remain implicit in much communities of practice work – a thread which is continued in the next chapter.

The first four chapters all draw out in different ways the value of developing a model of language use within communities of practice theory. In the fifth chapter, Maria Clara Keating develops this focus on language and discourse, extending it to include situated activity theory. A focus on activity complements the focus on practice, the 'person in the doing' in Keating's phrase recalling Holland and Lave's work on 'history in person', while showing how communities of practice are situated in broader social and discursive orders, and how the negotiations involved in the process of participation are discursive, semiotic and language-based. Keating draws on her own ethnographic research with Portuguese migrant women in London, which looked at their use of language and literacy practices in processes of creating and renegotiating identity. Focussing on discourse within this hybrid migrant situation is very different from looking at the more static communities described in Wenger (1998), since this hybridity brings to light discursive processes of conflict, instability and power negotiations which are easily overlooked in Wenger's model. The linguistic analysis of a research interview with one of the women she worked with shows how discursive activities are loci of tensions and contradictions. She demonstrates how the woman being interviewed drew on resources available to her from multiple communities of practice in her ongoing textual negotiation of self and shows through detailed analysis the discursive dynamics of participation and reification within this event, and how the woman repeats, recognises, reflects upon and recombines reifications in participation.

Deirdre Martin's chapter examines the communities in which a bilingual co-worker in a speech and language therapy department participates as she learns the practices of her job. In this setting, speech and language therapists are inducting the co-worker, through the use of English alone, to work in both Panjabi and English with clients. Martin suggests that sociocultural activity theory offers a theory of learning that accounts better for this innovative social *and* individual process, in which cognitions and skills are distributed across participants, and in which resources come both from the technical knowledge of speech and language therapy and from the tacit knowledge of the bilingual co-worker. In this situation, practices are generated through collaboration – "innovative expanded learning" – rather than being acquired by a newcomer moving into an existing community with established practices. While Lave and Wenger's model accounts well for the process by means of which monolingual assistants are inducted into the community, it accounts less well for the learning of bilingual co-workers, who need to draw on resources from a variety of people and communities, and also create new resources themselves, in developing their own innovative practices. As with other contributors to this volume, Martin shows that drawing on activity theory also allows the researcher to focus on the impact of macro-level social elements on learning and on the importance of language as a mediational tool.

Steven Harris and Nicola Shelswell describe the impact of introducing a communities of practice approach to teaching and learning in an adult basic education centre. They argue that Wenger's conception of learning can usefully be developed by drawing on ideas from cultural historical psychology, activity theory (cf. Keating, this volume, and Martin, this volume) and critical psychology – approaches which relate individuals and communities of practice to wider organisational and societal contexts. While their experience of implementing a design for learning drawing on the principles of communities of practice theory had many positive outcomes, issues also emerged around power, conflict, inclusion and exclusion, which are overlooked in Wenger's (1998) relatively benign model. They introduce concepts of *illegitimate peripheral participation* and *legitimation conflicts*, in which the legitimacy of a participant is explicitly brought into question by other members of the community (resonating with the conflicts over legitimacy and community membership described in Creese's chapter; see above). Sometimes this renders a participant increasingly marginal to its practice or even causes his/her complete withdrawal; at other times, it leads to more positive outcomes for the people involved. Conflicts also emerged between the development of communities of practice in the learning setting and the imperative to keep learning provision open to new participants, and between establishing communities of learners and individual progression beyond these communities – showing how becoming a central participant in a community of practice in the learning situation can bring its own problems.

Mary R. Lea's chapter continues to examine issues around introducing communities of practice as a model, this time in a different educational setting. She examines the way the concept has been taken up within Higher Education, in the context of shifts towards a broader concept of the field involving distributed and flexible (particularly on-line) learning. She argues for the need to return to using the concept as it was developed in Lave and Wenger's (1991) *Situated Learning*: that is, as a heuristic, a way of understanding learning in practice, rather than (in the way it has often been taken up more recently) as a top-down educational model, which paints a relatively uncritical picture of the academic community of practice. Lea draws on the field of academic literacies research to demonstrate the conflicts and contradictions within many academic communities of practice, which become evident through the study of language and literacy practices.

Greg Myers brings another set of questions to the concept: those which pertain to the production of risk, something which is not explored by Wenger's model in any detail. He examines one particular incident, the falsification of measurements at a nuclear plant in the UK in 1999. He shows what the communities of practice framework can offer in terms of developing an understanding of these events. Looking at the workplace in this way sensitises the researcher to the complexities of how events are produced through practice, as opposed to many of the official responses, which focussed only on whether or not correct procedures were followed. But Myers also demonstrates what the framework lacks, in terms of dealing with ambiguities of language and meaning, identities and localities in the production of risks. Concepts such as 'legitimate peripheral participation' are complicated by examining these events. For instance, what was 'legitimate' participation in the eyes of workers involved in the measurement of pellets was 'illegitimate' in the eyes of management, recalling the issues of legitimation conflict discussed in earlier chapters.

In the final chapter, James Gee moves beyond the theory of communities of practice by offering a new analytic construct, which he suggests might be a more fruitful alternative model. He defines a new term, the 'semiotic social space', referring to a space in which people interact with each other, getting and giving meaning to signs within it. While this focus on meaning is reminiscent of Wenger's 'negotiation of meaning', the focus on a 'space' rather than a 'community' means we avoid the difficulty inherent in communities of practice theory of talking about a *group of people*, rather than a space for activity, which immediately raises difficult questions about participation, membership and boundaries. Gee's principal research concern is education, and he uses the example of a science classroom to show what questions can be asked by exploring it as a semiotic social space, rather than a community of practice. Using the example of the real-time strategy game *Age of Mythology* to illustrate what he means by such a space, he defines one particular type, a relatively non-hierarchical interest-based 'affinity space', suggesting that these are especially common and important types of spaces in contemporary society, offering a powerful vision of learning, affiliation and identity, which young people encounter often in their everyday lives, but that school classrooms rarely demonstrate their positive features. He suggests that these concepts can do some of the work that the communities of practice concept is currently trying to do with respect to learning, but without some of its problems.

Across these chapters, three sets of common themes emerge, identifying areas in which we need to move beyond the current theory of communities of practice. Firstly, there is a call to incorporate a model of language-in-use, covering language, literacy and discourse; this is argued both on a theoretical level and with reference to a variety of examples. Secondly, there is the call for attention to issues of power and conflict within communities. This is expressed in different ways in different chapters (risk and stigma, diversity, equity, legitimation conflicts) but emerges throughout much of the work. Thirdly, there is the need to incorporate the broader social context in some way when researching communities of practice. These ideas are linked. As several of the previously described chapters show, attention to the detail of language-in-use draws out areas of conflict and negotiation around power; and these areas of conflict are often related to or driven by issues from the broader social context.

References

Chaiklin, S. and J. Lave (1996) *Understanding Practice: Perspectives on Activity and Context*. Cambridge: Cambridge University Press.

Eckert, P. (2000) *Linguistic Variation as Social Practice*. Oxford: Blackwell.

Gee, J. P. (2000) New people in new worlds: networks, the new capitalism and schools. In B. Cope and M. Kalantzis, *Multiliteracies: Literacy Learning and the Design of Social Futures*. London and New York: Routledge.

Gee, J. P., G. Hull and C. Lankshear (1996) *The New Work Order: Behind the Language of the New Capitalism*. Sydney and Boulder, CO: Allen and Unwin and Westview Press.

Goh, P., P. Thaxter and P. Simpson (2003) *Building Communities of Mission Practice in CMS*. London: Church Mission Society. Last accessed online 3 September 2003 at http://www.cms-uk.org/_pdf/ Building_ Communities.pdf.

Holland, D. and J. Lave (eds) (2001) *History in Person: Enduring Struggles, Contentious Practice, Intimate Identities*. Santa Fe: The School of American Research Press.

Holmes, J. and M. Meyerhoff (1999) The community of practice: theories and methodologies in language and gender research. *Language in Society 28* (2) 173–183.

Lave, J. (1988) *Cognition in Practice: Mind, Mathematics and Culture in Everyday Life*. Cambridge: Cambridge University Press.

Lave, J. and E. Wenger (1991) *Situated Learning: Legitimate Peripheral Participation*. Cambridge: Cambridge University Press.

Merriam, S., B. Courtenay and L. Baumgartner (2003) On becoming a witch: learning in a marginalized community of practice. *Adult Education Quarterly 53* (3), 170–188.

Prior, P. (2003) Are communities of practice really an alternative to discourse communities? Paper presented at the American Association for Applied Linguistics Annual Meeting, Arlington, Virginia, 22–25 March 2003.

Rogoff, B. (1990) *Apprenticeship in Thinking. Cognitive Development in Social Context*. New York: Oxford University Press.

Rogoff, B. (2003) *The Cultural Nature of Human Development*. New York and Oxford: Oxford University Press.

Rogoff, B. and J. Lave (1984) *Everyday Cognition: Its Development in Social Context*. Cambridge, MA: Harvard University Press.

Rogoff, B., C. G. Turkanis and L. Bartlett (2001) *Learning Together: Children and Adults in a School Community*. New York and Oxford: Oxford University Press.

Scribner, S. and M. Cole (1981) *The Psychology of Literacy*. Cambridge, MA: Harvard University Press.

Swales, J. (1998) *Other Floors, Other Voices: A Textography of a Small University Building*. London: Lawrence Erlbaum Associates.

Wenger, E. (1998) *Communities of Practice: Learning, Meaning, and Identity*. Cambridge: Cambridge University Press.

Wenger, E., R. McDermott and W. Snyder (2002) *Cultivating Communities of Practice: A Guide to Managing Knowledge*, Boston: Harvard Business School Press.

1

Literacy, Reification and the Dynamics of Social Interaction

David Barton and Mary Hamilton

INTRODUCTION

We work in Literacy Studies and approach the notion of community of practice to see how it can strengthen or challenge what we do. The field of literacy studies has developed in parallel with communities of practice work over the past twenty years. The two approaches have common roots in the work of Scribner and Cole (1981), but then the fields of situated learning and situated literacies largely developed separately. Our overall point is that the framings provided by theories of language, literacy, discourse and power are central to understanding the dynamics of communities of practice, but they are not made explicit in Wenger's formulations. These ideas form the basis of this and the following chapter. Our own work has examined the literacy practices of everyday life (as in Barton and Hamilton 1998; Barton, Hamilton and Ivanič 2000), and here we see that most social interactions in contemporary society, including those covered by Wenger, are textually mediated; this shapes, structures and constrains them. We will argue that the concept of reification in the communities of practice work is key to making the link with literacy studies.

In this chapter, we start out from the vignettes that form the data for Wenger's work in his 1998 book. We examine them through the lens of literacy studies, demonstrating the centrality of literacy practices and arguing that a textually mediated social world is revealed. This is a way of showing the potential contribution of literacy studies to the analysis of the social processes central to the communities of practice approach. It is clear from the examples of reification given by Wenger that he is sometimes talking about material artefacts and tools but also frequently refers to more abstract forms of semiotic representation, including many that involve literacy. Although he does not point this out, nearly all specific examples of reifications dealt with by Wenger in his data are in fact literacy artefacts of some kind. We therefore focus on the concept of reification as a way of developing both communities of practice work and literacy theory and identify some points of commonality between these theories and other social theories. In particular, we will refer to the work of Bruno Latour, Dorothy Smith and Dorothy Holland, all of whom have made theoretical observations that complement and further illuminate the analytic potential of the notion of reification.

LITERACY IN COMMUNITIES OF PRACTICE

Early on in the *Communities of Practice* book is a seventeen-page vignette entitled *Welcome to claims processing!* It is a synthetic composite example based upon Wenger's detailed ethnographic work in the claims department of a health insurance company. The vignette consists of a chronological description of a day in the life of Ariel, a claims processor, documenting her activities and with a running commentary of her thoughts and feelings. It is part ethnographic description, part fictional narrative. It follows her from leaving home in the morning through her work day and finishes with her driving home.

The vignette provides a clear description of the work lives of a group of people in a certain workplace at a particular point in time. Of course, it is meant as a prototypical community of practice, and the example is constantly referred to and used by Wenger to illustrate his arguments and to make particular analytical points. This main vignette is followed by a shorter four-page vignette, which is the analysis of a written text, a specific form used in the workplace, and there is a discussion of the ways in which it is referred to and talked about. Within the book, these two vignettes represent the main database upon which the theory is based. The first vignette can be summarised as follows:

Ariel leaves home and drives to work, thinking about traffic congestion and her physical appearance. She meets colleagues at the elevator and travels up to her workplace. When she arrives at work, Ariel signs in, checks her mail, logs on and works at her desk. Her work of dealing with insurance claims is a mixture of using computer data bases and forms, using print based documents, talking on the phone and talking to colleagues. Her activities are a mixture of informal activities and formal procedures. Her reading and writing activities go across print and screen and her writing appears to be mainly form filling and manipulating pre-written "pattern paragraphs".

She attends a meeting with colleagues of different status which has a formal agenda and where new procedures are explained. She has to fill out forms at the meeting and is invited to express her opinions on new work plans. There are also informal activities, such as celebrating a birthday by sharing a cake. Colleagues order their lunch ahead of time by phone and then take their lunch break together. Work passes more slowly in the afternoon, punctuated by a visit by senior staff. There is a description of training, where new procedures are taught. The phrase "Welcome to claims processing!", the title of the vignette, is uttered by a colleague to emphasise the point that formal procedures have to be backed up by the informal knowledge which other workers pass on.

Ariel keeps track of her activities throughout the day and her work is checked by the supervisor; she finishes the work day by filling in a production report detailing the work she has done and that she has achieved her targets. Then she leaves work, talks to colleagues in the elevator and drives home alone, worrying about traffic congestion and pollution.

The second vignette is less of a narrative. It concerns a form which is used by claims processors to calculate the co-ordination of benefits when customers are covered by more than one health plan. The form is called the Co-ordination of Benefit worksheet; the claims processors call it *'the C, F and J thing'*, referring to particular lines on the form. The vignette explains how the form was introduced in a training session to help processors calculate complicated benefits. They carried out exercises and could do the calculations. However, back in the workplace, they did not understand the basis of the calculations, and they would ask for reconfirmation from more experienced colleagues. When irate customers phoned them, the processors were unable to explain the benefit calculations to them. A further training session attempted to help processors deal with the customers, but it did not cover the reasoning underlying the calculations.

Literacy Studies research has often started out from the detailed study of particular social activities, and the first vignette is a familiar description to anyone who has been involved in ethnographic studies of literacy in the workplace. (See, for example, Gowen 1992, Hull 1997 and Belfiore et al. 2004.) Some researchers have studied particular genres of writing, examining the reading and writing around specific texts, as in the second vignette (although the reading and writing practices around forms, a common genre of writing, have not been studied extensively; see Wright 1981, Fawns and Ivanič 2001).

Ethnographers working in the general area of literacy have developed a distinct approach and have a particular lens for examining social activities. In our own work, mainly researching the literacy practices of everyday life and working within the framework of literacy as social practice, we earlier identified a set of propositions about the nature of literacy which guided our work and which can be seen as basic propositions for a theory of literacy (as in Barton and Hamilton 1998, pp. 6–13; Barton 2001). Drawing on this background, it is useful to apply the lens of literacy theory to Wenger's particular example. It is probably simplest to break our approach to literacy down into a set of points and then use the vignettes to illustrate the points. Although we deal with them separately, the points are in fact highly interconnected and build upon each other, and within each there are issues and debates which we will draw attention to. The points are as follows:

1. **The literacy events point.** The first point to be made about literacy is that a key way of understanding written language is to examine specific observable events and the role of texts in these events. The literacy event becomes a basic unit of analysis. In empirical research of everyday interactions, it is immediately apparent that literacy events are widespread. Whilst human social interaction may appear to be based upon spoken language, most contemporary interactions are, at the same time, literacy events. The interactions are about written texts. This is in two senses. Much spoken language is in the presence of texts and a large amount of spoken language makes reference to texts. The existence of these mediating texts changes what is said and

how it is said. Ordinary everyday spoken interaction – which is usually referred to as face-to-face and somehow viewed as 'natural' and unmediated – is in fact highly mediated, most often by texts, but also by other artefacts. There is no real distinction between face-to-face and mediated. This can be seen in the vignette, where even when the workers go off to lunch, although they are away from the workplace, they talk about texts.

Starting with this first point, the importance of literacy events as a unit of analysis can be clearly seen in the claims processing vignette. The work activities which are described can be seen as a chain of discrete literacy events. Ariel signs in, checks her mail, ignores some phone messages and logs on. The events may overlap, but there is clear signalling of the beginning and end of each one. Each literacy event is nested and can be broken down into a set of smaller activities like reading from a screen, entering a number on a form or signing a document. These go together to make up the meaningful event. The explicit analysis of literacy events provides a methodology for working with empirical data within a theoretical framework and deriving new insights about social interaction.

2. The literacy practices point. The second point is that specific events are made up of more general practices, that there are distinct, coherent configurations of practices which can be identified and named. These are often associated with specific areas of life. For example, the set of practices associated with writing an assignment in education is distinct from those associated with filing a safety report in a workplace or writing a personal diary in the home. In real life, such practices are hybrid and overlapping, with blurred edges, and people apply practices learned in one situation to new situations. This means that boundaries themselves are significant, generative spaces where resources may be combined in new ways or for new purposes.

In terms of the vignette, the specific activities of signing in, checking the mail and logging on are all identifiable, nameable, culturally recognisable practices with a cultural significance beyond the individual activities. Many of the activities are typical of workplaces, and it is helpful to talk in terms of workplace literacies. The vignette provides a clear example of specific practices associated with this sort of workplace. The writing, for example, is often the filling in of forms and using prewritten paragraphs. It is routine and repetitive.

The writing can also be seen as collaborative, where several people have been involved in the writing at different stages and there is no identifiable author. These are typical workplace literacies (and can be contrasted, for example, with the domain of education, where such activities of sharing, copying and collaborating are tightly controlled and policed, and often punished as plagiarism). Similarly, the range of reading activities in the workplace is formulaic, limited and constrained. In terms of the language used, this workplace has its own specific discourses, and ways of talking and writing, including a specialised vocabulary, such as 'a pre-exist', 'junk claims', etc. (see Chapter 2). Many of the workplace practices are those identified with the New Work Order (Gee, Hull and Lankshear 1996), with literacy used for close monitoring and self-regulation; in the vignette, there is a good example of a seemingly egalitarian meeting to discuss improving production which nevertheless has clear hierarchies across different grades. Other examples of workplace literacies described within a literacy studies framework can be found in Belfiore et al. (2004).

3. The social structure point. To understand particular literacy practices, we need to look beyond the observable social relations to broader social patterning. It is clear that some practices are more dominant than others, that literacy is significant to the institutions in which events are located and that issues of power are important. In fact, most literacy interactions involve unequal distributions of power between people. To address these issues, theories of literacy have to be located within broader social theories.

These power issues are not pursued in any depth in the *Communities of Practice* book. Wenger's focus is the local site of engagement and organisation rather than the field of business more generally; he deflects his focus away from power and the creation of higher level institutional structures. When referring to the company, "the formidable shadow of Alinsu is ever-present" (p. 79); however, it seems to exist in a separate world from the interminable shaping and reshaping of practice that goes on at the level of the claims processing department. Ariel and the other claims processors have some decision-making power, but only as a result of their positions in the tight work hierarchies. They exercise power, whilst at the same time they are incorporated into the practices of others. The practices of claims processing are presented to us as ready made, and there is little acknowledgement that the particular community of practice in the vignette is located in an institutional hierarchy, with the dominant form of the practices emanating from elsewhere. For example, their work is structured in terms of standardising quality systems that are part of a widespread audit culture which has been widely researched (as in Power 1999; Strathern 2000, for example). Complex forms and procedures are handed down to be locally negotiated and appropriated. Whilst this is a recognisable scenario, it is a particular and ahistorical vision of relations of power and authority within an organisation. There is some discussion of these issues in a footnote (p. 285), but they are not incorporated into the main argument of the book.

The vignettes are "days in the life of" not reflections back over broader spans of time that might include restructuring of the organisation or the sudden shifts of employment and life circumstances which characterise so many people's employment experience in the longer term (see point 4 below). Wenger presents a vision of the 'enchanted workplace' (Gee, Hull and Lankshear 1996) where workers participate freely and act democratically, whereas in reality their space for action is severely limited.

Another social structure issue not taken up in the book is that of gender, although there is clear gender patterning in the practices. The vignette is populated by at least fifteen women, whilst a small number of men have background roles in the story. Although we will not develop it here, the ways in which claims processing is typically women's work could be pursued (cf. McMahon et al. 1994).

4. The historical point. When examining practices at a particular point in time, it is clear that literacy practices come from somewhere. They exist within a cultural context and are built up from existing practices. Often, a key to understanding contemporary practices is to see what they are built upon; this provides another link between the local and the global and a way of understanding the power issues which we have drawn attention to.

The literacy events in the vignette are strongly anchored in a specific place and time. It is the United States with a privatised medical system at a point in the 1990s when computers were beginning to revolutionise office work. Since then, probably much of the work has been changed to on-line computing, maybe Ariel's workplace has been restructured with the work subcontracted to another company and she has lost her job, or perhaps the whole claim centre has been moved by the parent company to Latin America or Southeast Asia.

The historical basis of the practices described in the vignette can be clearly identified. We can see the ways in which the new computer-based practices draw upon and develop earlier print-based practices. For example, in the description of the activities of processing a claim, it appears primarily as a print-based activity, sorting and dealing with paper, augmented by computer records. The workers are in the middle of a gradual transition from the claims processor having responsibility for specific cases and individual relationships with clients to situations where any processor can deal with any case and the computer record is central. There is a small incident at the beginning of the vignette when it is pointed out that Ariel gets personally addressed letters as she gives her name out on the phone, whereas there is no need to do this as letters are now addressed to the company. The individual person becomes irrelevant as memory shifts from the individual to the computer.

5. The dynamic point. The next point is that literacy events are dynamic activities and that people are active participants in literacy events. One aspect of this is that literacy events have a point and a purpose for people. It is immediately apparent that literacy simultaneously serves both individual and social purposes and, in fact, there can be multiple and conflicting purposes involved in any literacy event. In the main vignette, there is a complex mixture of the workers' own purposes and the broader social purposes of the company they work for. There is regulation and surveillance at the same time as dealing with people's medical insurance claims. In the vignette, the claims processors are active in making the practices their own and in making them meaningful. They have vernacular responses to these dominant practices. We can see this illustrated in Ariel's situation where she has choice within a constrained space. She is assigned what work she has to do and what targets she has to meet, but within that she is able to prioritise her work and decide on the order in which she does things. She decides who to discuss cases with. Similarly, in terms of dress and other social markers of identity, she makes choices within predefined spaces.

Another aspect of the dynamic point is that change is important. Literacy practices change and are developed, and there is a certain amount of fluidity. There is constant change in the contemporary workplace and this is how learning becomes central and, in particular, informal learning. Literacy research has often identified the ways in which new practices are learned informally in everyday life, in workplaces and in education.

Wenger uses the first vignette to make the informal learning point repeatedly, how people learn from each other and how this is often superior to formal learning. The characters in the vignette are used to articulate the folk wisdom of the superiority of informal learning from colleagues over formal training courses. On-the-job informal learning is emphasised in the vignette, and the ways in which it interacts with more formal instruction, for instance where procedures learned in training are not effective in practice. In these examples, we can also see how there is a tension between the ways in which the written texts attempt to give permanent shape to and to synchronise activities and the constant change within the workplace. Often, the training events referred to in the vignette have the explicit aim of changing people's relationships to literacy artefacts. The second vignette exemplifies this: they are taught how to use a form but, back in the actual job, they support each other informally, especially where individuals are aware of gaps in their knowledge.

6. The multimodal point. The next point is important for understanding semiosis or meaning making. It is that print literacy always exists alongside a range of other modes of meaning making, in particular visual meaning making, and that literacy is but one part of a range of semiotic resources (Kress and van Leeuwen 2001), each with its specific affordances. The work of claims processing is highly multimodal, involving as it does an ever-shifting combination of speech, visuals, numerical information and other symbolic systems. Ariel is constantly bringing together written information, spoken information and visual information from printed material, computer screens, face-to-face conversations and phone conversations.

The vignette also provides a good illustration of the ways in which spoken language is constantly mediated by the written word, as mentioned previously. Much of the talk is about texts, and much of the workplace spoken language – such as answering the phone – is scripted, text-based language. There is also a subtle interplay of what is orally communicated and what gets written down, which would be worth further examination. For example, when workers receive warnings about not meeting their targets, these are often delivered orally and therefore are off the public record, whereas there are certain things within the claims process that for legal purposes they have to receive 'in writing'. Again, these practices have shifted with computer interactions and the routine recording of phone conversations at work.

One important aspect of multimodality is that the materiality of literacy is undergoing change, and this is central to discussions of reification. Social landscapes provide opportunities – things which can be done easily in them. The possibilities and affordances of literacy are associated with its material aspects. This includes the materiality of texts and the range of literacy artefacts which exist, their availability and expense. Whilst we are emphasising the importance of literacy as one of the factors which provide affordances and symbolic meanings and which shape interactions, other material aspects – such as the office layout – also do this (see Chapter 2). Focussing on literacy is particularly salient as the artefacts of paper, pen and printing provided a fairly stable set of textual affordances for five hundred years which have been disrupted by changes in technologies. New technologies shift the materiality of literacy, profoundly changing the semiotic landscape.

7. The recontextualisation point. The last specific point to be made is that texts can move across contexts, often changing their meanings and functions but nevertheless providing a fixed reference point in different events. Or, rather, to make this statement more active, people move texts across contexts. We refer to this as recontextualisation, and it is central to the activity of claims processing.

Texts provide constancy across events, for example, in the ways in which medical documents are put to new uses when they are used as evidence for medical claims. This workplace is held together in many ways by the texts which cross events, or which cross communities of practice. All the forms have different purposes as they pass through different events. Ariel fills in a form recording her output; this has another purpose when it is checked by her supervisor. In this way, texts can be a reference point for shared meanings and can synchronise activities. The form in the second vignette is a good example of this: it is used in training, it is used to make a calculation, it is checked with colleagues, it is then a record of that calculation and it is used to explain the benefits to customers.

There has been some work on how to analyse the ways in which texts are linked across contexts (e.g., Solin 2001). This is partly a question of intertextuality – how texts draw upon and relate to other texts (Ivanič 1998; Fairclough 2003). It also raises the issue of how texts and their meanings are reframed in different contexts. (See Bernstein on recontextualisation in relation to general processes of the classification and framing of knowledge, 1996, pp. 19–21, 47–48.) We will return to this important issue when discussing reifications.

TEXTUALLY MEDIATED SOCIAL WORLDS

Taken together, these points emphasise the centrality of literacy in the patterning of contemporary everyday activities and how people act within **a textually mediated social world** (cf. Smith 1990). The claims processing department of the insurance company can clearly be seen as a textually mediated world. It is full of texts, they have a central role and most communication is about texts. This is also a workplace which has been closely designed and highly scripted. Recent workplace studies have drawn attention to the roles literacy play in a variety of workplace interactions and to the idea that work itself has changed, becoming more textualised (Iedema and Sheeres 2003; Belfiore et al. 2004).

However, in their lives, people do not just act within the workplace. They act within a range of contexts. It is more accurate to talk in plural terms and to state that people act within textually mediated **social worlds**. These social worlds are not limited to highly scripted workplaces or workplace-like settings. They are constituted of many other domains and contexts. Social practices differ greatly across this diversity of contexts, and social interaction has different characteristics. It varies in terms of the degree of fluidity of social relations of power and authority, the types of historical structuring and change, the degree of formal framing or scripting and the degree to which its boundaries are agreed or contested.

The work on communities of practice starts out from constrained and well-defined task-oriented organisations such as individual workplaces. These ideas do not transfer so well to interconnected but dispersed networks – more loosely framed fields of social action – and they are weak on issues of power and conflict where groups do not share common goals and interests. In ethnographies of everyday literacy practices, such as those we have carried out (Barton and Hamilton 1998; Barton, Hamilton and Ivanič 2000), we encounter fields of social action that are not characterised by a stable or well-bounded shared purpose; they have diffuse and unclear membership without clear rights or direct channels of communication for negotiating meaning; there is often ambivalent engagement (which can also be seen in many classrooms and workplaces and other coercive communities) and incomplete repertoires of shared resources that leave many assumptions unarticulated. These features are not necessarily marginalising; rather, they are often the creative lifeblood of social change and challenge. Viewed like this, the social world is a long way from the prototypical community of practice. The social world is characterised by multiple membership; it has unresolved boundaries, with many different fluid communities of practice which exist in a variety of relationships to one another, both supporting and competing. As Holland and Lave point out in their discussion of the processes of social change, "much of what is contested in local struggles is the very meaning of what's going on. The world is not a 'given' in this perspective" (2001, p. 22). See also Scollon's notion of "nexus of practice", which describes a community of practice as one specialised form arising from the more general fluidity of social interaction (2001, p. 16).

REIFICATION

With these points in mind, we return to the notion of reification to see how it can be developed from a literacy studies point of view. As we have previously suggested, we also suggest that making links with the resources offered by other social theories could deepen our understanding of the implications of the concept of reification and help us take forward our analysis of it. People are utilising a range of such frameworks to move in the same direction. In particular, a major perspective is that of actor network theory and a number of

writers within both communities of practice/activity theory traditions and literacy studies have begun to point out the fruitfulness
of making links with it. (See, e.g., Miettinen 1999, Fox 2000, Pardoe
2000, Hamilton 2001, Brandt and Clinton 2002, Clarke 2002, Edwards
2003 and Wenger himself in many footnotes.) We will also briefly refer to the insights offered by the theoretical perspectives of Dorothy
Smith and Dorothy Holland. Each of these approaches talks of stable
but portable entities which cross contexts, and the overarching point
we want to make is that many of the most common and the most
significant stable entities are literacy related.

Wenger defines reification as "the process of giving form to our
experience by producing objects that congeal this experience into
'thingness'. In so doing, we create points of focus around which
the negotiation of meaning becomes organized.... Any community
of practice produces abstractions, tools, symbols, stories, terms and
concepts that reify something of that practice in a congealed form"
(pp. 58–59). Thus, reification is seen as both a process and a product. As Wenger describes it, participation in a community of practice
depends on reification. Neither is an optional feature, but they are
constitutive of each other. Reification entails not only the negotiation
of shared understandings but also enables particular forms of social
relations to be shaped in the process of participation. This approach
focuses on the positive and productive aspects of reification, although
he accepts, in a footnote (1998, p. 287), that negative aspects (such as
a tendency to confuse abstract concepts with material objects, a contribution to the process of commodification and the naturalisation of
meanings so that human agency is hidden) could still apply within
communities of practice.

In his general discussion on page 60, he explains the range of application of the term "reification". It can, he says:

cover a wide range of processes that include making, designing, representing, naming, encoding and describing as well as perceiving, interpreting
using, reusing, decoding and recasting ... from entries in a journal to historical records, from poems to encyclopedias, from names to classification
systems, from dolmens to space probes, from the Constitution to a signature
on a credit card slip, from gourmet recipes to medical procedures, from flashy
advertisements to census data, from single concepts to entire theories, from
the evening news to national archives, from lesson plans to the compilation of

text-books, from private address lists to sophisticated credit-reporting data-bases, from tortuous political speeches to the yellow pages. In all these cases aspects of human experience and practice are congealed into fixed forms and given the status of object.

Wenger's examples of reification include quite different kinds of rep-resentation, and the way he talks about reification here makes it equivalent to semiosis itself, that is, the sense-making and represen-tation of meaning that are an essential part of all discourse and social practice (see Tusting, this volume). Many of the reifications are lan-guage based, but the list also includes numerical databases, computer applications, monuments and architecture, visual images and dress codes. Some are numbers, and some are diagrams or images. Some are "objects" intentionally created for their symbolic significance, whilst others are the accidental traces of human activity or functional objects that have acquired symbolic meaning as well.

It is crucial to organise these things as semiotic markers and to name them as parts of different semiotic systems. To use Kress's term, they form a 'semiotic landscape' from which individuals in an inter-action make motivated choices of resources. This would allow us to differentiate much more finely between different kinds of reification and to clarify the powers of each. To make this connection is poten-tially to access a whole field of scholarship, a vocabulary and ana-lytical tools from social linguistics, discourse analysis and the new literacy studies that could strengthen the communities of practice framework.

Wenger usefully identifies four key features of reifications: (1) their succinctness and power to evoke meanings; (2) their portability across time, physical space and context; (3) their potential for physical per-sistence or durability and (4) their focussing effect – drawing atten-tion to specific features or distinctions within social reality. These four features of **succinctness, portability, durability** and **focussing** could help make important distinctions between reifications. We could observe, then, that some reifications are much more durable than others – but whilst a stone monument might rate highly on this di-mension, it would be low on portability. Spoken discourse may be extremely flexible and adaptable in focussing attention on new dis-tinctions and concepts, but is transient and (at least until recently) harder to make durable than written texts and numbers. Visual representations are not so good at fixing precise meanings, but can be powerfully evocative and succinct in communicating once an iconic meaning can be identified, as in logos.

Returning to issues of literacy, when he talks in a general way about reification, Wenger's description is extremely wide. This is in contrast, as we have seen previously, to his application of the idea of reification in the vignettes, where most reifications are, in practice, *literacy* artefacts. The examples he expands on involve written texts. Language is a powerful semiotic system, and it could be argued that written texts and numbers are so ubiquitous in Wenger's vignettes because they rate as highly powerful on all the dimensions of reification he identifies.

In summary, reifications vary in their ability to carry explicit and precise meanings; their durability, portability across time, space and cultural difference; manipulability; their accessibility and demands for specialist knowledge; their susceptibility to standardisation and audit and so on. Being able to describe and analyse these differences in relation to particular settings and social projects increases the theoretical power of the concept of reification. The expertise from literacy studies and the field of social semiotics more broadly, therefore, can be harnessed to particularly good effect to the idea of reification as used by Wenger. This relates to the insight offered by Dorothy Smith, who has pointed to the central role and especial characteristics of texts as active agents in solidifying and reifying power, through what she calls the relations of ruling:

I have come to see the text in its material as well as in its symbolic aspect as the bridge between the everyday/everynight local actualities of our living and the ruling relations. The text is a material object that brings into actual contexts of reading a standardized form of words or images that can be and may be read/seen/heard in many other settings by many others at the same or other times.... (Smith 1999, p. 7)

The notion of reification can be further strengthened by making connections with other theories that use a similar concept, but which name it differently. For example, the work of Bruno Latour and others, often referred to as actor network theory, offers a perspective from the sociology of science that has been used extensively to explore the development and history of scientific innovations. Actor network theory uses metaphors of "networks" and "nodes" rather than Wenger's notion of "communities". A network involves a mobilisation of resources or "agents", which typically includes physical materials, representations and people and the creation of what Latour refers to as "stable mobiles". These are representations of aspects of the world that are portable and thus can be accumulated and combined in new ways at a distance and used to co-ordinate action from within centres of power (see Latour 1987, p. 227ff and also Law 1994, p. 24). There is a strong parallel here with Wenger's use of the term reification.

Actor network theory challenges one of the current great divides in Western philosophy and science by insisting that agency resides in a combination of both human beings *and* non-human objects. This challenge is the key to understanding the analytical power of actor network theory, and it also makes the connection with reification. Within this perspective, humans and non-humans are not claimed to be identical, but aspects of human agency are delegated to objects. Latour's examples are of prosaic material objects such as a door opener or a sheep fold, which can act as substitutes for human beings in their absence, but the idea can be expanded to a wider range of social objects. For example, Hamilton (2001) has shown how the creation of a social object and its material forms – such as the language test used in the International Adult Literacy Survey – is a powerful example of an object acting on behalf of humans and which can eventually influence pedagogical practice in local settings far distant from the context in which the test was created. Similarly, it is possible to interpret some aspects of Wenger's vignettes using these ideas. For example, when Ariel no longer needs to respond personally to insurance claims, the database acts on her behalf as memory shifts from the individual worker to the computer. Actor network theory suggests, then, that objects can be seen to have agency in the sense that they can act in the place of human beings to mediate and co-ordinate the activities of others.

The power of a network derives from its size, the number and status of agents enrolled to its causes and its ability to stabilise meanings

in a contentious world. John Law (1994) has argued that accepted
social orders are created and stabilised through the assembling of
powerful networks. He and others use an ethnographic approach to
trace the flows or trajectories of social projects, following the chain of
events, actors and artefacts – including documents, institutional domains and activities (see also Marcus 1995). He suggests that a project
of social ordering generates and embodies characteristic forms of representation (including texts) that script the performance of those involved (Law 1994, p. 111). Like Wenger and Smith, then, Latour and
Law have pointed out how power accrues in networks through reifications. Like Wenger, although he uses a very generic term, many of
Latour's examples of stable mobiles involve written texts. Also, like
Wenger, he does not make explicit this connection between literacy
and the notion of stable mobiles.

Brandt and Clinton (2002) do make this link, however; they identify that literacy artefacts are a type of stable mobile that has a particularly important role to play in linking local and global practices because they serve to build and sustain long, stable connections and thus
networks across time and space. Literacy artefacts, in other words,
are particularly effective social agents in terms of making links across
contexts. Jones (2000), Tusting (2000) and other studies in Barton,
Hamilton and Ivanič (2000) also see literacy as crucial in linking local
and global practices. The material literacy artefacts stand in for absent but interested human actors and are the means by which people
and activities are incorporated into bigger networks of power. This
perspective invites us to trace the threads across contexts to detail
how local interactions are synchronised and orchestrated into bigger
patterns.

Dorothy Holland would also concur with this picture. Like other
Vygostskian activity theorists, she calls the reifications cultural artefacts and sees them as having a central role in developing new 'figured worlds' or in reinforcing existing ones. A figured world is a
socially produced and culturally constructed 'realm of interpretation' in which a particular set of characters and actors are recognised,
significance is assigned to certain acts and particular outcomes are
valued over others. Figured worlds are populated by a set of actors and agents who engage in a limited range of meaningful acts or
changes in a particular situation. Bartlett and Holland argue:

Cultural worlds are continuously figured in practice through the use of cultural artefacts or objects inscribed by the collective attribution of meaning. (Bartlett and Holland 2002, p. 12)

Within the perspective developed by Holland et al. (1998) and Holland and Lave (2001), the focus on reification is more on the ways in which cultural artefacts mediate the formation of identity and processes of social change and the possibilities of creative and generative change inherent in that process that are not foregrounded in Wenger's work.

As used by actor network theorists, the concept of reification takes on new dimensions. The link with power is much more explicit, and new theoretical tools are offered for analysing how reifications travel across time and space to accrue power; how social relations are involved in maintaining and promoting (or dismantling) particular reifications and who benefits from these activities. These tools include the concepts of **distribution, translation, framing** and **deletion; localising moves** and **globalising connects**. For example, from our work on literacy, we would identify localising moves such as exercising choice or preferences; interpreting general categories in the light of local contexts; appropriating texts to immediate and different purposes and recombining resources in novel ways. Similarly, globalising connects include being aligned with collectives, imaginatively entering figured worlds via texts and complying with text directives and affordances that synchronise actions with those of others. (See Hamilton 2001 for applications of the other terms to literacy, also Clarke 2002, and Brandt and Clinton 2002.)

In summary, it seems to us that sociological perspectives such as actor network theory can extend both communities of practice and literacy studies because they offer:

1. a more fluid and complex view of how social resources and interactions are connected and how people and texts move in and out of relationship with one another.
2. a clear picture of how power works in the social sphere, elaborating the connections between the accumulation of resources, the enrolment of agents and power and offering a methodology for analysing the trajectory of a social project – the flow and concentration of resources within it.

3. a whole new set of theoretical tools for analysing how these processes happen, how reifications travel across contexts and how local and time constrained interactions/moments are connected to broader, even global, practices.
4. analytical strategies for dealing with competing and conflicting enterprises, unstable or ambiguous social projects and the multiple and shifting perspectives that participants may have within a given social project.

CONCLUSIONS

We have argued in this chapter that theorists working from literacy studies and from the starting point of communities of practice have a common endeavour in understanding the dynamics of interaction and learning in the social world and that the insights they have developed in this endeavour can complement and strengthen one another. We have also argued that it is productive to link these perspectives with more macro-level social theory, such as actor network theory and by bringing in the work of theorists such as Scollon, Smith, Holland and the continuing work of Lave, which theorises the complexities of relationships between social structure and agency. These broader social theories need an understanding of how people act in groups and how learning and change take place. Both communities of practice and literacy as social practice are middle-level theories that have essential, detailed contributions to make to macro-level theory. Communities of practice is essential in that it provides a vocabulary for analysing socially situated learning. Literacy studies is essential because it enables a much closer and differentiated analysis of the power and affordances of different kinds of textual artefacts in mediating social interaction.

In particular, we have argued that Wenger's notion of reification is useful to pursue because it offers a specific analytical connection across communities of practice, literacy studies and broader social theory. In whatever way they are described, as cultural artefacts, mediating tools or stable mobiles, reifications are crucial for interactions across time and space, and often they are *literacy* artefacts. Reifications orchestrate and synchronise people's activities by stabilising meanings. They allow practices to travel across space and time. Different kinds of reifications have particular affordances and literacy-related ones are particularly powerful because of the semiotic resources they offer. The concept of reification adds to our understanding of the social construction of knowledge, the co-ordination of human activity and the role of institutions and cultural artefacts in these processes. It helps us focus, firstly, on the ways in which local situated practices and events are linked with other localities or with broader social formations; secondly, on what people bring in from elsewhere to a particular community of practice and thirdly, on the dimension of historical change, the origins of social formations and projects in different relationships to one another, whether these support, compete or conflict with one another.

References

Barton, D. (2001) Directions for literacy research: analysing language and social practices in a textually mediated world. *Language and Education 15* (2 & 3) 92–104.

Barton, D. and M. Hamilton (1998) *Local Literacies – Reading and Writing in One Community*. London: Routledge.

Barton, D., M. Hamilton and R. Ivanič (eds) (2000) *Situated Literacies: Reading and Writing in Context*. London: Routledge.

Bartlett, L. and D. Holland (2002) Theorizing the space of literacy practices. *Ways of Knowing 2 (1)* 10–22.

Belfiore, M. E., T. Defoe, S. Folinsbee, J. Hunter and N. S. Jackson (2004) *Reading Work: Literacies in the New Workplace*. London: Lawrence Erlbaum Associates.

Bernstein, B. (1996) *Pedagogy, Symbolic Control and Identity: Theory, Research, Critique*. London: Taylor and Francis.

Brandt, T. and K. Clinton (2002) Limits of the local: expanding perspectives on literacy as a social practice. *Journal of Literacy Research 34 (3)* 337–356.

Clarke, J. (2002) A new kind of symmetry: actor-network theories and the new literacy studies. *Studies in the Education of Adults 34 (2)* 107–122.

Edwards, R. (2003) Ordering subjects: actor-networks and intellectual technologies in lifelong learning, *Studies in the Education of Adults 35 (1)* 54–67.

Fairclough, N. (2003) *Analysing Discourse: Textual Analysis for Social Research*. London: Routledge.

Fawns, M. and R. Ivanič (2001) Form-filling as a social practice: Taking power into our own hands. In L. Tett, M. Hamilton and J. Crowther (eds), *Powerful Literacies*. Leicester: NIACE Publications.

Fox, S. (2000) Communities of practice, Foucalt and Actor-Network Theory. *Journal of Management Studies 37 (6)* 853–867.

Gee, J., G. Hull and C. Lankshear (1996) *The New Work Order: Behind the Language of the New Capitalism*. London: Allen & Unwin.

Gowen, S. G. (1992) *The Politics of Workplace Literacy: A Case Study*. New York: Teachers College Press.

Hamilton, M. (2001) Privileged literacies: policy, institutional process and the life of the IALS. *Language and Education 15* 178–196.

Holland, D., W. Lachicotte, D. Skinner and C. Cain (1998) *Identity and Agency in Cultural Worlds*. Cambridge, MA: Harvard University Press.

Holland, D. and J. Lave (2001) *History in Person: Enduring Struggles, Contentious Practice, Intimate Identities*. Santa Fe, NM: School of American Research Press.

Hull, G. (ed) (1997) *Changing Work, Changing Workers: Critical Perspectives on Language, Literacy, and Skills*. New York: State University of New York Press.

Iedema, R. and H. Scheeres (2003) Doing work to talking work: renegotiating knowing, doing, and identity. *Applied Linguistics 24 (3)* 316–337.

Ivanič, R. (1998) *Writing and Identity: The Discoursal Construction of Identity in Academic Writing*. Amsterdam: John Benjamins.

Jones, K. (2000) Becoming just another alphanumeric code: farmers' encounters with the literacy and discourse practices of agricultural bureaucracy at the livestock auction. In D. Barton, M. Hamilton and R. Ivanič (eds), *Situated Literacies*. London: Routledge, 70–90.

Kress, G. and T. van Leeuwen (2001) *Multimodal Discourse: The Modes and Media of Contemporary Communication*. Oxford: Oxford University Press.

Latour, B. (1987) *Science in Action*. Cambridge, MA: Harvard University Press.

Law, J. (1994) *Organizing Modernity*. Oxford: Blackwell.

Marcus, G. E. (1995) Ethnography in/of the world system: the emergence of multi-sited ethnography. *Annual Review of Anthropology 24* 95–117.

McMahon, M., D. Roach, A. Karach and F. V. Dijk (1994) Women and literacy for change. In M. Hamilton, D. Barton and R. Ivanič (eds), *Worlds of Literacy*. Clevedon, UK: Multilingual Matters, 215–224.

Miettinen, R. (1999) The riddle of things: activity theory and actor-network theory as approaches to studying innovations. *Mind, Culture, and Activity 6 (3)* 170–195.

Pardoe, S. (2000) Respect and the pursuit of symmetry in researching literacy and student writing. In D. Barton, M. Hamilton and R. Ivanič (eds), *Situated Literacies*. London: Routledge.

Power, M. (1999) *The Audit Society: Rituals of Verification*. 2nd edition. Oxford: Oxford University Press.

Scollon, R. (2001) *Mediated Discourse: The Nexus of Practice*. London: Routledge.

Scribner, S. and M. Cole (1981) *The Psychology of Literacy*. Cambridge, MA: Harvard University Press.

Smith, D. (1990) *Texts, Facts and Femininity: Exploring the Relations of Ruling.* London: Routledge.

Smith, D. (1999) *Writing the Social: Critique, Theory and Investigation.* Toronto: University of Toronto Press.

Solin, A. (2001) *Tracing Texts: Intertextuality in Environmental Discourse.* Department of English, University of Helsinki.

Strathern, M. (2000) *Audit Cultures: Anthropological Studies in Accountability, Ethics, and the Academy.* New York: Routledge.

Tusting, K. (2000) The new literacy studies and time: an exploration. In D. Barton, M. Hamilton and R. Ivanič (eds), *Situated Literacies.* London: Routledge.

Wenger, E. (1998) *Communities of Practice: Learning, Meaning and Identity.* Cambridge: Cambridge University Press.

Wright, P. (1981) Informed design for forms. *Information Design Journal* 2 151–178.

2

Language and Power in Communities of Practice

Karin Tusting

In this chapter, I argue that elements of theories developed within the field of the critical and social study of language could develop the theory of communities of practice, by offering a clearer understanding of the role of language within the process of negotiation of meaning. We have already mentioned in the introduction the need for a more fully developed theory of language within the theory of communities of practice. This chapter explores models from critical social linguistics which elaborate notions left unexplained in Wenger's model and offer theoretical and methodological tools for addressing some significant issues which remain unexplored, demonstrating this by reanalysing some of the example material from Wenger's 1998 book.

PRACTICE AND MEANING

I will begin by exploring the place of language within the theory as it currently stands, particularly the implicit importance of language as a form of meaning making within Wenger's development of the concept of practice. The concept of 'practice' is central to his conceptualisation of learning in communities. He defines practice as "doing, but not just doing in and of itself. It is doing in a historical and social context that gives structure and meaning to what we do" (1998:47). This concept of 'social practice' offers a way of analysing human activity which brings together the cognitive and the social aspects of human existence. Rather than focussing only on local activity, only on

structures of thought or only on broader social structures, it offers us
a way of conceptualising the socially situated nature of human activity. Wenger concurs with his collaborator Jean Lave's (1988) position
that "social practice is the key to grasping the actual complexity of
human thought as it takes place in real life" (Wenger 1998:281 n. 6).

Wenger develops this concept of practice and its implications for
understanding learning in communities in some detail, drawing for
illustration on empirical work carried out in an insurance claims processing office. He suggests that the central process involved in practice is the negotiation of meaning: *"practice is about meaning as an
experience of everyday life"* (1998:52, italics in original).

This 'meaning', for Wenger, is something experienced by people
engaging in the normal activities of everyday life. "It is not [...]
meaning as it sits locked up in dictionaries. It is not just [...] meaning as a relation between a sign and a reference. But neither is it [...]
meaning as a grand question – [...] the meaning of life as a philosophical issue" (Wenger 1998:51–52). In his example of medical claims
processing, the primary work activities engaged in by the insurance
workers he studied were classificatory ones. These were not seen –
at least by some – as being meaning-making activities; when Wenger
initially expressed an interest in working at Alinsu, senior management were surprised that he would want to look at learning in what
they called a "paper assembly line" (Wenger 1998:46). Nevertheless,
for each individual claims processor, what they are doing is experienced *by them* as an interaction which has some sort of meaning (even
if such work is repetitive and routine, and this meaning consists primarily of boredom). "Our engagement in practice may have patterns,
but it is the production of such patterns anew that gives rise to an experience of meaning" (Wenger 1998:52). 'Meaning' is therefore seen
as something which arises inevitably from the process of engaging in
living. He states: "Living is a constant process of *negotiation of meaning*. I will use the concept of negotiation of meaning very generally to
characterize the process by which we experience the world and our
engagement in it as meaningful. ... Human engagement in the world
is first and foremost a process of negotiation of meaning."

Despite its inevitability, this negotiation of meaning is not something which 'just happens', but something which people actively produce by engaging in all the activities which living entails: "My notion

[of negotiation of meaning] . . . is a fundamentally active, productive process", a process which "produces our being as an experience by making our living in the world meaningful" (1998:286n2). The term "negotiation" is used to convey a continuous process of the ongoing achievement of meaningfulness. Negotiation of meaning here refers to far more than meaning making through language. Since this construction of meaningfulness arises from everything that we do, it "may involve language, but is not limited to it" (1998:53).

This is a fairly broad understanding of meaning. In his development of the concept, Wenger offers analytical tools to explore this process as it is lived out by people and communities. He suggests that this 'negotiation of meaning' involves two constitutive, interlinked processes which he calls "participation" and "reification" and that it is in the convergence of these two processes that the negotiation of meaning takes place.

Participation refers to "a process of taking part and also to the relations with others that reflect this process. It suggests both action and connection" (Wenger 1998:55). Wenger uses this term to talk about involvement in communities, enterprises and activities. He limits the term only to actors who are members of *social* communities (in contrast, for example, to actor-network theory; see Chapter 1 this volume), suggesting that participation is characterised by the possibility of *mutual* recognition. It is broader than simply engagement in activity, incorporating notions of identity and community membership that still remain valid when the person concerned is not actively engaging. It therefore draws attention to the 'social-ness' of all sorts of activities which arise from particular identity and community affiliations, even when these activities may not appear in themselves social or participatory. (To illustrate this, Wenger uses the example of preparing slides alone in a hotel room for a conference presentation the next day; an activity performed alone, by a single individual, the meaning of which is inherently social (1998:57).)

The other half of the duality is 'reification', a term used to refer to the process of "making into a thing". Wenger suggests that "we project our meanings into the world and then we perceive them as existing in the world, as having a reality of their own" (Wenger 1998:58). Where participation relies on mutual recognition, reification is characterised by this notion of projection: "the process of giving form to our experience by producing objects that congeal this experience into 'thingness'" (1998:58). These objects may be material but are not necessarily so; the first examples Wenger uses to describe reification are abstract concepts: 'justice', 'the hand of fate', 'democracy', 'the economy'. These reifications congeal something of the practice that a community of participation engages in, but never all of it. He uses the term to refer to both the *process* of reification and the reified *products* that emerge from this, which can be as fleeting as a smoke signal or as solid as a pyramid.

Wherever negotiation of meaning is taking place, it involves both reification and participation. Even where reifications are imposed from above, they "must be re-appropriated into a local process in order to become meaningful" (Wenger 1998:60). It is in this *interplay* between participation and reification that negotiation of meaning takes place. A book (reification) is not involved in a process of negotiation of meaning until a person reads it (participation). An insurance claims form (reification) is not involved in negotiation of meaning until someone fills it in and processes it (participation). You cannot have a conversation (participation) without drawing on words, linguistic structures and ways of using language (reifications). Participation in meaning making always implies reifications and vice versa.

From this process of negotiation of meaning arise the three characteristics Wenger uses to define the 'community of practice': mutual engagement, joint enterprise and shared repertoire. Practice involves engaging with other people in the pursuit of some joint enterprise. Where this engagement is sustained over time, the people involved develop a repertoire of ways of engaging in practice, which includes ways of thinking, speaking, discourses, tools, understandings and memories which are to a greater or lesser extent shared amongst members of the community.

LANGUAGE AND MEANING MAKING

Despite the centrality of negotiation of meaning to the communities of practice model, and the key role of language within processes of participation and reification, Wenger does not draw out ideas about the relationship between language and meaning making more generally, beyond stating that meaning making cannot be reduced to language alone. However, while Wenger is careful to make clear that he is not just talking about language when talking about meaning, language is clearly central to much of the experience of negotiation of meaning we encounter in communities of practice. Although people make meaning in a variety of ways, language nevertheless has a privileged place in human communication. In Chapter 1 of this volume, we have seen how a close examination with a 'literacy lens' of the vignette at the beginning of the 1998 book demonstrates the importance of literacy events as part of the processes described. The same is true if this vignette is re-examined with a lens which focuses on the role of language in the events.

Language is one of the principal means by which meaning is reified, and the joint repertoires Wenger refers to which are built up in practice have many linguistic elements; his list (1998:83) includes "routines, words, tools, ways of doing things, stories, gestures, symbols, genres, actions, or concepts", most of which can be either partly or entirely linguistic in nature. One of the ways (although not the only one) of recognising whether a community has reified a particular element of its repertoire is whether it has been given a name within the community's practice, and the process of naming something is one of the significant ways in which that thing becomes reified. We see, for instance, within the repertoire of reifications which are drawn on in the vignette, the importance of a vocabulary particular to that practice which labels different types of people ('Level 6', 'supervisor'), the goals required of the processors (maintaining 'quality' while hitting 'production'), the particular ways in which medical conditions are redefined within this practice ('it's eligible') and the different types of claims locally recognised (with 'junk claims' being dreaded and 'easy claims' being prized).

The negotiation of joint enterprises routinely relies on linguistic communication. In the vignette, we see supervisors using a range of speech acts to attempt to control the way people go about their work, conveying new directives and organising people. They tell people that management will be logging their calls; they complain that there has been too much overpayment; they ask people to clean their desks in preparation for important visitors and they share a memo in a meeting that modifies codes. Language is also the way Ariel and the other processors negotiate with the powerful supervisors to attempt to re-shape the workplace's practices in their own interests: Ariel promises to make up ten minutes when she is late for work and pleads for an easy pile from the assistant supervisor.

Indeed, almost all mutual engagement involves language, to a greater or lesser extent. In the vignette, language is the principal means by which the processors share information and solve problems together, such as whether it is safe to assume that the date of emergency room treatment coincides with the date of an accident, whether circulatory conditions are covered, what 'incompetent cervix' means within the terms of this practice – eligible or not, how to cope with a form without a diagnosis or what the particular rules are for dealing with different company benefits schemes. Throughout the day, negative or difficult experiences are made public by being shared through language: "Here goes my quality!"; "What a way to start the day!"; "It's easy to explain here, but it's a pain to explain it on the phone"; "This guy's gonna yell at me"; "God, why is it so slow this afternoon". There are particular locally accepted 'facts' which are expressed in language: "You have to be well-organised in this job". The majority of the work that is done is language work: reading phone messages and claims forms, speaking to people on the phone, filling in forms on the computers, adding in 'pattern paragraphs' and entering notes on claims. Language is the principal means used by the processors to maintain their social relationships: greeting one another in the lobby, chatting about life outside work during the breaks, telling stories about adventures and relationships and gossiping about shared friends on the way home.

It is clear that language plays a central role in everyday activity within this community of practice. Therefore, understandings of the processes by means of which communities of practice are constituted and maintained require attention to the role of language within these processes. Research on communities of practice needs to include analysis of the language used. However, it is also clear that, within this model, language is only part of what is going on, and it is therefore necessary to draw on tools for this analysis which can deal with not only the language but also the relationships between language and other elements of the social process: the relationship between language and the other processes going on in interaction at the micro-level, and the role of language in the relationships between local communities and broader social processes.

LANGUAGE AND OTHER SOCIAL PROCESSES

To address the role of language within processes of communities of practice, we need a way of conceptualising the relationship between language and other social processes, together with an approach to analysing language data which can be situated within the broader communities of practice model. I will argue here that these issues have been addressed in the field of critical social linguistics. I am using this as an umbrella term to cover several areas within linguistics which are concerned with understanding the role of language as it is part of and woven into broader social processes, or 'language as social practice', including social semiotics, systemic functional linguistics and critical discourse analysis.

Critical social linguistics takes as a starting point an understanding of the world which sees all social practice as involving both semiotic (meaning making) and non-semiotic elements, with language as one of the principal semiotic systems drawn upon. In *Discourse and Late Modernity*, a significant recent theoretical work in this field, Chouliaraki and Fairclough (1999:23) argue that all practices "combine physical and symbolic resources, in varying degrees, and discourse is always a significant moment". They draw on a model developed by Harvey (1996) to identify semiosis, material activity, social relations and individual persons (minds, intentions, desires and bodies) as being the four significant different types of elements which are articulated in social practices, in relationships of 'reciprocal internalisation'. This means that semiotic events are not merely produced by semiotic systems, but co-produced by semiotic, material, personal and social systems – from which you cannot straightforwardly abstract merely the semiotic elements.

This understanding offers a model for situating semiosis within a broader social context. Within this model, meaning is produced by embodied, intentional, practically skilled actors, shaped by their whole history of interactions, engaging in material action. This action is situated within, and reproduces particular configurations of social relationships. This gives us a framework for understanding how the semiotic production of meaning is constrained and shaped by non-semiotic features of social structure, again, taking us a step beyond the model of the interaction of participation and reification that Wenger offers.

LANGUAGE AND BROADER SOCIAL STRUCTURES

The relationship between interactions in communities and broader social structures is not explored in detail in Wenger's model, and the tools developed within critical social linguistics can address this weakness.

Wenger's work provides a powerful demonstration of the fact that we all live out our lives and our learning within different configurations of communities of practice. Therefore, analysis of the workings of these communities can potentially give useful insights into the processes by means of which broader social structures are constructed and sustained. However, whereas the work Wenger published with Jean Lave (Lave and Wenger 1991) was explicitly driven by a critical social science agenda (particularly in studying learning in its relationship to social justice), the later work (Wenger 1998) seems more about understanding and facilitating learning for its own sake. Wenger's recent collaboration with McDermott and Snyder (Wenger, McDermott, and Snyder 2002), and his website CPSquare (http://www.cpsquare.com/), are very much oriented towards the corporate market, setting out the advantages for businesses in facilitating the growth of communities of practice in the workplace.

In contrast, critical social linguistics seeks explicitly to understand and challenge the role of discourse in perpetuating broader relations in contemporary society. Detailed analysis of discourse – i.e., 'language as social practice' (Fairclough and Wodak 1997) – is used to identify the broader patterns which constitute and sustain social relations, particularly relations of inequality. To see 'language as social practice' is to understand variations in language as being structured not merely through the syntactical and lexical constraints of language itself, but also socially. Fairclough (2003) argues that, in different social settings and within different networks of social practices, there are particular configurations of genres: ways of acting and interacting, discourses: ways of representing, and styles: ways of being or identities. Discourses, genres and styles all influence one another within and across particular networks of social practices. He refers to this combination of discourse, genre and style in a particular social field as its 'semiotic order', the possibilities and constraints of which have a powerful effect on the semiosis which is actualised.

This model therefore gives a framework for the analysis of semiosis as it is socially structured and for relating local semiotic interaction and the mechanisms and processes of more global social orders. Examining local interaction in communities of practice with this model in mind would enable us to develop clearer understandings of how these processes reproduce and change structures and processes in the broader social order, in a way which Wenger's analyses currently do not address.

INTERACTION AS THE 'NURSERY FOR CHANGE'

In addition, the critical social linguistics model of the relationship between language and broader social structures does not assume this is a stable relationship. Wenger's work has been criticised for offering a fairly static model of the communities of practice (Engeström et al. 1999, Contu and Willmott 2003). Despite developing a detailed conceptualisation of the processes by means of which individuals engage in learning and move in and out of communities of practice, the theory offers a fairly unchanging image of the communities themselves. While communities of practice are understood as being centrally about ongoing processes of negotiation of meaning, much more attention is given to how these processes maintain communities in existence than to how communities themselves change.

Of course, ideas about learning are at the heart of the communities of practice model, and learning is always about change in some respect. Fairclough, Jessop and Sayer (2002) draw on Wenger's work, as well as on that of Jean Lave (1988), to argue that learning – as they conceptualise it, as "active participation in the innovative meaning-making practices of a community" – can be seen as productive of change in knowledge, social relations and social identities and therefore in semiotic form in discourses, genres and styles. But again, the attention is more on how individuals learn to become members of particular communities. The processes by means of which communities of practice change, and the ways these communities are affected by and affect change in the social order more generally, are not explored in depth.

This is brought into relief by comparing it with Fairclough's dialectical conceptualisation of social practice, in which social practices are seen as inherently unstable, and the dynamics of social change are a central concern. A significant motivation for critical social linguistics is to understand and potentially influence processes of social change, and it is argued that attention to discourse gives particular insights into their workings. One of the reasons given for this is that, following Volosinov, Chouliaraki and Fairclough argue (1999:48) that the "analysis of the discourse moment of a social practice can give insights into its dynamism which are not available from other moments". This is because discourse is shaped both by the social order, and by the ongoing activity and struggle involved in every interaction. This activity and struggle cause transformations in discourse which reflect and construct change in the social order more broadly. Since social practices depend on social interaction for their continuation and transformation, Chouliaraki and Fairclough describe interaction as 'the nursery for change' (1999:38). It is therefore argued that analysing discourse in interaction gives a useful handle on the analysis of processes of broader social change and transformation.

This gives both a rationale for the analysis of processes of local interaction and a means through which this analysis can be used to offer insight into broader processes of social change, which the communities of practice model does not currently offer.

APPROACHING LANGUAGE ANALYSIS

To summarise, the argument is that critical social linguistics offers some ways of conceptualising and analysing the role of language in communities of practice which could potentially extend the theory. The linguistic aspects of the participations and reifications identified by Wenger are understood as being situated within a particular semiotic order, which shapes (and is shaped by) the way meaning is negotiated in the community of practice. The local and the broader social orders are understood to be articulated in inherently unstable

ways, and the focus on language gives us a way of understanding
the role of negotiation of meaning both in sustaining communities
and as the 'nursery for change'. The relationship between semiosis
and other elements of social practice is understood in terms of reciprocal internalisation. This model enables us to extend the theory
of communities of practice by addressing the relationship between
the language used in the immediate situation of the community of
practice, and the broader social forces and structures within which
the community is situated.

These concepts remain on the theoretical level without analytical
tools by means of which the way language can be said to 'reciprocally
internalise' the other elements of social practice can be addressed. I
will close by briefly returning to the Alinsu vignette to demonstrate
how these ideas could be operationalised in looking at data from this
particular community of practice, to show the role of language in constructing and maintaining the relationships within this community
of practice, the way this community of practice is related to broader
social trends such as the introduction of 'new work order' practices
(Gee, Hull and Lankshear 1996) and how focusing on language can
bring out some of the tensions and contradictions involved in this process. This analysis will draw largely on the framework developed by
Fairclough, most recently outlined in a work aimed at non-specialists
(Fairclough 2003).

Fairclough describes a variety of tools that can be used to approach
the analysis of texts from the perspective outlined above. He suggests a model of social life which sees what actually happens, 'social
events', as being shaped by more abstract and general potentialities,
'social structures'. The relationship between events and structures is
mediated by networks of 'social practices', patterns and regularities
which make some possibilities more likely to occur than others in
a given context. Events are constructed by people – social agents –
involved in events, who draw on practices to shape their behaviour.

Written and spoken language texts are one of the elements of social
events, and Fairclough's approach to textual analysis starts from this
perspective, looking at texts as they are involved in social events.
(I have already made the case for looking at language in particular
above and will not reiterate it here.) He suggests that there are a
range of ways of using language associated with any network of

social practice and refers to this discursive aspect of social practice as its 'order of discourse'. This order of discourse is what social agents draw on to mediate between the potentialities of language structure and the actualities of what ends up being said or written in any given event.

Drawing on ideas from systemic-functional linguistics (see, e.g., Halliday 1978, 1985), Fairclough identifies three key functions which language fulfils. Language is used to represent the world in some way (Representation), language is used to express personal and social identities (Identification), and language is itself part of what is going on, the action of the event (Action). As mentioned above, at the level of the possibilities of the order of discourse, he labels these 'discourses' (potential ways of representing things), 'styles' (potential ways of expressing identity through language) and 'genres' (potential ways of using language in the situation). He suggests a range of ways of analysing aspects of texts related to genre, discourse and style.

In terms of discourses, Fairclough suggests that we think about the way social events are represented in texts – and the way different groups of people associated with different social positions represent the world – by examining questions such as what is excluded or included in texts; the relative abstractness or concreteness of representations; and the way processes and relationships, social actors, time and place are represented.

In terms of styles, he suggests that we examine aspects of identification such as modality, that is, what people commit themselves to in a text, with respect to truth (epistemic modality), with respect to obligation (deontic modality) and with respect to values (evaluation, including both explicit evaluative statements and perhaps, more importantly, implicit value assumptions, which are often the main sources of value judgements in texts).

In terms of genres, we can look at the generic structure of texts – there exist some highly standardised genre structures, such as the newspaper article patterning of 'headline, lead paragraph, satellite paragraphs', or the classroom discourse patterning of 'elicitation, response, evaluation'. However, there also exist far less standardised ways of using language, in less ritualised activities, which can be examined in terms of genre. Other aspects of the way language is used in the interaction include things like the types of exchange which are used in a given setting (whether information or knowledge is being exchanged through statements and questions, or whether the exchange is oriented to action through offers and demands) and the grammatical mood of the language (declarative, imperative and interrogative).

Fairclough suggests that, by taking this approach, the analyst can bring together examination of the 'internal relations' of the text (the way the text is constructed semantically and grammatically), and its 'external relations' with the other elements of the social events concerned (how texts figure as part of the actions, identifications and representations that are going on), to allow us to answer broader questions about the role of language in social life.

RE-EXAMINING ALINSU FROM A LANGUAGE PERSPECTIVE

The previous chapter in this volume has already explored the way in which the situation described in Wenger's initial vignette is distinctive, as a 1990s office work environment, showing tensions between the 'new' and the 'old' work orders. We see the introduction of 'total quality management' practices, with the joint emphasis on processors meeting 'quality' and 'production' targets, and each processor being expected to monitor their own performance against these criteria. The social relations enacted through practice show an attempt to introduce egalitarian practices (decisions taking place in regular 'team meetings', for instance), but examining the language used shows that hierarchical relationships clearly structure much of what is going on. Looking at genre aspects of the team meetings, they are used principally as ways in which the supervisor conveys information and directives to staff. Looking at the discourses of the workplace, the way participants are represented is by means of their labels as a particular 'level' of processor, and a clear distinction is made between those who are called 'processors' and those who are called 'supervisors'. In terms of 'style', a great deal of deference is expected from, and shown to, the important visitors in the afternoon.

In more general terms, this interaction is framed within a capitalist context in which people's economic survival depends on them selling their labour to a powerful employer, who defines the work that they need to do, its value and the hours in which they need to do it. We see elements of the resulting alienation from work in the understandings the processors share about clock-watching; in the separation bet-ween the tedium of 'work' and the exciting stories shared about 'life', where the weekend becomes a privileged space for 'escapades' which are then recounted as entertainment in the workplace during breaks and lunch hours; in the way people look forward to their breaks and carefully negotiate as much time as possible away from their desks; in the pressure people feel to meet their 'production' and 'quality' targets; and in the stress that they encounter when they do not do so and their job is threatened.

A focus on the way language is used is one way of gaining insights into the way these tensions are played out in interaction. I will take the example of the use of language in the unit meeting described on pp. 24–26 of Wenger (1998). While the possibilites for linguistic analysis are limited by not having a transcript of a meeting to work with and the fact that this is a constructed vignette rather than a representation of actual events, looking at it in this way nevertheless gives an idea of what can be achieved through focussing on language. We will see in particular how the hierarchical power relationships which structure this workplace are constructed and maintained by the way language is used in meetings.

The unit meeting is an event in which language is central. Using Fairclough's term, the meeting is an accepted 'genre' of activity, one in which there are shared understandings about the ways people in the meeting act, interact and use language. The participants know where and how to sit, who can speak at which points and who is in control of turn-taking and of opening and closing the 'official' parts of the meeting. Before the official start, there is "a mixture of local chat with interjections across the semi-circle. The atmosphere is generally relaxed and the talking as well as the configuration convey a sense of familiar conviviality." At this point in the meeting, language is serving the identificational function of expressing friendliness and interest in one another, as well as the representational one of sharing news and information. The processors are positioned by their use of language as equals and as friends; the hierarchies of 'Level 5' and 'Level 6' processors are not made salient by their use of language at this point.

However, there is one clear demarcation, between processors and supervisors. It is the supervisor, Harriet, who checks whether every-one is there, and it is Harriet who has the right to use language to

redefine the starting point of the meeting: "We'll wait for her." The beginning of the meeting is signalled when Harriet starts giving people
instructions: asking them to clear their desks for the visit of the important clients and asking them to make sure they don't 'fool around'
while the visitors are there. This both conveys information (Representation) and positions Harriet as being in a position of superiority,
having the right to issue instructions and expect that they will be
obeyed (Identification and Action). The expression 'fool around' is
an informal one but also one which positions the processors in a
somewhat childlike way.

The hierarchical arrangement of the processors into levels is then
made salient when Harriet announces that the vacation list needs to
be filled out in order of seniority. The relations of power in the workplace are reinforced when Harriet tells people about the problem with
the toll-free number being used for personal calls and informs them
that calls longer than fifteen minutes will be monitored. The response
to this is grumbling and defensive remarks, which are acceptable
within the context of the meeting. Active resistance, however, is not
expressed; within what it is acceptable to say during a meeting of this
kind, a position of explicit rejection of the surveillance would be less
easy to take up.

There follows a discussion about the introduction of a dedicated
telephone answering unit, and Harriet invites contributions from the
processors about this. Ariel, along with many of the other processors, has ambivalent feelings about this. However, Harriet does not
ask people whether or not it should happen; she "asks for sugges-
tions, and requests that processors think about how they would want
to go about implementing such an idea". It is made clear that the
decision-making power is held higher up in the hierarchy and that
the contribution required from processors is merely to work out ways
in which the decisions taken above them can be enforced.

A memo is circulated which modifies the codes processors are
supposed to use, and Harriet goes through it orally, paraphrasing
each item and allowing people to ask questions. She retains control
of the interaction by working through the memo in this way. Whatever impact such a change may have on processors' work, the only
response they can express, without explicitly challenging Harriet's
interactional control, is to learn and understand the new codes.

It is only when Harriet's business is concluded that other people are permitted to speak, demonstrating her power in controlling the agenda of the meeting. The hierarchy is maintained by the fact that the next person to speak is the assistant supervisor, who complains about there being too many overpayments and blames this on a deficit in the processors, assuming that they do not check eligibility carefully enough. Only then is it time for the other processors to contribute. There is a reminder from Nancy about physical therapy, and finally Beliza asks about a specific issue she is having difficulty with: "Well, for me, it's just this deductible".

At this point, the nature of the interaction shifts. It is instructive to compare the description of this discussion with the discussion about the new codes. Whereas in the discussion about the codes, Harriet was in control of the interaction, of who speaks and when, and of what is spoken about, when Beliza asks her question about the deductible, "an animated discussion ensues with everyone contributing examples and partial explanations until Beliza seems satisfied." This is a different type of spoken interaction, where turn-taking decisions are distributed among the group as a whole, and no single individual is in control of the interaction.

The final event of the meeting is a cake-cutting ceremony, in honour of the recent birthday of Sara, the assistant supervisor. This shifts the genre of the interaction from 'meeting' to 'celebration', and the sorts of speaking that are expected are different: applause and cheers, rather than questions and answers. But this is taking time away from work, and within this capitalist work culture, the processors are paid on the understanding that their work time is spent actually engaged in processing. The supervisor's conclusion of the meeting, "Well, it was nice seeing all your faces again", is consonant with this, as is the processors' discussion afterwards about "whether the cake-cutting part of the meeting should be considered morning break".

Note, too, that Harriet's remark is an implicit closure of the meeting, relying on processors' shared understandings of what counts as a 'close'. The relationships between supervisor and processor are constructed as being informal enough that an explicit close of the meeting is not necessary; but the hierarchy remains, with the supervisor expecting people to 'read between the lines' and understand what this remark means, and also expecting them to return to their desks before they have finished eating the cake. This underlines the fact that, although the cake-cutting ceremony shows elements of a social situation, the dominant genre is still that of 'meeting'and the dominant values are those of 'work'; in a purely social situation, it would be unacceptably rude to cut into people's eating time in this way.

We see here how language use both constructs and internalises the social relationships of the workplace, and the way processors' time and work are controlled by those higher up the hierarchy. We see the unstable articulation of the social order in the workplace here in the contradictions between the egalitarian social relationships of chat and cake-cutting and the hierarchical power relationships of an-nouncing surveillance of people's telephone calls – limiting people's responses to the introduction of a phone unit and chiding proces-sors for allowing overpayments. The potential for interaction to act as a 'nursery for change' is controlled here by Harriet's control of the agenda of the meeting. Nevertheless, we see joint sense-making taking place among the processors following Beliza's query, and it is possible to see how such a group could potentially develop new ways of doing things and resistance to practices imposed from above in similar interactions.

However, as is clear from the rest of the vignette, this interaction takes place within a setting where for the processors to keep their job they have to fit in with the stringent criteria of 'quality' and 'pro-duction' that management require of them. Processors who do not achieve the goals set by management are placed on warning; and if they do not improve, they lose their jobs. Given this control of peo-ple's livelihoods, within a system where not only income but also health and other social benefits depend on a steady job, the hierar-chical control which management can display over workers and the playing out of this control within interaction become easier to explain.

CONCLUSION

In this chapter, I have argued that since Wenger's model of the com-munity of practice places the negotiation of meaning at the heart of his understanding of practice, it is an omission not to consider in more depth the role of language and other forms of semiosis within this, and the relationships between processes of meaning making and other social dynamics. An examination of the vignette which opens Wenger's 1998 work demonstrated the centrality of language to the processes of negotiation of meaning which construct and maintain communities of practice. I have argued that critical social linguistics offers a fruitful way of conceptualising the role of language within this situation, giving us better understandings of the relationships between language and other social processes, and between local interaction and broader social structures. I have argued that attention to language use within communities of practice offers a better understanding of the dynamics of participation and reification, and in particular that the lens of critical social linguistics can offer ways of conceptualising the role of local interaction in sustaining broader social structures and relationships and give us ways to see interaction as the 'nursery for change', as well as the means by which communities of practice are continued. Finally, taking a 'language look' at the team meeting described in the vignette was used as an example to demonstrate how paying attention to language use can give us insights into the way in which broader social structures and power relationships are played out and maintained within the dynamics of participation and reification in a particular community of practice.

References

Chouliaraki, L. and N. Fairclough (1999) *Discourse in Late Modernity: Rethinking Critical Discourse Analysis*. Edinburgh: Edinburgh University Press.

Contu, A. and H. Willmott (2003) Re-embedding situatedness: the importance of power relations in learning theory. *Organization Science* 14 (3) 283–296.

Engeström, Y., R. Miettinen and R.-L. Punamäki (eds) (1999) *Perspectives on Activity Theory*. Cambridge and New York: Cambridge University Press.

Fairclough, N. (2003) *Analysing Discourse: Textual Analysis for Social Research*. London and New York: Routledge.

Fairclough, N., B. Jessop and A. Sayer (2002) Critical Realism and Semiosis. Department of Sociology, Lancaster University. [On-line] Available at: http://www.comp.lancs.ac.uk/sociology/papers/fairclough-jessop-sayer-critical-realism-and-semiosis.pdf.

Fairclough, N. and R. Wodak (1997) Critical discourse analysis. In T. van Dijk (ed), *Discourse Studies: A Multidisciplinary Introduction*, vol. 2. London: Sage.

Gee, J. P., G. Hull and C. Lankshear (1996) *The New Work Order: Behind the Language of the New Capitalism*. Sydney: Allen and Unwin.

Halliday, M. A. K. (1978) *Language as Social Semiotic: The Social Interpretation of Language and Meaning*. London: Edward Arnold.

Halliday, M. A. K. (1985) *An Introduction to Functional Grammar*. London: Edward Arnold.

Harvey, D. (1996) *Justice, Nature and the Geography of Difference*. Oxford: Blackwell.

Lave, J. (1988) *Cognition in Practice: Mind, Mathematics and Culture in Everyday Life*. Cambridge: Cambridge University Press.

Lave, J. and E. Wenger (1991) *Situated Learning: Legitimate Peripheral Participation*. Cambridge: Cambridge University Press.

Wenger, E. (1998) *Communities of Practice: Learning, Meaning, and Identity*. Cambridge: Cambridge University Press.

Wenger, E., R. McDermott and W. M. Snyder (2002) *Cultivating Communities of Practice: A Guide to Managing Knowledge*. Boston: Harvard Business School Press.

3

Mediating Allegations of Racism in a Multiethnic London School

What Speech Communities and Communities of Practice Can Tell Us About Discourse and Power

Angela Creese

INTRODUCTION

In this paper, I will examine two approaches to the study of community to understand what kind of purchase they can give on a small piece of ethnographic data from a large multicultural London secondary school. The first approach has emerged from linguistic anthropology and is the notion of a *speech community* developed by Hymes (1968, 1972, 1974) and Gumperz (1972, 1982, 1999). The second is the *community of practice* developed by Lave and Wenger (1991) and Wenger (1998), and emerging from psychology and education, but also widely used today in management studies and by the commercial sector and its consultancies.

An argument is made that, despite its concern with *shared repertoire*, the learning theory of communities of practice lacks a coherent theory of language in use. Despite its emphasis on negotiation of meaning, we are given little insight into how meanings are made and interpreted. It lacks the infrastructure to explain the role language plays in social life. The notion of speech community, on the other hand, stems from the tradition of linguistic anthropology which has developed a coherent theory of language and the tools to describe and explain language use. Within the linguistic anthropological tradition, language is seen as working through a complex interplay of signs and symbols. Language is fundamentally social and performs a variety of functions, all of which define it as a cultural artefact which has its foundations in the organization of humankind and its culture. In the words of Sapir, language is "able to ticket off experience associated with whole groups, delimited classes, or experience rather than with the single experiences themselves" (Sapir 1921:8). Sapir views language as social action; most particularly, as communicative action (Lucy 1993:18). Language relies on interpretants through which the sign-referent relationship is mediated. Meaning is not transmitted but is actively created through the interpretation of 'signs'. Nothing is a sign unless it is interpreted as a sign (Sapir 1921, Peirce 1955). I will show that the notion of speech community is more able to give a purchase on the data presented because of its ability to show how language functions within a context. It is able to describe and explain how participants come to share a particular repertoire and how a discourse comes to dominate.

The chapter is organised along the following lines. Firstly, a selective overview of the two theoretical positions underlying the terms 'speech community' and 'community of practice' is set out. Secondly, data from an ethnographic study of a multilingual London secondary school is presented, the bulk of which comes from two student-produced texts regarding an accusation of racism. Thirdly, a discussion section examines the descriptive and explanatory power the two different theoretical positions bring to explaining the ethnographic data from an urban multicultural and multilingual school.

THEORETICAL BACKGROUND: SPEECH COMMUNITY
AND COMMUNITY OF PRACTICE

Both approaches to the study of community have their tradition in a resistance to notions of a normative human subject. In the case of speech community, this has already been well documented. Hymes accused linguistics of taking a 'Garden of Eden' view of language which presented an ideal speaker – an unmotivated cognitive mechanism, not a person in the social world (Hymes 1972:273). At the time, Hymes rallied against not only linguistics in failing to incorporate a sociocultural standpoint, but also anthropology for its failure to utilize speech as a means of explaining social behaviour. He described the role of speech in human behaviour within anthropology as being 'honoured in anthropological principle, if sometimes slighted in practice' (Hymes 1968:99). Out of these debates, Hymes developed the ethnography of speaking (and later ethnography of communication) (Hymes 1968, 1974). The ethnography of communication combines an etic framework which consists of a list of universal components and functions constituting speech events alongside an emic focus which aims to describe and understand the local meaning-making processes of participants' language in use. It is this emic perspective which defines the ethnography of communication as a departure from earlier normative and functionalist models of language use.

Similarly, communities of practice have their tradition in resisting normative approaches to teaching, learning and assessment. Lave explored and developed the term *'practice'* as an argument against functional theory.

[t]he functionalist position contains a theory of learning: in particular, that children can be taught general cognitive skills if these 'skills' are disembedded from the routine contexts of their use. Schooling reflects these ideas at a broad organisational level, as it separates children from the contexts of their own and their families' daily lives. At a more specific level, classroom tests put the principle to work: they serve as a measure of individual, 'out of context' success (Lave 1988:8–9)

In contrast to functionalist theories, Lave sought to develop a theory of learning that would accord legitimacy to different knowledges. Vann and Bowker (2002) give an interesting account of how this led Lave and later Lave and Wenger and Wenger to work towards an ethnographic methodology which could understand and account for individual differences in learning.

'Practice' emerges as an instrument of a de-reifying, critical social theory crafted to problematize the prominence of normative functional models as formal educational assessment techniques. It is de-reifying precisely in how it distances itself from the normative impositions of 'structure' as found in the functionalist framework, through an appeal to a living process that such impositions would have obscured. . . . To study practice is to study a lived-in world. It is to see the reality that the normative model will have missed. It is an ethnographic seeing that does not impose normative reifications and as such sees a kind of pre-reified knowledge-bearing subject. It is to build a new scientific object. The object of this science is practice. (Vann and Bowker 2002:6–8)

In 1991, Lave and Wenger developed their investigation of 'practice' as a scientific object through their study of apprenticeships. This work emphasised the seemingly invisible character of learning and work practices and helped to make obvious the deeply social nature of learning and knowing. Communities of practice therefore draw on theories of learning which place social practice at the centre of learning. Learning is viewed as situated, distributed and shared.

So far, I have shown what the two approaches to the study of community share in terms of a commitment to non-normative positions. They also share a commitment to ethnography as a research methodology. Below, I begin to outline where the two views of community differ. I do this first by revisiting definitions of the terms speech community and community of practice.

DEFINITIONS

Within the ethnography of communication, a speech community is defined as 'a community sharing knowledge of rules for the conduct and interpretation of speech. Such sharing comprises knowledge of at least one form of speech, and knowledge also of its patterns of use' (Hymes 1974:51). And, similarly from Gumperz (1982:24), 'a group of speakers who share rules and norms for the use of language'. Although there has been a recent softening of the phrase 'rules of language use' to 'patterns of language use' (see Erickson, 1990, 1996), ethnographers of communication continue to use Hymes and Gumperz's original work to look for continuities and patterns in how a community is shaped by language use and how language use shapes a community. This is achieved by approaching the study of community as if it is complex and diverse.

If one analyses the language of a community as if it should be homogenous, its diversity trips one up around the edges. If one starts with the analysis of the diversity, one can isolate the homogeneity that is truly there. (Hymes 1972:276)

One starts with a social group and considers the entire organisation of linguistic means within it (Hymes 1974:51)

In Hymes and Gumperz's work on speech community, the study of communication is culturally framed and communicatively constituted. It is the speech activity of a community which is the primary object of attention. Rampton (1998:3) points out that, for Hymes and Gumperz, speech community functions as an ontological marker, "a necessary primary term in that it postulates the basis of description as a social, rather than a linguistic entity". Indeed, Hymes' concern with the social in linguistics has driven his other key analytical tools, such as communicative competence, speech situations, events and acts. The speech community provided the starting point for Hymes to look at ways of speaking within it.

The ethnography of speaking is concerned with the situations and uses, the patterns and functions, of speaking as an activity in its own right. (Hymes 1968:101)

Others have pointed out the problems of operationalizing 'speech community' (Irvine 1986, in Wolfson 1989; Wolfson 1989; Eckert and McConnell-Ginet 1998). Irvine asks, 'What are the social characteristics of a social unit? I would suggest that the concept of the speech community is still an abstracted, idealised notion that runs into practical problems when you try to opertionalise it in conducting fieldwork' (1986, in Wolfson 1989:51). Eckert and McConnell-Ginet (1998:490) argue that, by choosing a location to study, rather than practice as social engagement, we fall into the danger of defining communities in terms of abstracted characteristics, such as age, gender, ethnicity or social class. "We are then forced into reconstructing the social practice from which the characteristics and linguistic behaviour in question have been abstracted."

Wolfson summarises Hymes as arguing, 'The simplest answer is to begin by looking for groups that have some sort of pre-existing definition apart from speech usage' (Wolfson 1989:50–52). What Hymes is suggesting then for his speech community is an already socially organised unit formed around either location and/or (non linguistic) social practice and activity.

A community of practice is defined in different terms. Lave and Wenger (1991) define community of practice as "a set of relations among persons, activity, and world, over time and in relation with other tangential and overlapping communities of practice" (1991:98). In 1998, Wenger built on this work where he made explicit the association between practice and community. His concern was partly to show how communities are coherent through their practices. The dimensions of community practice are:

- *mutual engagement* in which participants are engaged in actions whose meanings they negotiate with one another,
- *joint enterprise* which is the result of a collective process of situated negotiation which feeds back into practice and
- *a shared repertoire* which results in the creation of resources and artefacts belonging to the community and used for negotiating meaning (1998: Chapter 2).

The defining feature of this view of community is around social practice and activity. An existing social unit located geographically is not the starting place; although, of course, participants may very well be located in one particular setting.

This view of community also comes with its critics. Eraut (2002:3) argues that very little attention is given to how the communities themselves change, and that Lave and Wenger consistently emphasise commonalities rather than diversity. Engeström (1999:12) argues, "the instability and inner contradictions of practice are all but missing from Lave and Wenger's accounts". Those who criticise Wenger argue that his theory cannot account for how a set of relations among persons changes as contradictions appear in the practice.

DIFFERENCES

The two views of community come from different academic traditions and have as their unit of analysis a different focus. The Ethnography of Communication (together with its micro-partner, interactional sociolinguistics) comes from a tradition of anthropology and the study of culture. It is dedicated to explaining situated language use and is concerned with the communication activity of a community and how that community (and its culture) is constituted and constitutes itself through its participants' language use. Importantly, this description is achieved through reaching for the emic perspectives of the discursive practices among community participants; that is, through understanding how participants come to collectively presuppose or articulate discursive patterns themselves in their community practices. This tradition looks at how meanings are represented, nego-tiated and interpreted in discourse. It attempts to capture both the dis-cursive rituals and practices of a community, and also the processual formation of context and the significance of language as contingent phenomena in creating meaning and calling up social knowledge (Gumperz 1999).

Communities of Practice theory has emerged from the academic tradition of psychology. Not surprisingly, this tradition has focussed on the role communities play in learning. Here, communities are cen-tral to explaining how learning happens through increasing partic-ipation and engagement. The object of study or unit of analysis is learning in practice. The community is therefore defined in terms of the practice work it does. It is constituted through its practice and extended through the development of this practice.

Participation within the community is a core element of this learn-ing process and is reproductive in nature. Newcomers are inducted into communities of practice and continue to acquire competence and status within them. The terms 'newcomers' and 'old-timers' are cen-tral to Lave and Wenger's learning theory which argues that learning happens best through participation in a community of practice (1991). Wenger (1998) developed the notion of participation in his later work, where non-participation is added to participation in the shaping of identities. He argues,

We not only produce our identities through the practices we engage in, but we also define ourselves through practices we do not engage in. Our identities are constituted not only by what we are but also by what we are not. (1998:164)

Wenger goes on to develop 'non-participation' within communities of practice and refines the term by distinguishing between *peripherality* and *marginality* (1998:167). In the former, non-participation is a less than full participation, and it is the non-participation itself which is the enabling factor of participation.

For instance, for a novice not to understand a conversation between old-timers becomes significant because this experience of non-participation is aligned with a trajectory of participation. It is the interaction of participation and non-participation that renders the experience consequential. (1998:167)

In the latter case of marginality, non-participation prevents full participation.

Here it is the non-participation aspect that dominates and comes to define a restricted form of participation (1998:166).

From this perspective, learning takes place through a process of increasing participation in communities of practice.

In Section 1, I have outlined what I consider to be the main tenets of the two approaches to the study of community. I have argued that speech community and communities of practice share an opposition to normative views of the human subject. They are both fundamentally concerned with the role language plays in negotiation and interaction. However, their unit of analysis is different. Those studying speech communities are interested in studying the communicative practices of participants in order to describe both cultural patterns and emergent identity positions. Those studying communities of practice, on the other hand, are interested in how learning is constituted through the practice of community participants. The first is concerned with reading off from discursive practice, cultural understanding and emergent meanings, whereas the second is concerned with presenting a social model of learning.

In Section 2, I present some ethnographic data from a one-year ethnography. The data drawn upon are field notes and site documents from a week-long incident at one school in a much larger and longer study. The incident was an accusation of racism made by one group of girls against another and some of the teachers in the school. It was an explosive event which stopped much of routine teaching of Year 10 (14– to 15-year olds) girls for one day and which continued to create waves of anger throughout the week. Following the presentation of these data, Section 3 is used to consider how the two theoretical positions outlined above can give us a purchase on the school community described.

SKONNINGTON SCHOOL AND ITS
TURKISH-SPEAKING STUDENTS

The school is a lively mixture of colours, cultures, languages and differences housed in an old and rather bleak Victorian building on the side of a busy road. The school is a single-sex girls' school. Over 90% of the students are listed as having English as an additional language (EAL). The largest linguistic minority during the data collection period was Turkish-speaking.

The Turkish-speaking minority consist of an older more established Turkish Cypriot community and newer Turkish/Kurdish-speaking refugees. Both have settled in the same areas of London. The more recent group has come to Britain as political refugees caught in the cross-fire of the Turkish Government's battle with the separatist Kurdistan Workers' Party, a left-wing Kurdish revolutionary group fighting for an independent Kurdistan. Those seen as promoting or even supporting any form of Kurdish autonomy or rights within Turkey are dealt with harshly by the Turkish state (see Amnesty International report indexes: EUR 44/87/95 and EUR 44/80/95; Refugee Council Factsheet 1995). Since the late 1980s and increasingly so in the 1990s, large numbers of Turks and Turkish/Kurdish-speaking Kurds from mainland Turkey arrived. The group tended to be highly politicised (Campbell 1994). Despite the numbers of people involved, very little research exists on the Turkish-speaking communities in London (Ladbury 1977, Mehmet Ali 1991, Institute of Education 1999).

We now move to look at how a particular incident in the school impacted on the school community. Data consist of two student-produced texts distributed to passersby and visitors to the school, and ethnographic field notes written up as analytic vignettes of the two-day event (Erickson 1990).

INSTITUTIONAL RACISM OR EQUAL OPPORTUNITIES?

On 12 October 1994, at 8:45 a.m., I entered Skonnington School as I had done for the previous five weeks to collect data for the ethnographic study I was conducting on the relationships, roles and talk of EAL teachers and the mainstream subject curriculum teachers with whom they worked. However, this day was immediately different. It started with a demonstration of 20–25 bilingual (Kurdish)Turkish/English-speaking girls from the school who were outside the school gates with banners and a loudhailer saying 'Black and White Unite Against Racism' and 'Beep your Horn if you are Against Racism'.

The girls were also distributing the following text to passersby and to teachers who had gone out to speak to them.

Text One

**WE WANT TEACHERS NOT TO DIVIDE US
BUT TO GIVE BETTER EDUCATION**

On 11 October a group of students started arguing with the other groups of Turkish and Kurdish students.[1]

They all forced them to get into a room and blackmailed, so that they don't tell the teachers about this. There wasn't a good reason for this. But only prejudice. That is not the first time its happened, it continues for years and years in our school. Also we are aware of that the students in schools of Borough X are facing the same problems. And attacks on the students is not the only problem in our school. Briefly the problems we are facing are;

1. When there is a complain about the foods we get, what staff tell is if the food is cleaner in your country then go back to your own country.
2. Some of our teachers e.g. the English teacher Miss X is insulting the students especially refugees.
3. The teachers in Skonnington school and other schools are treating to the students depending on their nationalities. While the other students get rid of everything, some students especially Turkish and Kurdish students are being blame.
4. By this they are trying to divide the students into aparts. We know that all the problems that we are facing can be solved. The teachers and the management of the school do not want to solve the problems deliberately.

The students have nothing to attack each other. We only want to study and be educated in better methods. Students should be united against all other problems we are facing in our school. But the school management is avoiding this by dividing the students

---

[1] According to the girls demonstrating outside, the 'group of students' with whom they were arguing were African Caribbean, and it was also this group of girls which the demonstrating girls felt were being given preferential treatment by the teachers.

in spite of their nationalities. We don't want our teachers to divide us, we just want better education. We don't want racism in our schools, we want to unite with all black and white students. That is why we are having the boycout in our school and our demands are as follows.

1. We don't want any racist teachers in our school, especially, Mrs X.
2. We don't want teachers and managements to divide students by their nationalities.
3. we want them to consider all the complaints that we have e.g. foods, bullying.
4. Our only demand is to have friendly and egual education for all students

(Spelling and punctuation as in the original.)

Later in the day, this was followed by a second text, written by a different group of girls, African Caribbean and black mixed heritage, who were contesting the writers of text one's account. This text was distributed to students and teachers within the school community and also to the local BBC network who had arrived at lunch time.

Text Two

STOP FOOLING AROUND

Due to recent letters that have been received by the students outside of Skonnington that are against your silly boycott we feel that you are making a mockery out of yourselves.

Nothing will be resolved if you carry on acting like immature little 5 year olds. This is only to make you see what fools you are. Some of us think that you are right to appeal against your rights but not in this manner. By holding up banners and posters saying that **'black and white unite'** has no meaning because most of the people or students like each other and have no means for racism so we all think by what you are doing is wrong.

You are making our school reputation go down and you are hurting a lot of peoples feelings by what you are doing although you might have already noticed. Maybe what you are doing is right but you have no feelings and consideration of what other people think of you. Many turkish and kurdish people are not protesting because they feel that nothing will not be resolved and that they also think it is wrong.

   We gather that some people are racist but a fact is that everybody in a way is racist and that includes all of the kurdish and turkish people. Fair enough we admit some of the students can be rascist but that does not allow you to bring any of the teachers into it and by doing that you have made things worse.
   STUDENTS THAT CARE !!!

(Spellings, bold and punctuation as in the original.)

It is clear from even an initial reading that the writers of texts one and two present the school community and teachers very differently in the two accounts.

Text one constructs the teachers as racists and divisive:

Teachers:
- insult refugees
- treat students differently depending on their national backgrounds
- single out Turkish and Kurdish pupils for blame
- divide students against one another
- let problems go unsolved and do not follow up complaints

While text two constructs the teachers as victims.
Teachers:

- have been hurt
- are having their reputation damaged
- are the same as anyone else

In text one, the writers present themselves as united with the rest of the student community.

Students
- should not attack one another
- are united in their need for better and fairer education

In text two, on the other hand, present the student writers of text one as different from the rest of the student community.

Student writers of text one are:
- silly; immature; like five-year-olds; fools; wrong; hurtful
- not supported by other Turkish/Kurdish-speaking students
- have no feelings and show no consideration

In text one, claims of difference are highlighted, particularly ethnic difference and unfair treatment by the school of these differences. Text one writers bring to the fore ethnic identity markers. Much is made about the differential treatment of different ethnic groups in the school. The writers present themselves as fighting against the 'establishment'. They index particular genres of writing. Text one reads as a revolutionaries' political manifesto in which the unfair treatment of different ethnic groups is central.

Text two exemplifies an equal opportunities discourse. It builds upon the notion of a school community to which both teachers and students belong and within which they are all equal. In this text, only one group is held outside it: the writers of text one. The writers of text two attempt to isolate these students, not only from their ethnic group who they aspire to represent, but also from the rest of the school community.

Text two endorses the school's discourse of 'we are all the same' under a rubric of equal opportunities and distances itself from the discourse of challenge put forth in text one. The student writers of text two use a very different genre from the 'political manifesto' of text one. Rather, they appear more to be writing in the style of a letter to a media editor of some kind. Indeed, the BBC was one of their intended audiences because at the time of writing the girls knew the film crew would be visiting the school. Moreover, little is made of difference of any kind within the school. Ethnicity is played down, as are differences between teachers and students, being mentioned only to claim that the dissonant group is not representing the Turkish/Kurdish group. It is shared agendas which are constructed here with racism attributed to everyone rather than a particular group.

LEGITIMATE AND NON-LEGITIMATE PROTESTS

The school has a clearly preferred message in text two. This message presented the school as a community in which all its participants were treated equally around issues of learning, discipline, procedure, ethnicity and race. It was this message, via text two, which was handed to the local BBC network when the camera crew turned up just after lunch. The head teacher herself was advised by the local educational officers not to speak to the BBC film crew. However, she did arrange for the writers of text two to speak with the press. I was not present at this meeting. Despite the fact that the head teacher had avoided making direct commentary to the media, she had gone some way towards effectively managing the kind of messages which the outside world would hear about the school given the rather uncomfortable accusations made by the student writers of text one. In the final event, the local BBC current affairs programme did not run this news item.

The work which went into producing a united community discourse was orchestrated by the head teacher and senior managers, but this is only part of the truth. Their position was not simply 'imposed' from above on the rest of the school community, but also emerged from the teachers and the students themselves, to differing degrees. The writers of text two and many of the teachers recognised the discourse of equal opportunities as being an important ideology in the school community. It was nonparticipation in this discourse which saw the students of text one as (temporarily at least) outside the school 'community'.

STAFF MEETING

During and following the demonstration, the head teacher held a series of ad hoc emergency staff meetings. One of these is reported in detail below:

> *Fieldnotes, 13th October:*
>
> The whole staff is assembled and school is to start late. The headteacher narrates the incident. A lot is made about the reputation of the school. She talks about the successes of the school; names some 'Turkish' girls who have been successful; and what a good reputation the school has for integrating all races. She explains

there have been racist incidents in other schools in the borough but not in this school.

She thanks the staff repeatedly for their support and says she does not want to see staff turn against one another. After she has finished speaking several teachers are selected to give their opinions. She starts with Mr Hakan and Miss Zengin. Both bilingual teachers support the Head's arguments that the group of girls were organized by outside groups; that there is a girl who has been trouble ever since she arrived, agitating the others. Both the bilingual teachers support the school's line that the girls, even if they have grievances should have gone through the regular channels. The majority of teachers who speak, say that girls should be disciplined, that they were lying if they say they did not know about the anti racist policy.

The teachers react angrily to the girls' accusation that the teachers treat the Afro Caribbean girls differently from the Turkish girls because they, the teachers, are afraid of confrontation. The physical education teacher is really angry and says, "that's a load of rubbish."

In the main it is only those who are taking the same line as the headteachers who speak out. Only one teacher offers an alternative view when he says that 'we' the teachers should admire the girls for demonstrating, because we have all done this in our lives, "After all they wouldn't be able to do this in Turkey." While he is speaking, the teacher accused of racism gets up and walks out. He continues saying that we must look into the comment that the girls don't know about the anti racist statement. He is the only teacher to take a different line. Following his comment there is uncomfortable silence. The meeting is near the end and the head teacher tells her teachers she will keep them fully informed.

(Spellings and punctuation as in the original.)

This vignette makes salient some of the interpretations made by the head teacher and her teaching staff of the accusations made in text one. The head teacher developed three arguments against the girls' behaviour. One theme which the students of text one had raised was the lack of follow-up by staff of their grievances when racist incidents occurred. The head teacher did not address this directly, but she (and her teachers) were adamant that the students themselves had not followed the correct procedures. This was central for the head teacher, as it allowed her to show the school as having equal measures for all when dealing with racism. There seems to be little awareness that the students might not have followed normal procedure because of their frustrations in the past or that the school had not been successful in making its procedures known.

Related to the discussion of procedures is the second theme the head teacher developed which was the description of the girls as rude and heavily influenced by outsiders. This interpretation of the girls' behaviour was similar to that made by the students in text two. The demonstrators were presented as foolish and easily influenced by others. They were stripped of their intentionality. The girls were presented as outside of the school community because of their rudeness and lack of willingness to play by the school's rules.

A third theme apparent in the field notes is the reaction to accusations of racism and the argument that teachers treat different ethnic groups differently in the school. Teachers were outraged by this suggestion, and a discussion about the feasibility of this could not even be developed in the staff meeting – such was the anger it created. The general consensus was that all groups were treated equally and in the same way within the school.

The interpretations the head teacher and the majority of teachers choose to take up around the event are parallel to those developed by the student writers of text two. Both the staff meeting and text two develop a position of shared and equal agendas. Diversity is celebrated in the same way, with each "multi"-culture treated as if it were equal and the same. Only those teachers who were seen to be central in supporting this discourse were recruited to help in its endorsement. Some teachers were silenced either because their views were considered to be too dangerous or not seen to be relevant. The two bilingual teachers were seen as central to supporting the school's central message and were actively recruited during the staff meeting to lend their voices to the head teacher's.

DISCUSSION

In this section, I apply the theoretical positions implied by the concepts of *speech community* and *community of practice* to the data described in text two. It should be said, in fairness, that the data presented previously was collected using the ethnography of communication/interactional sociolinguistics, and my focus from the start was on ways of communicating within the schools which made up my study and not on how participants learned to become productive participants within that community. It is only after the data collection period ended that I used the communities of practice literature to revisit the data.

In the data I have presented in this chapter, I have used a definition of community built upon location and discursive practice. Firstly, the schools were chosen because they were located in areas of London where the largest linguistic minority were Turkish-speaking and, even more specifically, employed Turkish-speaking EAL teachers operating some form of partnership teaching with the colleagues. Secondly, schools provided the clearest forum to understand how participants interpreted an educational policy in context. From the onset, I constructed Skonnington school as a community as it allowed me to start with an already formed social unit in which I could capture participants' ways of communicating. I went on to consider how these were positioned differently within the school community. Through focussing on the school, I was able to make a social analysis of communication within it and come to an understanding of which discourses were privileged by the school and which were contested. A focus on the sociolinguistic allowed me to reach conclusions about issues of power and dominance in discursive practices (Creese 2003). It allowed me to view the school community as at times conflictual as well as communal.

This view of community was established through a focus on how meanings were created and interpreted by participants from within. In the previous analysis, I have attempted to link a micro-analysis of language functions and forms in the two student-produced letters to an analysis of the wider societal context. I have tried to show how the 'equal opportunities discourse' of the school came to dominate and silence other narratives. To do this, it was necessary to look at the interactions of different participants around the event (see Creese 2002, 2003 for further examples). This involved working within a view of language and interaction as both patterned and influenced by the context in which it took place, but also as flexible and non-deterministic. As Erickson has argued,

We are not just typecast by a single category of social identity throughout an entire encounter. Our social identity is situated in the interaction at hand; we perform it as we go along and we do so conjointly with the other interactional partners. Culture and language style differences, in other words, sometimes made a big difference for the way interaction happened, and sometimes it did not. (Erickson 1996:295)

And similarly Ochs argues,

... in any given actual situation, at any given actual moment, people in those situations are actively constructing their social identities rather than passively living out some cultural prescription for social identity.... A social constructivist perspective allows us to examine the building of multiple, yet perfectly compatible identities – identities that are subtle and perhaps have no label, blended identities, even blurred identities. (Ochs 1993:296, 298)

In the data and analysis I have presented, I have shown that participants' language use indexes particular histories, discourses and written genres. I have also argued that the identities which participants take up through and around the two texts are not fixed around social categories. Thus, ethnicity and linguistic heritages were less important in explaining events than the notion of belonging to the school's speech community. We see participants taking up different alignment positions around the school's response to the two texts. By examining language-in-use through the event, we can understand how participants use language (signs) to mediate and create their contexts. Through analysing the language used in the two texts and around the two texts, we can come to understand how a dominant discourse became contextualised, and how different participants played peripheral and central parts in the construction of marginal and dominant discourses. We come to understand the processes of creating and interpreting particular signs by different participants. We see variety in interpretation but also the building of shared interpretations as one particular discourse comes to dominate. We also see how this impacts on the creation and interpretation of other communicative exchanges.

Wenger (1998) is also very much concerned with negotiation of meaning. We see this in his interest in shared repertoires. According to Wenger, learning happens through participating in particular kinds of social practice which allow for maximal negotiation of meaning. However, he provides us with few tools to describe or understand how this actually happens. We are left without an account of how meanings are made between old-timers and newcomers through negotiation.

Wenger appears to project a view of meaning making which is predominantly concerned with the symbolic and referential functions of language (lexicalised propositional content). He is concerned with participants' shared understanding of practice, that is, how participants come to agree on the meaning of symbols they use to communicate their practice. Like others concerned with learning theories, he can be criticised for privileging the symbol or how signs come to be shared between participants in their teaching and learning of new knowledge (Hasan 2003), that is, through mutual engagement and joint enterprise between old-timers and newcomers. This social activity results in a shared repertoire. However, what is missing from this account is the workings of the actual negotiation process itself and how these micro-processes feed back into bigger discourses and vice versa. Thus, although Wenger professes to be interested in negotiation, he is not able to offer an account of the role it plays in constituting a community. He has much less interest in the indexical/interpersonal nature of language. The notion of indexicality within language provides a tool for understanding how negotiation unfolds. Indexicality allows for an understanding of the contextualisation processes between interactants. It describes how linguistic forms become associated with particular culturally recognised types of communicative events (Silverstein and Urban 1996, Wortham 2003).

The notion of speech community is embedded in a theory of meaning making which sees language use as both patterned and fluid. It offers an account of how participants come to read metapragmatic cues within context. It looks at language as indexical and symbolic and shows how participants use their language to construct new contexts and identities while also working within contextual constraints. It allows the researcher to move between micro- and macro-discourses and offers an explanation of mutuality informing the other. Speech communities are places where identities are situated and in process.

In this chapter, I have argued that the ethnography of communication and interactional sociolinguistics provide the tools of analysis for an understanding of negotiation within community which is lacking in the communities of practice paradigm. Negotiation of meaning and the building of shared repertoires need sociolinguistic explanations in order to account for participants' performance within their social context. Categories such as old-timers and newcomers and their resulting joint repertoires do not capture the complexity of positionings that the student participants took up around the social event described previously. Through the use of analytic tools found within the ethnography of communication and interactional sociolinguistics (such as speech event/act, language function, symbolism, indexicality, contextualization cue and emic perspectives), we can offer an explanation of how participants interact and negotiate their various positions through events and how one particular discourse comes to dominate. The notion of speech community is embedded in a theory of language use which allows the researcher to capture both the patterns and heterogeneity of language use. Views of community which are unable to describe the complexity of language use will not capture diversity, contestation or issues of power.

References

Amnesty International (1995) Turkey: Unfulfilled promise of reform. September. *AI Index: EUR 44/87/95*.

Amnesty International (1995) Turkey: Families of "disappeared" subjected to brutal treatment. September. *AI Index: EUR 44/80/95*.

Blommaert, J. and J. Verschueren (1998) *Debating Diversity: Analysing the Discourse of Tolerance*. London: Routledge.

Campbell, D. (1994) Kurds campaigner escapes shooting. *The Guardian*. December 31. p. 3.

Creese, A. (2002) The discursive construction of power in teacher partnerships: Language and subject specialists in mainstream schools. *TESOL Quarterly 36* (4) 597–616.

Creese, A. (2003) Language, ethnicity and the mediation of allegations of racism: Negotiating diversity and sameness in multilingual school discourses. *International Journal of Bilingual Education and Bilingualism 6* (3–4) 221–236.

Eckert, P. and S. McConnell-Ginet (1998) Communities of practice: where language, gender and power all live. In J. Coates (ed), *Language and Gender: A Reader.* Oxford: Blackledge.

Engeström, Y. (1999) Innovative learning in work teams: analysing cycles of knowledge creation in practice. In Y. Engeström, R. Miettinen and R.-L. Punamäki (eds), *Perspectives on Activity Theory.* Cambridge: Cambridge University Press.

Eraut, M. (2002) Conceptual analysis and research questions: do the concepts of 'learning community' and 'community of practice' provide added value? Paper presented at AERA, New Orleans, LA; April 2002.

Erickson, F. (1990) Qualitative methods. In R. L. Linn and F. Erickson, *Research in Teaching and Learning,* vol. 2. New York: MacMillan Publishing Company.

Erickson, F. (1996) Ethnographic microanalysis. In S. L. McKay and N. H. Hornberger (eds), *Sociolinguistics and Language Teaching.* New York: Cambridge University Press, 283–306.

Gumperz, J. (1982) *Discourse Strategies.* Cambridge: Cambridge University Press.

Gumperz, J. J. (1972) Sociolinguistics and communication in small groups. In J. B. Pride and J. Holmes (eds), *Sociolinguistics.* Harmondsworth: Penguin, 203–224.

Gumperz. J. J. (1999) On interactional sociolinguistic method. In S. Sarangi and C. Roberts (eds), *Talk, Work and Institutional Order.* Berlin: Mouton de Gruyter, 453–471.

Hasan, R. (2003) Semiotic Mediation, Language and Society: Three Exotripic Theories: Vygotsky, Halliday and Bernstein. [On-line] Available at: http://web.uct.ac.za/depts/pgc/sochasan.html. Accessed January 14, 2003.

Hornberger, N. H. (1995) Ethnography in linguistic perspective: understanding school processes. *Language and Education 9* (4) 233–248.

Hymes, D. (1968). The ethnography of speaking. In J. Fishman (ed), *Readings in the Sociology of Language.* The Hague: Mouton, 99–138.

Hymes, D. (1972). On communicative competence. In J. B. Pride and J. Holmes (eds), *Sociolinguistics.* Harmondsworth: Penguin, 269–293.

Hymes, D. (1974) *Foundations in Sociolinguistics: An Ethnographic Approach.* Philadelphia: University of Pennsylvania Press.

Institute of Education (IOE) (1999) *Turkish Cypriot Children in London Schools: A Report for the Turkish Cypriot Forum by the International Centre for Intercultural Studies and the Culture, Communication and Societies Group.* London: University of London Institute of Education.

Ladbury, S. (1977). The Turkish Cypriots: ethnic relations in London and Cyprus. *Between Two Cultures.* Oxford: Basil Blackwell.

Lave, J. (1988) *Cognition in Practice: Mind, Mathematics and Culture in Everyday Life.* Cambridge: Cambridge University Press.

Lave, J. and E. Wenger (1991) *Situated Learning; Legitimate Peripheral Participation*. Cambridge: Cambridge University Press.

Lucy, J. A. (1993) *Reflexive Language*. Cambridge: Cambridge University Press.

MacLure, M. (2003) *Discourse in Educational and Social Research*. Buckingham: Open University Press.

Mehmet Ali, A. (1991). The Turkish speech community. *Multilingualism in the British Isles*, vol. I. London: Longman.

Ochs, E. (1993) *Constructing Social Identity: A Language Socialization Perspective. Research on Language and Social Interaction*. Hillsdale, NJ: Lawrence Erlbaum Associates.

Peirce, C. (1955) *Collected Papers II*. Philosophical writings of Peirce. Selected and edited with an introduction by J. Buchler. New York: Dover. Orginally published as 'The Philosophy of Peirce: Selected Writings. London: Routledge and Kegan Paul, 1940.

Rampton, B. (1998) Speech community. In J. Verschueren, J.-O. Ostman, J. Blommaert and C. Bulcan (eds), *Handbook of Pragmatics*. Amsterdam/ Philadelphia: John Benjamins.

Refugee Council (1995) Kurds: Turkish Kurdish refugees in the UK/Kurds in Turkey. *Refugee Council Factsheet*. January.

Refugee Council (1995) Persecuted at home: destitute in the UK: don't put asylum seekers out on the streets. *Flyer, Refugee Council*.

Sapir, E. (1921) *Language: An Introduction to the Study of Speech*. London: Hart-Davies.

Shaffif, W. B. (1991) Managing a convincing self-presentation: some personal reflections on entering the field. In W. B Shaffif and and R. A. Stebbins (eds), *Experiencing Fieldwork*. Newbury Park: Sage Publications, 72–81.

Silverstein, M. and G. Urban (eds) (1996) *The Natural History of Discourse*. Chicago: University of Chicago Press.

Vann, K. and G. C. Bowker (2002) Instrumentalizing the Truth of Practice. Paper presented at ISCRAT, Amsterdam, the Netherlands, 2002.

Wenger, E. (1998) *Communities of Practice: Learning, Meaning and Identity*. Cambridge: Cambridge University Press.

Wolfson, N. (1989) *Perspectives: Sociolinguistics and TESOL*. Cambridge, MA: Newbury House Publishers.

Wortham, S. (2003) Linguistic anthropology of education: an introduction. In S. Wortham and B. Rymes (eds), *Linguistic Anthropology of Education*. Westport: Praeger Press, 1–30.

4

"I've Picked Some Up from a Colleague"

Language, Sharing and Communities of Practice in an Institutional Setting

Frances Rock

This chapter examines interfaces between the notion of *community of practice* and the sociolinguistic study of a workplace. The workers are all police officers, and the chapter focuses on one tiny aspect of their working lives: the statement and explanation of the right to silence to people under arrest. This focus makes it possible to see how a routine, pervasive work task permeates and becomes permeated by communities of practice. By focussing on one discrete activity which is common to a large organisation, and performed through talk, I am also able to demonstrate how close study of language data can be informed by the community of practice framework and can, in turn, enrich the framework.

INTRODUCTION

Community of practice is an elusive term[1]. Clearly, the term involves *communities* – collectives of people – and *practices* – frameworks of doing. However, those who articulate each concept, typically in oppositional terms, illustrate how far beyond these notions the concept goes. *Community*, here, does not denote socially recognised

---

[1] The term has been appropriated inconsistently. Scollon criticises its use as a common-sense label for computer-mediated collectives (2001:146). Studies of police organisations have tended towards such appropriation in the UK (Allen, Nulden and Sørensen 2002), the Netherlands (Laat 2001; Laat and Broer 2004) and Australia (Andrew 2002): this sense is ignored here.

categories (Wenger 1998a) or relationships; rather, these communities are "'about' something" (Wenger 1998b:4). This makes the concept useful for *socio*linguists, who propose that language serves such 'about-ness' or social engagement, "not the place and not the people as a collection of individuals" (Eckert and McConnell-Ginet 1998:490). *Practice* too conveys more than shared "behaviours" (Meyerhoff 1999:226) or shared ways of "doing things" through talk, convictions or norms (Eckert and McConnell-Ginet 1998:490)[2]. Its extra signification centres on its potential for enabling learning and changing identity (Lave and Wenger 1991:53).

The term, as a whole, presents a particular combination of *practice* and *community* (Holmes and Meyerhoff 1999:174, Eckert and McConnell-Ginet 1999:190) being "defined simultaneously" by each (Eckert and McConnell-Ginet 1998:490) and underpinned by social negotiation (Wenger 1998a:73). Consequently, the framework informatively represents social practices as:

- developing in the habitus over time through sequences of social or mediated actions (Scollon 2001:141)
- transitory and inevitably "unfinalisable" (Scollon, after Bakhtin 2001:167).

The concept thus articulated is highly relevant to the study of police officers who work together in a "dynamic and rapidly changing environment", where legal and regulatory novelty create ever-increasing complexity (Laat and Broer 2004) in settings like the one used for illustration here, the police interview room (see Figure 4.1). It also has "obvious appeal" for sociolinguistic enquiries about how discourse facilitates membership diachronically (Holmes and Meyerhoff 1999:175).

Community of practice further eludes definition because writers tend to downplay (Laat and Broer 2004), even dismiss (Scollon 1998:14), discussion of whether particular collectives constitute such

---

[2] Wenger uses *practice* somewhat erratically, as a mass and a count noun, and in labelling a community of practice. Scollon refines the term which extends the descriptive apparatus. Noting that for Bourdieu, *practice* is most often a "loose, large, and ambiguous" mass noun (2001:143), he uses the term for "a narrowly defined count-noun entity", introducing *nexus of practice* to describe recognisable bundles of practices (2001:147).

FIGURE 4.1. The police interview room – "where the rubber meets the road" (Eckert and McConnell-Ginet 1998:491–492).

communities. Lave and Wenger themselves present the concept as largely "intuitive" (1991:42), Wenger denouncing "a simple metric" which would specify "exact ranges of size, duration, proximity, amount of interaction, or types of activities" of a 'true' community of practice (1998a:122; see also Scollon 1998:14, 2001:146). However, in resisting "encumbering the concept with too restrictive a definition", Wenger instead advocates exploring "the perspective that underlies" it (1998a:122). Following this line, this chapter does not use the framework as a diagnostic to identify five, ten or twenty officers who might be said to form a community, and explore the extent to which they do. Instead, it exemplifies how an interactional sociolinguistic take is enriched by and enriches the community of practice concept. This dialogue has two sources in sociolinguistics. Firstly, membership of communities of practice is "accomplished", put "on the table" and "ratified" through talk (Scollon 1998:52), so the study of talk illuminates community in its diversity. Secondly, sociolinguistics has considerable experience of studying collectives. Indeed, specific aspects of the community of practice framework recall established sociolinguistic frameworks for examining social worlds as Bucholtz (1999:202–208), Holmes and Meyerhoff (1999) and Scollon

(2001:142–158) have illustrated (summarised in Table 4.1). Holmes and Meyerhoff provide a useful summary comparison of assumptions underlying use of each framework (1999:179).

Communities of practice are "not a new kind of organisational unit" but "a different *cut* on the organisation's structure" (Wenger 1998b:2). This cut is guided by members' reflexivity about "what [their community] is about" (joint enterprise), "how it functions" (mutual engagement) and "what capability it has produced" (shared repertoire of resources) (Laat 2001:2; see also Wenger 1998b). I therefore use these three features to explore police practice, drawing on officers' introspection about their practices and on exchanges between officers and detainees within police interviews – practice itself. Allen, Nulden and Sørensen (2002) note the challenges of research with or on police in which formal access must be negotiated and informal access to "the backstage" earned. They describe this backstage as "the hidden transcript, a discourse not meant to be publicly uttered or printed." Indeed, by seeking to investigate officers' communities of practice, one craves access to both front and backstage (Goffman 1959). Within this study, that access has been invaluable[3]. I collected the data discussed here between 1999 and 2001 around England and Wales within a larger study on communication between police and lay people[4]. They reveal that language is crucial to workers' own notions of both *community* and *practice*.

JOINT NEGOTIATED ENTERPRISE

Holmes and Meyerhoff (1999:175) suspect that Wenger's *joint enterprise* is too loosely specified to assist sociolinguists. Nonetheless, its central concepts "stated, shared goal" and "mutual accountability" (Holmes and Meyerhoff 1999:175) are extremely relevant here, particularly in combination with other aspects of the framework, notably reification and boundary objects, incorporated below. Wenger locates joint enterprise squarely with community members who define it in

[3] I am indebted to the many police forces, police officers and detainees around England and Wales who have generously given their time and enthusiasm to this study. All participants are given pseudonyms here, ultimately, to anonymise police forces.
[4] I am grateful for the support of an Arts and Humanities Research Board grant (BA98/3092) in that larger study.

TABLE 4.1. *Examinations of the Relationship Between Community of Practice and Other Frameworks*

Author	Has Compared Community of Practice to...	Source of Comparison Framework
Scollon (2001)	discourse community universe of practice (capital 'D') Discourse reality set	Swales (1990, 1998), Bourdieu (1977, 1990), Gee (1990, 1996, 1999) Scollon and Scollon (1979, 1981)
Holmes and Meyerhoff (1999)	social identity theory	Tajfel (1978); Tajfel and Turner (1986)
	speech community	For example, as articulated by Labov (1972), Gumperz (1971) and Preston (1989)
	social network theory	After Milroy (1987) and Kerswill (1994, for example)
	various social constructionist approaches, particularly to language and gender	Such as Crawford (1995) Hall and Bucholtz (1995)
Bucholtz (1999)	praxis	Marx (see, for example, the second and eleventh theses on Feuerbach)
	investigations of social structure and agency	Giddens (1979)
	attention to the connectivity between language and other social practices, indeed to language "as a social phenomenon" (1999:204–205)	Bourdieu (1978, 1991), Certeau (1984)

pursuing it. He describes enterprise as "their negotiated response to their situation [which] thus belongs to them in a profound sense, in spite of all the forces and influences that are beyond their control" (1998a:77).

The forces and influences beyond officers' control in relation to delivering the right to silence are articulated mainly in police officers' *Codes of Practice* (Home Office 2003:76–80), which explains that the right should be stated using a prescribed wording known as the *caution* (Gudjonsson and Clare 1994; Kurzon 1995, 1996; Cotterill 2000; Russell 2000; Fenner, Gudjonsson and Clare 2002). The caution can be compared with the American *Miranda warnings* which state the right to silence along with other rights (Shuy 1997). Inevitably, the *Codes* focus on why and when to caution, outlining the circumstances in which a caution is required and those in which it is not and, in a recent addition, the circumstances in which a novel wording should be used. They also provide two institutional goals concerning linguistic aspects of cautioning and reformulating whilst being audio- or video-recorded before interview:

- **Cautioning**: Officers should use the words specified in the *Codes* although "minor deviations" from that wording are tolerated (Home Office 2003:77–78). The wording reads:

  You do not have to say anything. But it may harm your defence if you do not mention when questioned something which you later rely on in court. Anything you do say may be given in evidence.

- **Reformulating**: Officers should explain the caution "in their own words" "if it appears a person does not understand" (Home Office 2003:80). Officers typically check whether detainees understand the caution, using a yes/no question before and after explaining it.

Both of these stated goals reify, conferring "thingness" (Wenger 1998a:58), through which "aspects of human experience and practice are congealed into fixed forms" (Wenger 1998a:59) using naming, encoding, interpreting, reusing, decoding, representing and recasting. Reification of the caution's official wording enables that wording to *do* arrest, transforming addressees from 'free' to 'detained'

(Austin 1962, Searle 1969) and transforming talk from 'informal' to 'in interview'. Officers recognise this functionality, characterising the caution with the metaphor "a tool of the trade". Reification of the cautioning procedure enables that whole procedure to become a 'thing' for being seen to have administered rights fairly and unambiguously.

Reifications can be 'frozen' into "monuments" which can "be reintegrated as reifications into new moments of negotiation of meaning" (Wenger 1998a:60). By audio- or video-recording cautioning and, indeed, by simply making it obligatory within detention procedure, cautioning can be revisited subsequently, most notably in court. Reification represents the caution as a boundary object, serving "as a coordinating mechanism between . . . [an institutional group] and different – and largely disjoint – constituencies" (Wenger 1998a:106). Boundary objects are often standardised, meaning that "the information . . . is in a pre-specified form so that each constituency knows how to deal with it locally" (Wenger 1998a:107, after Star 1989). The caution is certainly standardised which helps one constituency, police officers, to know how to deal with it; indeed, their dealings with it rest on its standardisation. However, for some detainees, who officers describe as *switching off* when cautioning begins, standardisation may be distracting.

Joint negotiated enterprise suggests that officers, provided with institutional goals around a reified boundary object, do not simply adopt those goals but negotiate a response to them. Some officers presented their cautioning as meeting institutional requirements, directly and inevitably, observing, for example:

HELEN: we like to get interviews in as evidence and in order to do so we have to comply with PACE and that's the tool to do so - so that's all

Helen's caution, a performance of compliance, illustrates how reified boundary objects like the caution can connect or not do so, because they "enable coordination" but possibly "without actually creating a bridge between the perspectives and the meanings of the various constituencies" (Wenger 1998a:107). Meeting goals around cautioning is not always about unblinking compliance, however. Officers problematised stated goals in various ways, showing that negotiated enterprise can take forms which the institution has not determined (Wenger 1998a:79) or even anticipated. Mac exemplifies:

MAC: sometimes I almost feel I'm almost apologising for have to - telling them all this stuff because they might want to get on with it and I really deep down want to get on with it

He identifies tensions around the stated institutional goals, which conflict with interactional goals and indeed with other institution goals, particularly, timely investigative interviewing. Of course, officers could not negotiate a response to such conflicts which involved ignoring cautioning's stated goals, but Mac's frustration evidences a common negotiated response. McElhinny describes, after Bourdieu (1977), officers' "occupationally conditioned habitus" which is realised as an economy of affect leading them to exhibit and indeed experience affective responses as if "on a limited budget" (1998:314–315). The data I investigated suggest some officers are aware that such an economy might influence their cautioning, leading them, like Mac, to negotiate a response to the goals around cautioning which uses only their available resources:

SUE: I stand there in - parrot fashion like I reel it all off like a robot... because I want to get on with it I don't relate to what they're listening to

Mutual accountability, in this setting, is not simply getting police work done, but also making a way through complex, often conflicting demands around applying legal requirements to a 'real world' in a way which fits with officers' own personal and collective notions of self and of that endeavour. It has led Sue to prioritise institutional goals over interactional or interpersonal ones. As Wenger explains, "relations of accountability include what matters and what does not,... what to pay attention to and what to ignore,... when actions and artefacts are good enough and when they need improvement or refinement" (Wenger 1998a:81). For Sue, ignoring how she has cautioned allows her to focus on whether she has cautioned and what will happen next. Other officers, too, problematised their own practice:

TIM: you make your stab at it and you go for it but there's nobody dragging you back saying "oh you did that wrong" sometimes I've no doubt I've pitched things at certain levels and it's been totally inappropriate but it's the best level that I've got

For Tim, like many officers, 'good' cautioning was variable, dictated by his interlocutor. Joint negotiated enterprise had enabled Tim to review but not improve his own practice in relation to this standard.

Defining a joint enterprise is a process, not a static agreement. It produces relations of accountability that are more than norms. These relations are manifested not as conformity, but as the ability to negotiate actions as accountable to an enterprise. Clearly, officers negotiate accountability differently from one another, although in this case in response to related joint negotiated enterprise around shared goals. Here, speakers' comments on their own practices and those of colleagues make it possible to draw out layers of the community of practice framework very clearly.

MUTUAL ENGAGEMENT

Mutual engagement enables action (Wenger 1998a:73), typically through "regular interaction" (Holmes and Meyerhoff 1999:175). The key to recognising mutual engagement seems to be openness to its variability. As Wenger points out, no rules govern the form that it may take, indeed "[w]hatever it takes to make mutual engagement possible is an essential component of any practice" (1998a:74). Mutual engagement might happen anywhere from casual, informal encounters, as people "pass in the corridor or share morning tea", to formal, work-oriented settings (Holmes and Meyerhoff 1999:175).

Examples of mutual engagement abound in officers' descriptions of cautioning practices. Officers describe appropriating new methods of, and approaches to, explanation, by observing, either formally – within mentoring relationships – or informally, particularly if moving to a new team or gaining a new colleague. However, learning within a community is not simply about copying others, but instead "occurs through centripetal participation in the learning curriculum of the ambient community" (Lave and Wenger 1991:100). So, many officers presented learning to caution as a constantly ongoing process of fit-finding between their own professional identity, the institutional requirement to caution and the demands of specific situations. Some officers caution every day, others very occasionally, yet a constant is that their learning does indeed happen anywhere, from the interview room to the canteen. I asked Harry, a uniformed patrol officer with 28 years experience, about how officers learned to caution. He explained:

HARRY: occasionally you get it back to front and things and we have a laugh about it afterwards
FRANCES: that's training itself isn't it?
HARRY: yeah that's true actually yeah I mean going afterwards in the canteen "ah you made a right mess of that didn't you?" "but - I got it back to front"

Excerpts like this suggest that *community* may be a disingenuous label. Barton and Hamilton urge caution about this "cosy and beguiling word" because "closely structured local social relations can also be oppressive, disruptive or resistant to individuals' needs" (Barton and Hamilton 1998:16). Wenger, too, stresses repeatedly that community should not be romanticised, as it can reproduce such "counterproductive patterns" as injustice and prejudice and is indeed likely to be "the very locus of such reproduction" (1998a:132, see also 1998a:77). We could thus see this "having a laugh" as a dangerous trivialisation of an important speech event, potentially generating counterproductive patterns. Atherton (2002) points out that Lave and Wenger do not clearly distinguish legitimate peripheral participation, through mutual engagement, from occupational socialisation. He goes on to criticise such socialisation, particularly police "canteen culture"[5], presumably with the sort of incident which Harry has described in mind. However, officers' talk suggested that incidents like this are more accurately viewed as ways of identifying and rectifying problems informally. In imagining an officer who "got it back to front", Harry does not present an indifferent or sneering individual, celebrating in his/her own incompetence, but one with reflexivity. Officers seemed to use informal talk to address trouble without, perhaps, having

[5] *The New Oxford Dictionary of English* (1999) gives the following definition for *canteen culture*: "a set of conservative and discriminatory attitudes said to exist within the police force".

obviously done so. Those who described similar incidents illustrated how informal interactions scaffold social participation.

Their negotiation is attributable to mutual engagement in that "[b]ecoming good at something involves developing specialised sensitivities... that are brought to bear on making judgements about the qualities of a product or an action" (Wenger 1998a:81). Like Sue, in the previous section, Don problematised the possibility that detainees might miss the caution's warning perlocution, due to its delivery, pointing out that officers often fail to "say it with meaning". Unlike Sue, who responded by simply disregarding the negotiated goal of administering a meaningful caution, Don's response invoked that goal:

DON: a lot of coppers [quickly] "you know don't have to say anything but it may harm your defence rrrr rrrr rrrr" and you think "well I didn't hear that so what chance-?" and in fact I've said-when I've been with an officer and he's said it like that I'll I've actually said "look just say that again but say it like I could hear you as well as him there" and they've sort of laughed and (.) embarrassed about it (.) but they've said it again

Alan similarly felt that 'good' cautioning was part of being an officer, he was adamant that officers who are "unable to explain [the caution]... shouldn't be giving it in the first place". Other officers, too, presented explanation as a reified 'skill' which all officers should 'have' (Scollon 2001:156):

CARL: I've sat in on interviews with other officers and I've heard their explanations of the caution and I'm thinking to myself "it's not wrong but it's hard to understand what he's saying"

Unlike Don, who intervened, seeking to improve practice, Carl simply looked on, unable to articulate how his colleagues' explanations deviated from the negotiated goal of demonstrating competence through reformulation.

SHARED REPERTOIRE OF RESOURCES

Shared repertoire concerns the emergence of "joint resources for negotiating meaning" (Holmes and Meyerhoff 1999:176), including, of great relevance to cautioning, words, ways of doing things,

actions, concepts (Wenger 1998a:83), along with "specialised ter-
minology and linguistic routines" which may prove "especially
fruitful" for language analysts (Holmes and Meyerhoff 1999:176).
Indeed, *repertoire*, selected "to emphasise both ... rehearsed character and ... availability for further engagement in practice" (Wenger
1998a:83) characterises cautioning well. Resources are adopted (from
outside, like the caution's official wording) or produced (internally,
like officers' responses to that wording) by the developing community. These data demonstrate that officers share resources for both
understanding and explaining the caution.

Resources for Understanding and Planning Explanations

Many officers described being initially baffled by the caution. Some,
who use it rarely, accordingly simply memorised the wording, almost ignoring its meaning. Wenger anticipates such approaches, describing "understanding in practice" as "the art of choosing what to
know and what to ignore in order to proceed with our lives" (Wenger
1998a:41). Those who could not live with such confusion devised
ways to understand. For some, like Emma, learning was solitary:

EMMA: when you're learning the law ... the easiest way to learn
     things is obviously to break it down and formulate your own inter-
     pretation of that law um or else otherwise you would never ever
     be able to apply the law to the situations that you go and deal with

Emma presents isolated learning as necessary, bringing confidence.
For her, nonetheless, "learning is about becoming a practitioner, not
about learning about practice" (Laat and Broer 2004). Other officers,
like Tom, invoked communities for learning:

TOM: when I first read it I didn't understand it I thought "well I
     don't know what the middle bit means" but as soon as somebody
     explained it it was fine

Officers' explaining task not only requires understanding, officers
also described working on the nexus of practice (Scollon 2001:142)
around explaining itself. Some described formal, classroom-based
instruction as central here:

CHRIS: people should be trained and I think are trained in the importance of the caution and um how to bring it across in your own words

Others described similarly institutionally sanctioned learning, delivered more informally:

PAUL: when you join the police you get tutored by experienced officers... you take them probably literally to begin with and then you probably modify into your way of doing it

Gavin too appropriated resources for explanations from colleagues but quite informally from the outset:

GAVIN: I interview along with a lot of different people you know we often go in pairs... and you listen to their ways of explaining it and you think "oh that's a good way" and sometimes you pinch stuff

Gavin's picture of ongoing learning was repainted by many officers who tend to work with each other and figure out *"oh I'll do it like that"*. Colin, for example, presented this sharing as particularly reciprocal:

COLIN: I've picked some up from a colleague when I came back [from a different station] and some have maybe picked things up from me (.) I think it's only natural that you do "well I don't like doing that I'm never going to do that but [pointing] I'll abstract that and I'll abstract that and I'll abstract that"

This dissemination illustrates brokering – transferring "some element of one practice into another" (Wenger 1998a:109), potentially promoting homogeneity amongst officers' reformulations. Such transfer may map change, as Wenger explains, "the geography of practice reflects histories of learning" (1998a:127).

Officers who learn through such direct legitimate participation in communities of practice, be it peripheral or more central (Lave and Wenger 1991:29), felt such learning was important to their work, as Terry explained when I asked him what kind of training in cautioning he or colleagues might appreciate:

TERRY: well you're probably asking the wrong person about training um I think after your initial training you learn out there (.) that's

where you learn how to pick up what's - you get the vibrations if
you like um it's just experience it's like everything else in life

For Terry, like Lave and Wenger, learning cannot be uncoupled from
practice. McElhinny explores how learning 'out there' becomes incorporated into police training describing guidance on a police training
video as less like "directives for police behaviour than as a distillation
of officers' experiences of what works . . . encoded in their training"
(1998:318). This too blurs neat divisions between 'training' and 'doing
the job' which are both central to the framework and particularly
evident in many officers' talk about ongoing learning.

Resources for Explaining

Having looked backstage at officers' talk about cautioning, we now
move to the performance of cautioning. Recall the caution's middle
sentence:

(But) it may harm your defence if you do not mention when questioned
something which you later rely on in court.

Now consider one officer's explanation of that:

OFFICER: 1 the middle part (.)
              2 it may harm your defence
              3 if you do not mention when questioned
              4 something which you later rely on in court (.)
              5 that means (.)
              6 if I ask you a question now in the interview (.)
              7 and you refuse to answer it (.)
              8 and then at a later date in court
              9 actually give an answer
             10 for the same question (.)
             11 the court can think to itself
             12 "well why didn't you answer the question
             13 in the first place?"
             14 alright?
DETAINEE: 15 yes
OFFICER: 16 and that could ((use)) against you
             17 or it could be (.) in your favour
             18 alright?

DETAINEE: 19 yep
OFFICER: 20 also (.) if you answer a question that I put to you now
21 and then at a later date - uh later date
22 you change what you've answered (.)
23 so you - you change your story so to speak
24 again if it goes to court the court can think
25 "well why have you changed your story?" (.)
26 and it might be f- in your favour
27 or it might go against you
28 alright?
DETAINEE: 29 yeah

Excerpt 1 – An Officer Explains the Caution's Middle Sentence. This officer has transformed the official wording in various ways. Whilst officers explain the caution very differently from one another, a number of resources for explaining appear to emerge repeatedly, clustering in particular police forces. My discussion of this excerpt will explore some of these resources. I will then ask whether these shared ways of explaining might be seen to evidence communities of practice or something different. First, a structural overview:

- **Orientation (lines 1–5)** – The officer begins this section of his reformulation by framing (Bateson 1972, Goffman 1974, Tannen 1993) or focussing through a metalinguistic label *the middle part* (line 1) which explains the upcoming talk's anaphoric relationship with the official wording and its cotextual place within the reformulation. He then restates the official wording's relevant section (lines 2–4) before introducing his own gloss through further metalanguage, *that means.*
- **Inference-drawing scenario 1 (lines 6–17)** – The officer illustrates a possible sequence of events which may lead a court to draw inferences, centring on possible silence during interview.
- **Inference-drawing scenario 2 (lines 20–27)** – Finally, the officer hypothesises a different sequence of events which, he suggests, may also initiate inference-drawing. In this scenario, inferencing may happen despite talk in interview.

These moves are punctuated with comprehension checks in which the officer uses *alright?* to challenge the detainee to attend and reflect, dialogically drawing him into the explanation. At this level then, the officer says much more than the caution's official wording, explaining, through metalanguage and inventive illustrative examples, features which are ubiquitous amongst officers. A more detailed examination also reveals "multiple uses of particular linguistic resources" (Eckert and McConnell-Ginet 1998:487) amongst officers.

Restatement

The officer's repetition of the official wording (lines 2–4) is characteristic of these data, where officers more frequently used such repetition when reformulating the middle sentence than any other part of the caution. Such repetition may be productive, as Norrick explains: "[o]n the one hand, the repeat borrows recognisable elements from its original, but on the other hand, it differs from that original, if only through reference to it and contextual separation from it" (1994:15). Specifically, through restatement the repeated text is:

- *recontextualised* (Linell 1998) – placed in a new context, within the activity of explaining, rather than that of reciting an official wording;
- *recontextualised* – extracted from the official wording, isolated, then inserted into a new context, forming new textual relations;
- *repeated* – with two potential consequences. Firstly, repetition allows detainees to take different or additional semantico-pragmatic information from the text. Secondly, it marks the repeated text. In this case, the officer does not say why this sentence might be marked. Other officers explain marking through evaluative metalanguage, describing the sentence as *the difficult bit*, for example.

No aspect of this shared resource of repetition is exclusive to this officer.

Adding Detail Through Local Knowledge

The officer's 'own words' reformulation begins in line 6, with a conjoined *if-* clause, prospecting his imminent activity (*ask you a question*) and the detainee's possible response (*refuse to answer*) (Saville-Troike

1985, Jaworski 1993, Kurzon 1995). This has a clear source in the original wording:

... it may harm your defence if you do not mention **when questioned** something...

The officer thus explicates *when questioned*, stating that questioning is pursued:

- by one particular individual – *I*, not other officers inside or outside interview;
- at a particular time – *now*, not later within detention, with an associated 'now or never' implicature;
- during a particular speech event – *in the interview*;
- in a particular way – through the whole string, the officer implies that the court can only draw inferences if the detainee avoids a specific question in interview but responds to that *same question* in court. So, he presents 'questioning' as the asking of particular questions, not the whole questioning interaction during which the detainee may raise issues of his own volition.

In his second scenario, the officer similarly specifies *when questioned* as *if you answer **a question** that I put to you now* (line 20). Other officers particularise by adding detail, too, but do not all add the same details. Some imply that 'questioning' is abstract, continuing throughout detention, others that multiple officers might question, and others that detainees' spontaneous talk is as important as answers to specific questions, for example. Finally, some do not disambiguate *when questioned* at all.

Adding More Than Detail?

In line 7, the officer substitutes a verb phrase:

do not mention   →   becomes   →   *refuse to answer*

The resulting representation is rather loaded. It suggests that silence is active (refusal) rather than passive (neglecting mention) and thus presents someone who avoids even one question during interview as rather uncooperative. Emphatic *actually*, later in the turn (*in court actually give an answer*) additionally implies that silence in interview, followed by talk in court, is inexplicable. One could claim that the official wording discourages silence, for example, by following *You do not have to say anything* with *but* (see Winter 1979). Representing silence as a refusal to participate could be seen as an attempt to intensify this possible perlocution; more charitably, as an attempt to highlight silence's consequences. Either way, this representation adds something quite specific to the official wording – again something not unique to this officer.

Although the official wording avoids naming *inference*, the concept underlies the medial sentence[6], yet many officers express reservations about explaining inferencing. This officer personifies, representing inferences as emanating from an incredulous court, collectively asking *well why didn't you answer the question in the first place?* (lines 12–13)[7], an animated depiction which could be said to further encourage talk. Other officers similarly personalise the court.

Officers explain the caution apparently with scant regard for its strict legal meaning. This said, it would be totally nonsensical for them to explain the full implications of relevant complex, rapidly evolving law. In explaining, officers must steer a course between stated goals and meaningful practice, with their decisions about how to do this having major implications for detainees. A shared repertoire of resources potentially influences this activity, interacting with a "perspectival framework" emanating from membership of the occupational group of officers. This chapter has shown that officers draw on both, enhancing some matters whilst structuring the world in ways that render others almost invisible (Goodwin and Goodwin 1997:303). Officers thus offer a particular institutional view, sometimes the only perspective available to

---

[6] This middle sentence is intended to convey roughly that, if a detainee only introduces a defence in court, the court may be permitted to infer that that account might be less than completely truthful. This aspect of the wording was introduced in 1995, to a legal system which had previously allowed an unfettered right to silence, in an attempt to reduce 'ambush defences' in which detainees' defence teams introduce information when it is too late for prosecutors to investigate.

[7] The officer's presentation of inference-drawing in his second scenario mirrors that of the first, so I will draw examples only from the first scenario, lines 6–17.

detainees. Awareness of this was a feature of officers' joint negotiated enterprise:

MARK: the police have got to be careful what they say so that they don't give the impression that they're influencing the suspect as to what he says

DISCUSSION

Although officers are "a group of people oriented to the same practice," they will not necessarily orient "in the same way" (Bucholtz 1999:210; see also Wenger 1998a:79). Yet, in discussing joint negotiated enterprise (Section 2) and mutual engagement (Section 3), we saw patterns in officers' orientations to the two institutional goals around cautioning. Then, in discussing shared repertoires of resources (Section 4), we saw that officers explain the caution differently from one another, but that various sets of commonalities exist between some officers despite their geographical spread. What can this tell us about the framework? The first possibility is that we might see all officers, united by shared institutional membership, as one huge community of practice. Eckert and McConnell-Ginet suggest that a whole profession can share such membership even if their "size and dispersion means . . . that face-to-face interactions never link all the members" (1999:189)[8], as do Goodwin and Goodwin (1997:292; see also Swales 1990:25 for discussion of the related 'café owner problem'). In contrast, Wenger warns that this misses "crucial discontinuities among the various localities where relevant learning takes place" (Wenger 1998a:125). A related second possibility is that all officers constitute a community of practice because they share the task of delivering the right to silence. Meyerhoff demonstrates that, even if speakers share a "linguistic and behavioural repertoire", they do not necessarily share community membership or lack heterogeneity or social diffusion (1999:237) – community of practice is not about institutional affiliation or shared institutional demands.

---

[8] Elsewhere, Eckert and McConnell-Ginet suggest that groups as small as pairs of officers working together as partners exemplify community of practice (1998:490).

The influence of police force-level initiatives on communities of practice is, nonetheless, apparent in these data. Some forces encourage officers to reformulate, some even provide explanation resources, particularly printed specimen formulations, whilst others discourage reformulation altogether. Officers' cautioning practices and their introspection reveal that such generalised policies are influential; crucially, however, their only certain influence is in providing a stated goal for officers to negotiate. Keith's rejection of such guidance exemplifies this:

KEITH: we're given a sheet of A4 paper with printed out a full page of
    A4 but to sit there and read that out is probably more complicated

Questions about whether an institution constitutes a community of practice ultimately impose artificial problems, because boundaries of communities of practice "may or may not coincide with institutional boundaries" (Wenger 1998a:119, 1998b:4). Rather than attempting to force existing institutional structures into the framework, I propose that these language data invoke Wenger's view of constellations of interconnected communities. Through constellations, we can view police forces comprising many communities of practice which, whilst of different sizes and kinds, may share historical roots, enterprises, institutional affiliation, working conditions, members and artefacts (Wenger 1998a:127)[9]. Thus, similarities and differences between officers' practices can be seen as the result of their many memberships of many communities of practice, creating the appearance of patterns at the macro-level of police forces or above, but actually the result of micro-level groups, like those that officers have described, sharing problems and ideas, routinely.

These data also highlight another aspect of the multiplicity of communities of practice, that each individual simultaneously inhabits different communities of practice. Both Ehrlich (1999:251) and Ostermann (2003), investigating legal workplaces, have found that

---

[9] The view of multiplicity which emerges in this aspect of communities of practice affords the framework some advantages over others such as *reality sets* (Scollon and Scollon 1979, 1981) which describe the "interaction among worldview, socialisation practices, forms of discourse and social relationships", but which less successfully present the possibility that individuals might participate in multiple reality sets (Scollon 2001:144).

legal specialists' linguistic behaviour is more influenced by work-based communities of practice than ways of being arising through gender. By acknowledging such multiple memberships and their fluctuating influence, individuals no longer appear subsumed in "totalising entities" of communities of practice (Scollon 1998:13) which might be expected to generate homogenisation instead as constantly negotiating membership (Eckert and McConnell-Ginet 1998:491) and participation. *Participation* usefully illustrates this multimembership being "a constituent of our identities... not something we turn on and off" (Wenger 1998a:57). Accordingly, multimembership influences participation across communities, as officers explain:

TONY: you can't sit there to a 12 year-old using the same sort of attitude and demeanour and language as you would with a 45 year old (.) and - they just don't understand it um so you bring it down to their level and you use different - sort of - ways of explaining it because (.) at the end of the day I'm a father (.) I know the way you have to speak to children to get it over to them and it's just because they've been out stealing or whatever (.) it doesn't make them not a child

Multimembership can have diverse results as particular memberships become salient unpredictably when participation places "negotiation of meaning in the context of our forms of membership in various communities" (Wenger 1998a:57). For Tony, membership of communities of practice around fatherhood, life outside work, has affected work participation.

The notion of multimembership fits police forces well. Particular communities within forces connect with others through various trajectories of membership[10]. For example, those on peripheral trajectories might include regular detainees; others, like probationary officers, have inbound trajectories, joining a particular community, intending and intended to become full members, negotiating place

---

[10] Eijkman (2002) takes a rather unusual stance by problematising multiple membership of communities of practice, presenting it not as a given, but a potential site of tension. He illustrates that police officers engaged in academic study might experience a conflict between these two memberships, centring on different values attached to particular forms of participation, even when studying for an in-service police diploma.

and identity within a partnership, rank, role and branch. Multi-membership also illuminates cautioning. Study of language data around cautioning has been revealing here because, as Scollon observes, "some practices are homologous straight across... circles into other circles" (2001:156). Cautioning is one such practice in which a specific, comparable formulation and, often, a resulting interaction permeate an organisation, offering a particular view of that organisation.

PRACTICAL IMPLICATIONS

This final section illustrates how the implications of the preceding analysis might inform 'real world' decision, having implications for officers, detainees and the police organisation. Interpersonally, the extent of variation in practices between workplaces has implications for all newcomers (Holmes and Meyerhoff 1999:177). Institutionally, Wenger recommends that organisations attend to "what emergent communities of practice indicate with regard to potential strategic directions" (1998b:4) because "the knowledge that companies need is usually already present in some form" (1998b:4). This certainly applies to cautioning, where, as we have seen, some officers resist institutional guidance having already tackled the challenge of explanation themselves. Additionally, the framework offers insight into:

- **Provision of an official caution wording** – "Reification shapes our experience" (Wenger 1998a:59), so the Home Office influences the nature of police work by providing a caution, the particular caution and procedure which they have. Furthermore, reification has a double-edged power (Wenger 1998a:61). In the caution, reification renders the right to silence pocket-sized, summarisable and discrete. However, in doing so, it divides the caution's concepts from actual interactions, abstracting them until the wording's implications are implicit and lexicalising in ways which foregrounds certain possibilities, such as an imminent court appearance, at the expense of others.
- **The provision of explanations to accompany the official wording** – Reified boundary objects can travel without "the physical limitations of mutual engagement", but "if unaccompanied

by people" risk "divergent interpretations", "possible misunderstandings and incompatible assumptions that can remain undetected" (Wenger 1998a:111). If this holds for cautioning, a caution unaccompanied by spontaneous explanation risks denying rights. Wenger proposes that "[a]ccompanied artefacts have a better chance of bridging practices . . . a person can help interpret the document and negotiate its relevance" (Wenger 1998a:112). Such observations have implications for the institution in deciding whether to recommend reformulation and for individual officers' decisions about whether to explain.

- **Responses to official formulations** – Reified boundary objects potentially drive people to "take a stand by requiring interpretation". For example, the language of a new policy might be seen as "typical of its authors' reputation . . . [serving] only to confirm the cynicism of the intended audience" (Wenger 1998a:111):

CLIFF: we shouldn't have to explain should we? it should be so easy to understand
POLLY: the people that have said to us "this is your new caution get on with it" . . . they probably haven't really thought about how can we put this in layman's terms

These officers were antagonistic towards explaining, not (only) because they found it difficult, but also nonsensical. As Scollon explains "any action positions the social actor in relationship to others who are engaged in the practice. Poor performance in the practice might signal many things – novice status, cynical disdain of practice, temporary inattention" (2001:141). Wenger suggests that boundary objects should be designed for "participation rather than just use" (Wenger 1998a:107). Participation in cautioning involves officers' engagement in practices around cautioning. A caution which is designed without the complexity of this engagement in mind, in view of the myriad resources which have only been sketched here, will not necessarily adapt well to use. Scrutiny of the caution's appropriation by constellations of communities of practice may be risky, Wenger warns, indeed, that "[m]any [communities of practice] are best left alone – some might actually wither under the institutional spotlight" (Wenger 1998b:3). However, observing language practices through and beyond the communities of practice framework has immense potential implications.

CONCLUSION

The community of practice offers a novel way into questions about language in institutional settings and, in turn, close scrutiny of speakers' comments on their language practices, and of those practices, contributes to examination and application of the framework. This chapter has asked what might evidence communities of practice in language data. Officers' reformulations do share surface realisations but, perhaps more revealingly, practices of devising and using an extended cautioning routine, as well as keeping that routine updated and orienting in relation to institutional and negotiated goals around that routine, all appear to be accomplished, by some officers, communally. In discussing how they caution, officers acknowledge and exhibit community in their practice to different extents. This complex of shared and different cautioning practices and representations of those practices makes for intriguing challenges for the community of practice position and its fit with language data.

References

Allen, D., U. Nulden and C. Sørensen (2002) *e-policing on SafeStreet*, Workshop Presentation at IRIS25 (Information Systems Research in Scandinavia), August 10–13, 2002, Bautahøj, Denmark. [On-line] Available at: http://www.iris25.cbs.dk/panelsandworkshops/epolicing.pdf.

Andrew, I. (2002) Networking and Communities of Practice. [On-line] Available at: http://www.reframingthefuture.net/Action_Plans/2002/files/cp247.html. Accessed June 20, 2003.

Atherton, J. (2002) Learning and Teaching: Situated Learning. [On-line] Available at: http://www.dmu.ac.uk/%7Ejamesa/learning/situated.htm. Accessed June 20, 2003.

Austin, J. (1962) *How to Do Things with Words*. Oxford: Clarendon Press.

Barton, D. and M. Hamilton (1998) Local Literacies: Reading and Writing in One Community. London: Routledge.

Bateson, G. (1972) Steps to an Ecology of Mind. New York: Ballantine.

Bourdieu, P. (1977) *Outline of a Theory of Practice*. 'Richard Nice' tr. Cambridge: Cambridge University Press.

Bourdieu, P. (1978) *Outline of a Theory of Practice*. Cambridge & New York: Cambridge University Press.

Bourdieu, P. (1990) *The Logic of Practice*. Stanford: Stanford University Press.

Bourdieu, P. (1991) *Language and Symbolic Power*. Cambridge, MA: Harvard University Press.

Bucholtz, M. (1999) "Why be normal?": language and identity practices in a community of nerd girls. *Language in Society 28 (2)* 203–223.

Certeau, M. de (1984) *The Practice of Everyday Life*. Berkeley: University of California Press.

Cotterill, J. (2000) Reading the rights: a cautionary tale of comprehension and comprehensibility. *Forensic Linguistics 7 (1)* 4–25.

Crawford, M. (1995) *Talking Difference: On Gender and Language*. London: Sage.

Eckert, P. and S. McConnell-Ginet (1998) Communities of practice: where language, gender and power all live. In J. Coates (ed), *Language and Gender: A Reader*. Oxford: Blackwell Publishers, 484–494.

Eckert, P. and S. McConnell-Ginet (1999) New generalisations and explanations in language and gender research. *Language in Society 28 (2)* 185–201.

Ehrlich, S. (1999) Communities of practice, gender and the representation of sexual assault. *Language in Society 28 (2)* 239–257.

Eijkman, H. (2002) Reframing the first year experience: the critical role of 'recognition work' in achieving curricular justice. Paper presented at The 6th Pacific Rim First Year in Higher Education Conference 2002: Changing Agendas – Te Ao Hurihuri, University of Canterbury, Christchurch, New Zealand, 8–10th July 2002.

Fenner, S., G. Gudjonsson and I. Clare (2002) Understanding of the current police caution (England and Wales) among suspects in police detention. *Journal of Community and Applied Social Psychology 12* 83–93.

Gee, J. (1990) Background to the "new literacy studies". In Gee, J. (ed), *Social Linguistics and Literacies: Ideology in Discourse*. London: The Falmer Press.

Gee, J. (1996) *Social Linguistics and Literacies: Ideology in Discourse*. (Second edition). London: The Falmer Press.

Gee, J. (1999) *An Introduction to Discourse Analysis: Theory and Method*. London: Routledge.

Giddens, A. (1979) *Central Problems in Social Theory: Action, Structure, and Contradiction in Social Analysis*. Berkeley: University of California Press.

Goffman, E. (1959) *The Presentation of Self in Everyday Life*. New York: Doubleday.

Goffman, E. (1974) *Frame Analysis*. New York: Harper Colophon.

Goodwin, C. and M. Goodwin (1997) Contested vision: the discursive construction of Rodney King. In B. Gunnarsson, P. Linell and B. Nordberg (eds), *The Construction of Professional Discourse*. London: Longman, 292–316.

Gudjonsson, G. and I. Clare (1994) The proposed new police caution (England and Wales): how easy is it to understand? *Expert Evidence 3 (3)* 109–112.

Gumperz, J. (1971) *Language in Social Groups*. Stanford: Stanford University Press.

Hall, K. and Bucholtz, M. (eds) (1995) *Gender Articulated: Language and the Socially Constructed Self*. London: Routledge.

Holmes, J. and M. Meyerhoff (1999) The community of practice: theories and methodologies in language and gender research. *Language in Society 28 (2)* 173–183.

Home Office (2003) *Police and Criminal Evidence Act, Codes of Practice, Code C*. London: HMSO.

Jaworski, A. (1993) *The Power of Silence: Social and Pragmatic Perspectives*. London: Sage Publications.

Kerswill, P. (1994) *Dialects Converging: Rural Speech in Urban Norway*. Oxford: Clarendon.

Kurzon, D. (1995) The right of silence: a socio-pragmatic model of interpretation. *Journal of Pragmatics 23 (1)* 55–69.

Kurzon, D. (1996) To speak or not to speak. *International Journal for the Semiotics of Law 9* 25.

Laat, M. (2001) Learning in a community of practice: creating and managing knowledge through networked expertise. Paper presented at the 2nd World Conference on Organized Crime, Modern Criminal Investigation and Human Rights, Durban, 3–7th December, 2001.

Laat, M. and W. Broer (2004) CoPs for cops: managing and creating knowledge through networked expertise. In P. Hildreth and C. Kimble (eds), *Knowledge Networks: Innovation through Communities of Practice*. London: Idea Group Publishing.

Labov, W. (1972) *Sociolinguistic Patterns*. Philidelphia: University of Pennsylvania Press.

Lave, J. and E. Wenger (1991) *Situated Learning: Legitimate Peripheral Participation*. Cambridge: Cambridge University Press.

Linell, P. (1998) Discourse across boundaries: on recontextualisation and the blending of voices in professional discourse. *Text 18 (2)* 143–157.

McElhinny, B. (1998) I don't smile much anymore: affect, gender and the discourse of Pittsburgh police officers. In J. Coates (ed), *Language and Gender: A Reader*. Oxford: Blackwell Publishers, 309–327.

Meyerhoff, M. (1999) Sorry in the pacific: defining communities, defining practices. *Language in Society 28 (2)* 225–271.

Milroy, L. (1987) *Observing and Analysing Natural Language*. Oxford: Blackwell.

New Oxford Dictionary of English, The (1999) Oxford: Oxford University Press.

Norrick, N. (1994) Repetition as a conversational joking strategy. In B. Johnstone (ed), *Repetition in Discourse: Interdisciplinary Perspectives*, vol. 2. Norwood, NJ: Ablex Publishing Corporation, 15–29.

Ostermann, A.C. (2003) Communities of practice at work: gender, facework and the power of *habitus* at an all-female police station and a feminist crisis intervention centre in Brazil. *Discourse and Society 14 (4)* 473–505.

Preston, D. (1989) *Perceptual Dialectology: Non-Linguists' Views of Areal Linguistics*. Dordrecht: Foris.

Russell, S. (2000) "Let me put it simply": the case for a standard translation of the police caution and its explanation. *Forensic Linguistics 7 (1)* 26–48.

Saville-Troike, M. (1985) The place of silence in an integrated theory of communication. In D. Tannen and M. Saville-Troike (eds), *Perspectives on Silence*. NJ: Ablex Publishing Corporation.

Scollon, R. (1998) *Mediated Discourse as Social Interaction: A Study of News Discourse*. London: Longman.

Scollon, R. (2001) *Mediated Discourse: The Nexus of Practice*. London: Routledge.

Scollon, R. and Scollon, S. (1979) *Linguistic Convergence: An Ethnography of Speaking at Fort Chipewyan, Alberta*. New York: Academic Press.

Scollon, R. and Scollon, S. (1981) *Narrative, Literacy and Face in Interethnic Communication*. Norwood, New Jersey: Ablex Publishing Corporation.

Searle, J. (1969) *Speech Acts: An Essay in the Philosophy of Language*. Cambridge: Cambridge University Press.

Shuy, R. (1997) Ten unanswered language questions about Miranda. *Forensic Linguistics 4 (2)* 175–195.

Swales, J. (1990) *Genre Analysis: English in Academic and Research Settings*. Cambridge: Cambridge University Press.

Swales, J. (1998) *Other Floors, Other Voices: A Textography of a Small University Building*. Mahwah, New Jersey: Lawrence Erlbaum Associates.

Tajfel, H. (1978) Interindividual behaviour and intergroup behaviour. In Tajfel, H. (ed), *Differentiation Between Social Groups: Studies in the Social Psychology of Intergroup Relations*. London and New York: Academic Press, 27–60.

Tajfel, H. and Turner, J. (1986) The social identity theory of intergroup behaviour. In Austin, W. and Worchel, S. (eds), *Psychology of Intergroup Relations*. Chicago: Nelson Hall, 7–24.

Tannen, D. (ed) (1993) *Framing in Discourse*. Oxford: Oxford University Press.

Wenger, E. (1998a) *Communities of Practice: Learning, Meaning and Identity*. Cambridge: Cambridge University Press.

Wenger, E. (1998b) Communities of practice: learning as a social system. *Systems Thinker 9 (5)* 2–3 (June/July 1998).

Winter, E. (1979) Replacement as a fundamental function of the sentence in context. *Forum Linguisticum 4 (2)* 95–188.

TRANSCRIPTION KEY

- (.)   A pause (timings have not been analysed here)
- -   A halt or abrupt cut-off
- ...   Hesitation features have been removed from the transcript to aid reading
- " "   Words inside quotation marks are reported speech or thought
- [ ]   Words inside square brackets are comments
- (( )) Unclear words

5

The Person in the Doing: Negotiating the Experience of Self

Maria Clara Keating

If the world is held together by communicative acts and connected through communicative channels, to speak means to choose a particular way of entering the world and a particular way of sustaining relationships with those we come in contact with. It is then through language use that we, to a large extent, are members of a community of ideas and practices.

(Duranti 1997:46)

INTRODUCTION[1]

This chapter engages in a critical assessment of some of the concepts underlying the Communities of Practice approach to social life and suggests ways of complementing it with theories of language (Halliday 1993), discourse (Chouliaraki and Fairclough 2000) and with an approach to situated activity (Engeström, Miettinen and Punamäki 1999). To focus on the person in the doing from a language and discursive perspective implies that "participation in practice" is far from being a consensual and adaptative process of apprenticeship, but a conflicting and problematic process of negotiation of meanings, where mental, psychological, social and discursive aspects are revealed in the person's own process of making signs (Kress 1997). In particular, dynamics such as *participation* and *reification* are not merely

[1] This research could not have been carried out without the full support of the Calouste Gulbenkian Foundation, Lisbon Portugal and the Centre for Social Studies at the University of Coimbra, Portugal.

located in communities of practice but are also language-based and *situated* in broader formations of practice and discourse, immersed in social, structural and historical orders (Barton et al. 2000).

The present chapter draws on ethnographic research into the routes through language and literacy practices experienced by a group of Portuguese women who have migrated to London. It focussed on the role of language and literacy in people's processes of creating identities in migrant situations[2]. This was a dynamic process where people played their own active role, located in the changing environment of the Portuguese community in London that saw its profile shift rapidly from that of 'migrant' (with all the restrictions that 'being a migrant' implies) to that of 'European citizenship' since 1986 (with all the apparent social and economic possibilities that 'European citizenship' implies). Social transition opened space for conflicting, ambiguous and hybrid ways of doing that overlapped the old and the new. New ways of understanding business, work, education, community associations and public institutions were emerging for the Portuguese in the city of London, but they did not replace the restrictions (in terms of language, work or social welfare) that people still experienced in their daily lives and that confined a vast majority of them to the traditional places of social activity (usually, domestic help and the service sector). The study focussed on the mechanisms of agency, resistance and transformation revealed by personal experiences with language and literacy as these experiences emerged from the changing structural and historical factors that configured them in many faceted ways (Keating 2001).

PEOPLE, COMMUNITIES AND PRACTICES IN
MIGRANT SETTINGS: AMBIVALENT TENSIONS
IN THE PROCESSES OF "BEING"

Etienne Wenger's definition of practice within the framework of Communities of Practice is a helpful analytical tool to establish the link between individual doings and understandings and cultural/social

---

[2] Migration is a key factor in the social and economic profiles of Portugal. Its semi-peripheral position in the world both as a country hosting immigrants and as a country exporting emigrants gives Portugal a unique profile, of being both a 'centre' and a 'periphery'. This allows an interesting analytical position that can take hybridity as a starting assumption for social research (Santos 1993, 1995, 2001).

ways of using literacy. Shared "doings" (practices), shared "understandings" (learning) and shared "senses of one's own self" and of the other (identities) forge each other within the frames of certain communities or groups that exist because their members have common interests and aims (Wenger 1998:47). "Doings" imply explicit representations and materialities (including print or handwritten materials) and yet also tacit or implicit assumptions about these doings. In fieldwork, I found myself involved and immersed in the posters, billboards, flyers and flags, colours, smells, music, Portuguese-based talking styles like loud laughs, overlaps or *talking bad* (Goldstein 1995). These were some of many other materialities that constructed the settings where the women in the study participated as being public, Portuguese, church, association, travel agency or driving school. Tacit and implicit assumptions about "migrant things" also existed in the minds of the people who gathered around the common aim of maintaining these settings. People acted accordingly, motivated by the wish to meet a shared aim, with shared sensitivities and "embodied understandings" of the practices. In this sense, the social and the intuitive, the material and the assumed, the explicit and the tacit met to be part of a sense of 'wholeness' that only came into being through shared activity and participation. The flexible and dynamic aspects of communities of practice (together with their degree of shared history and joint enterprise that allow them some kind of stability that supports the existence of such groups) highlighted two facts about the field. Firstly, the Portuguese community in London existed in spite of the mobility of the Portuguese coming to and fro from Portugal and the UK, because there were groups of people who practiced Portuguese ways of doing on a regular and a local basis. Secondly, the routes through literacy practices of the women in the study were somehow based on the existence of communities of practice that they entered at some point, with which they learned something, eventually changed their ways of doing things, and in this process created new aims for themselves (Keating 2001).

Applying this approach to a general migrant setting might run the risk of distorting its very definition. Wenger focuses on local gatherings of individuals within regulated organisations such as the claims processing department where he has done his ethnographic work – not on mobile, ever-changing settings such as Portuguese migrant associations, or hybrid offices where travel agency, driving school and interpreting office overlap in order to meet the unexpected needs of people in their migrant, foreign, highly informal and subordinate situation. In this, Wenger's concept of *community* became somewhat misleading. People in migrant settings actually lived, worked and learned in Communities of Practice as they are defined by this author, and yet, a very different notion of community lingered on; one that implied political, historical and discursive configurations that went beyond people's own doings and yet were present in their minds and lives through values, attitudes, representations or artefacts that constructed these people's identifications and identities as Portuguese in London.

Wenger establishes the link between local ways of doing and broader social and historical structures by considering practice as "that level of social structure that best reflects shared learning experiences" (Wenger 1998:126). In participating in everyday social action, individuals change to meet other individuals' ways of doing things, in a constant negotiation of meanings that implies *participating* in practice and *reifying* it, or producing reifications about it. Individuals and practices (and indirectly communities) constitute each other in mutual and dynamic ways, both changing in this process. Underlying this social approach to learning is a consensual view on social interaction, where people act to reach a space of *shared* understanding between people (i.e., a space of intersubjectivity that allows development (cf. Rogoff 1990)). It is based on a model of apprenticeship (Lave and Wenger 1991) that focuses on people's learning events as "integrated into the formation of practices and identities" (Wenger 1998:125). Practices exist as coherent and established wholes, with their "insides" and "outsides", even when sustained over time by continuities and discontinuities that allow them the possibility of change and transformation (Wenger 1998:129). As a consequence, the tense, conflicting, ambiguous process of the discursive and power negotiations implied in the construction of these centres and boundaries is silenced *as if* it were a settled process. Who defines the unitary entity, how it is defined and in whose interests it is defined as a whole does not appear in the foreground, making it into a somewhat "ideal" approach (Swales 1998:196–208).

In part, the peripheral role that language and discourse play in this social approach to learning leads to this consensual model. "Discourse" is defined as a "social, interactive resource for constructing statements about the world and coordinating engagement in practice, reflecting an enterprise and the perspective of a community of practice" (Wenger 1998:289). Defining "discourse" as "resource" is as far as the author goes. Language is repertoire and "available material" that travels from practice to practice, forms continuities and discontinuities and is reinterpreted and adapted to other practices (Wenger 1998:129), but not social practice itself. In Wenger's view, establishing relationships between things and making meanings of them are the basic foundations of learning (i.e., *participating* and *reifying*). In the alternative view expressed here, participating in the process of establishing relationships to constitute the reified resources is social semiotic action, including language and linguistic action. Meaning-making mechanisms sustain the acts of creating stable meanings, linguistic forms or language styles; they also sustain the acts of constructing, deconstructing and reinventing these meanings, thus acknowledging their instability. Language and meaning-making mechanisms are an intricate part of learning and the latter cannot be properly considered without the former. To look at these negotiations as 'discursive' complements yet challenges Wenger's consensual definition of 'practice' and 'the social'. It acknowledges the existence of conflicts and ambivalences and searches for the mechanisms that handle and underlie these tensions. In that sense, it brings a dynamic view to the act of negotiating meanings, deeply permeated by issues of power and ideology.

THE PERSON IN THE DOING: LANGUAGE, DISCOURSE, PARTICIPATION AND ACTIVITY

To think about participation in social practice implies thinking about the ways people act in social settings and thus relate to the practices of their everyday lives. Usually, one thinks about participation in terms of people's doings and the ways these doings fit into ways shared by groups or communities. On the one hand, social approaches to learning look at the ways in which people change their terms of participation in the attempt to participate fully in social practices (cf. Chaiklin and Lave 1993, Wenger 1998). On the other hand, language research with a focus on speech in social interaction sees participation in terms of the sequences and units of speech that give expression to particular social roles, sustained by social organisations and institutions, that people use as resources. This provides a link between people's uses and the ways these are socially constituted and forged (cf. Duranti 1997).

A further development of this is to locate these uses of language as practices sustained by discourses and discursive fields, to which people relate in the act of utterance. In this sense, participation is seen as the extent to which people can use discourses coming from different fields and reproduce them or bring them together in acts of creativity, thus providing openness in the construction of social representations and realities (Fairclough 1989, 1992; Fairclough and Wodak 1997; Chouliaraki and Fairclough 2000). Chouliaraki and Fairclough's view of discourse as a "semiotic moment of social practice" provides a position from which one can understand not only the learning mechanisms going on as people participate in social practice, but also the semiotic and the discursive mechanisms that these participations imply. (For a full discussion of this link, cf. Chapter 2, this volume.) First, it defines language as an ongoing process of being styles and resources, able to be rearticulated with others and thus prone to 'gaps' for creativity and renewal. Second, it situates the person's "ways with words" in discursive forms and fields that open particular subjectivities from which the person departs, to which she orients and of which she becomes aware in the process of participation in social practice. As Chouliaraki and Fairclough point out, people's positions depend on the access, the lived experiences with the available discourses and the social orders and structures that configure these positions. This "affects the degree of openness or closure of the practices in which they are involved" (Chouliaraki and Fairclough 2000:121)[3].

---

[3] Insights into the openness of the social world would need the sort of analysis which cannot be made here. What matters for this purpose is the insight that ways that people have of relating to discourses imply argumentative positions (cf. Billig 1991, 1996) at the moment of negotiation and meaning making in situated activity that vary according to people's own histories, past experiences, motivations, resisting or aligning attitudes and ways of envisaging their own aims and future outcomes as they engage in activity. With what tools is the person engaging in situated activity, thus participating in practices and using the discourses (and the literacies) around her? How does the person recognise and use the strategies provided by language and discourse to engage in aligning or transformative modes of participation? These are questions underlying the analysis of the data, and they remain to be answered in its full complexity. They provide a structural determination that should not disappear in the analysis.

Participation can imply actions and doings, as well as linguistic acts of representation of these doings. It thus emerges in the tension between social action and the semiotic mechanisms that bring meaning to (and in a way constitute) this social action. This is particularly relevant in Halliday's language-based theory of learning that sees learning as semiosis, best analysed through a systemic-functional approach that implies multifunctional dimensions of linguistic use (Halliday 1993):

I have suggested that learning consists in expanding one's meaning potential, and up to this point, meaning potential has been defined in terms of the ideational (experiential plus logical) and interpersonal meta-functions. The interpersonal component of the grammar is that of "language as action"; this builds up into a rich array of speech functions, modalities, personal forms, keys and various dimensions of force and attitude by which the speaker enacts immediate social relationships and, more broadly, the whole pattern of the social system with its complexity of roles, statuses, voices, and the like. The experiential component of the grammar is that of "language as reflection"; this expands into a theory of human experience, construing the processes of the "outside world", as well as those of inner consciousness, and (in a related but distinct "logical" component) the logical-semantic relations that may obtain between one process and another. Together these make up a semiotic resource for doing and for understanding **as an integrated mode of activity**. (Halliday 1993:107)

In Halliday's terms, the ideational meta-function (i.e., the "inner and outer" representations of the world) and the interpersonal meta-function of language (i.e., the speaker's resources for enacting social relations through language) constitute "an integrated mode of activity", in which doing and understanding intermingle in simultaneous and complex ways. Halliday goes on to introduce the "textual" meta-function as the way through which language creates semiotic relations of its own that function as coherent models or "metaphors" for action and experience (i.e., 'meaning worlds' that will allow the space for theoretical knowledge (cf. Halliday 1993:108). Essential as it is to explore adults' learning further, this issue will be set aside for the time being in order to concentrate on the tension between ideational and interpersonal. By highlighting ideational or interpersonal modes of meaning, translated by any linguistic items that convey the tension between the speaker's distance or proximity to what she is 'trying to say', the person complexifies her understanding and resolves the tensions that exist between the subject positions being brought into the utterance. In this language activity, the person reifies, participates and reifies again, in a constant process of negotiation of meanings. Also, as people use language in particular ways, they go through personal processes of *becoming* particular identities. Underlying this process of *becoming* are individual acts of appropriating the subjectivities offered by the language, the artefacts, the resources, the communities of practice and all other factors shaping the situated event. Again, to forge particular identities or senses of self depends on the ways individuals are participating in the activity, use the resources at their disposal (and the subjectivities that they carry) and do something about them.

This engagement in doing may be analysed by focussing on individuals' *activities* as they happen in *events*. This highlights the creative processes of negotiation and argumentation that the person uses in her everyday doings. It opens up new paths to explore people's participation in *practices* and the *communities* that these practices imply. Insights about this from *Activity Theory* are particularly useful in this process. Activity theory (originating from the work by Vygotsky, Leont'ev and Luria in the 1920s) develops ideas about the social nature and formation of the human mind, in which the relation between individuals and social environments is best seen through the ways individuals act upon objects in the world, mediated by tools, signs or artefacts – shaped by the social and cultural environments where these actions are taking place. Actions also imply collective activities and thus social relations and interactions. Human action as mediated activity transcends the dualism between thought and action and, one could add here, between actual deeds and semiotic representations, as they imply one another in dialectic ways (Engeström and Miettinen 1999:5). Of the five themes of debate within activity theory outlined by Engeström (1999:21–28), three seem to be particularly relevant for a framework that tries to apply insights about activity to studies of language and literacy. Firstly, activity theory and theories of mediated action give emphasis to issues of language as tools and artefacts. Since Vygotsky, signs and language have been seen as mediating tools in object-oriented action. The tension rises according to whether one wants to concentrate on the role that signs have in the production and achievement of goals or on the forging of the means of expression and communication proper, as these are mediated by signs[4]. Secondly, activity theory has focussed mainly on the ways in which the sociocultural context of the activity impinges on individual and mental processes of internalisation. This is inspired by Vygotsky's original interest in issues of internalisation and the development of higher psychological functions. Engeström, however, suggests that complementary views of externalisation and creativity are crucial to contemporary research, particularly as it becomes gradually more important to establish links between individual human agency and the transformation of the structural organisation of societies[5]. To focus on the ways new artefacts and new social patterns are created can thus allow researchers to understand in more depth these mechanisms of personal and social change. Thirdly, activity theory gives particular relevance to issues of historicity. To look at actions as they are situated in the intersection of the histories of the various components that interact in a particular activity provides a manageable approach that acknowledges both social and individual processes of change (ontogeny and phylogeny):

Historical analyses must be focused on units of manageable size. If the unit is the individual, or the individually constructed situation, history is reduced to ontogeny or biography. If the unit is the culture or the society, history becomes very general or endlessly complex. If a collective activity system is taken as the unit, history may become manageable, and yet it steps beyond the confines of individual biography. (Engeström 1999:26)

Acting in the social world, then, implies the interplay of a number of factors that have their own history of engagement in previous

---

[4] Links between activity and language need further empirical research and provide connections between linguistic, discursive, semiotic and sociocultural mechanisms that are in urgent need of being brought together in a systematic way.

[5] The need for creativity and inspired new ideas is turning into a commodified asset that individuals need to display as they enter the labour market, and the mechanisms through which this is appropriated and 'managed' would need further understanding and critical awareness. One example of the way activity theory has been appropriated by management studies and sociology of organisations is Frank Blackler's research on the "management of change" (i.e., "how to manage change"). Blackler looks at how individual people act within organisations, and how, by participating in local activities, they change both themselves and the broader organisation (Blackler 1992, 1993).

activities. As they meet in a particular time and space configuration, they produce outcomes that will determine future activities. Engeström has thus developed activity theory by including other aspects that in his view determine the ways individuals act upon the world (such as *informal rules, institutional structures* and *communities of practice* – all of them with their own "histories of being" located in previous activities), thus devising what he has called an *activity system* (cf. Engeström 1999).

In my own research, this focus on individual people through the activity system was helpful in accounting for the historicity of the person's experiences with literacy. It added a historical focus both to the individual's developing ways with literacy and to the changes happening within the Portuguese community, as individuals engaged in situated activities. Even though uniquely positioned in their own historical configurations, the women in the study shared common ways of experiencing the environments that they met upon their move to Britain and common ways of handling, coping with and developing their reading and writing practices, in both Portuguese and English. When relating to social practices of literacy, these women seemed to *repeat*, to *recognise*, to *reflect* upon and to *recombine* ways with literacy and, in this process, *reinvent* these practices for themselves. More than being simple and straightforward, these women's experiences were kaleidoscopic, personal and social, stable and changing, particular yet general – implying the workings of language, literacy, mental processes, ideologies, social structures and histories (Keating 2001).

A focus on *activity* complements the focus on *practice*. On the one hand, *practice,* and participation in practice in particular, involves sedimented ways of doing, talking, reading, writing and being – in sum acting in the social world, sustaining and sustained by social organisations and structures, and yet open for change and transformation by the people that reproduce, resist or enact these social actions. On the other hand, *activity* brings in the person's engagement in a focussed and microscopic way, involving the person in the doing, her own history and her own processes of negotiating the aims, the tools and artefacts used in the doing. It thus provides a systematic view on the ways the person reacts to locally configured environments, draws from the resources that she evaluates as being there at reach and finds new ways of relating to them. As activities are *loci* of tensions and contradictions that derive from the components at play, and from the histories of participation that each component carries, activities are also sites of negotiation of voices that interact with each other in polyphonic ways. Tensions and contradictions are thus discursive, solved as people act and thus enhance or silence particular words and associations to reach the discursive moment of social practice.

There are ways in which a focus on activity adds to studies of literacy as a social practice. Literacy can be seen in terms of its multiple materialities, social practices, discursive configurations and people's participation – doings and learning (Barton et al. 2000, Keating 2001). Firstly, materialities of language can be seen as being forged in activity and used as artefacts for further action. Secondly, practices are configured in activity in the sense that they are being appropriated, used as resources and reproduced in local events. They are thus configured in unique ways that affect the practice and might change it in the long run. Thirdly, identities are being forged in the tension between the subjectivities that emerge from the way the activity is being performed at a particular time, space and social configuration. Finally, changing participation by individuals in actions (i.e., learning) emerges in people's negotiations as they engage in activities. Again, these negotiations can be seen only as social actions or also as linguistic and discursive doings.

These insights will be further illustrated by looking at the ways in which one of the women in the study, Isaura, negotiated meanings and senses of self in an event where she compared two women's magazines, one in Portuguese and the other in English. By engaging in this act of comparing, Isaura drew on resources of very different kinds to make sense of both magazines and her self in the course of the conversation with the interviewer.

NEGOTIATING THE EXPERIENCE OF 'SELF':
ISAURA READING MAGAZINES

Isaura, Novels and Gendered Magazines

The use of gendered literacy materials was a lasting influence in Isaura's ways of making sense of herself and her environments since childhood. Apparently, Isaura followed a number of literacy patterns that echoed a recognised stereotype of the female roles and behaviour around literacy. They resonated with the findings in the British national survey of adults and children's reading, in which women's reading practices were said to be attached to the use of genres like romances, sagas and fiction and implied an overall attitude of "escaping to another world" and "exercising imagination". Behind this use, however, is a complex negotiation between people's inner motivations and the ways they handle the ideologies at play in the contexts in which they have been socialised (Barton and Hamilton 1998:170–176). In Isaura and other women in the study, these motivations and emotional responses seem to have been based on "the different experiences and cultural knowledges that they brought to the reading"[6] and used in different modes and with different aims. Over time, Isaura used gendered literacies to escape the pressures of her family in Portugal and workplace in Britain, get information, learn English or find references that would enable her to evaluate the world around her (Gray 1992, Hermes 1995, Ang and Hermes 1996, Barton and Hamilton 1998:170–176).

The literacy event about to be described took place in Isaura's living room. Isaura compared two women's magazines, one in English and the other in Portuguese. In the course of engagement in this, Isaura textually negotiated her sense of self by using particular meaning-making mechanisms and by drawing upon the resources that she had available at that moment and place. Before introducing the event, there will be a short description of the magazines and of the sections that Isaura picked up in the course of her comparison, where the researcher brings her own perspective and experience of these artefacts and texts as a fieldworker. They will provide a context of dialogue between what I have seen and learned from these texts and the ways Isaura appropriated them in her own evaluation and comparison.

Material Artefacts as 'Resources': 'Take a Break' and 'Maria'

Large in size, and printed on cheap paper, *Take a Break* (Figure 5.1) is considered one of the most widely read housewives' magazines, usually associated with others like *Bella* and *Chat*. It is largely made

---

[6] Cf. Gray (1992), cited in Barton and Hamilton (1998).

FIGURE 5.1. *Take a Break*, issue no. 28, 11 July 1996, H. Bauer Publishing.

up of "true stories" and photographs of "real people" that readers sell to the editor for prices between £50 and £200. Other women in Isaura's Portuguese-speaking networks in London mentioned it, and one of them sold the story of her experience as the wife of a Portuguese migrant to this magazine. This was taken as an example for Isaura, who mentioned in our interview the possibility of publishing her own story about her daughter's health problems. Photographs on the front page depict family scenes – mainly heterosexual couples, parents and children – sitting indoors on couches. Screaming headlines – in which words associated with "war" and "violence" like "torture", "front-zone", "dare" and "destroyed" – catch the eye of the reader. Marked lexical items, like "nan" and "toyboy", describe family or close relationships. *"Readers' reality"* (Figure 5.2) is *Take a Break*'s

FIGURE 5.2. *"Readers' reality"* page, *Take a Break* 11 July 1996, H Bauer Publishing.

section that Isaura picked up as "the problem page". It consists of two and half pages of "real life stories". Topics in this issue ran along the lines of sexual harassment and persecution at work, death of a parent, extra-marital affairs, negative experience of an interracial and inter-cultural close relationship and terminal illness caused by smoking. All of these stories showed disturbed feelings and drastic attitudes towards close relationships, together with an emphasis on the effect of these on the narrator. The stories usually had the same type of narrative scheme: presenting a state of affairs, bringing change or disturbance in this state of affairs and concluding with solutions that kept the balance and conformed to the norm. In the end, characters were "disturbed" but got over it. The stories ended with moral issues and were taken as "learning experiences".

FIGURE 5.3. *Maria* magazine, issue no. 922, 10–16 July 1996, Grupo Impala.

Maria (Figure 5.3) is one of the most popular magazines published in Portugal and widely read by the female population, both in Portugal and in the migrant communities. It has a small A6 manageable size and is published by a professional team and by people hired for their particular expertise. Reader's collaboration is allowed in writing only in "the reader's page". The front page of this issue depicts a young popular Portuguese football player on the beach, thus bringing in two stereotypes of Portuguese social and economic life – football and tourism. Surrounding the photograph, and also in primary colours, are titles describing the contents of the magazine. A game of words with the title of the most popular Brazilian soap opera at the time, *"Explode coração"* (Explode heart), represents Dani,

FIGURE 5.4. *"Consultório íntimo"*, Maria magazine, issue no. 922, 10–16 July 1996, Grupo Impala.

the "football player", as a "heart exploder". The semantic environment of this front page is limited to heterosexual relationships and marriage made explicit by the use of words like "heart, marriages and quick sex". *"Consultório íntimo"* (Figure 5.4) is the section pointed out by Isaura as *Maria's* problem page. Visual representations of ordinary people are absent, and the one photo in the four pages embraces the topic as its icon. The main textual format is the conventional question and answer genre, where 'the expert' (in this case, a middle-aged Portuguese man in a passport photograph, named with the professional title of "Dr.", meaning that he has acquired a higher education degree) gives advice about experiences shared by the female reader. Topics are limited to intimate relationships and heterosexual marriage reinforced in the 'expert's' voice: "this section is for you and your [male companion]". These textual positions, together with the formal division between a three-page section "for her" and a one-page section "for him", reinforces the reader identity as female, heterosexual, involved in a clear sexual division of labour. For women, problems included adultery, rape, falling in love with a priest, an older man or a husband's friend, controlling passionate feelings and being jealous. For men, problems oriented to the physical performance of sex.

Sexuality is constructed in both magazines in an interesting game of hide and seek. In *Take a Break*, it hides under the index titles of stories of disrupted relationships, disguised under the neutral tone of a Health section. In *Maria*, it is overt and linked to "how to's", performance and women's active role and responsibility in it. Representations of gender and sex seem to be as obvious, overt and explicit in the Portuguese magazine as they are disguised or implicit in the English magazine.

THE EVENT

Isaura first mentioned *Take a Break* by assigning it to "the stuff that she usually read" and decided to go to her room to fetch it. She left the living room declaring that *Take a Break* was better than *Maria* and came back with a copy of each. With this, Isaura created the space to compare the two magazines as an instance of her reading practices, and thus prepared the ground for the event that followed.

As Isaura entered the room with the two artefacts, I first picked *Take a Break* and looked at *Maria*. Isaura held *Maria* in her hands as she mentioned that it had nothing of worth in it. I shifted my attention from *Take a Break* to *Maria* and asked why. Isaura took *Take a Break* out of my hands and stated that "this one was good".

As she focussed on *Take a Break*, Isaura highlighted a particular section, the one on "real lives". This one was "different" because it provided her with more relevant information. She stopped at the *"Readers' reality"* page and expanded on this difference in general terms. By engaging in a personal narrative about her difficulties in dealing with medical discourse, and the ways she used this magazine as a source of information, Isaura concluded with one word, *"esclarece-se"* (one gets information), left the English magazine and picked up the Portuguese one.

Isaura then described how she usually read *Maria*. As she turned the pages, she selected the relevant sections to illustrate her points, using action verbs in the simple present. She used this verbal strategy to recognise and reflect upon the existence of a certain practice around the act of reading this magazine.

The activity changed as Isaura stopped at the *"Consultório íntimo"* page that she considered "too explicit". She shared worries about children's access to public representations of sex and the body. Once, Isaura realised that her daughter had been handling, together with her teenage cousin, a copy of *Maria* with explicit photos of childbirth, thus getting the information about "where babies came from". Isaura used this narrative as an example of how children "get to know things parents don't expect them to", as they handle the literacy materials available in the environment. This set up the topic of children's access and reactions to certain materials and from there the topic of particular media representations. Isaura first assessed the distribution of general as opposed to sex magazines in England and evaluated *Maria* as a 'hybrid', one that brought together features of both genres (combining explicit photos with cooking recipes) that she disliked. She then associated her son's learning experiences at home and school, and her own past school experiences. She finally generalised by associating magazines with TV, sex with violence and her son's once situated reaction to a particular set of explicit photos with children's reactions to media representations. Isaura mentioned the need to be careful about keeping the balance between avoiding certain representations, and dealing with children's reactions and curiosity when that happened. Isaura then *recombined* these issues as parts of her worries, as a mother, about her children's sex education.

Mapping the Event: Resources, Actions and Meaning-Making Mechanisms

For reasons within this interaction, Isaura felt it was relevant to engage in the act of comparing her two favourite magazines that she

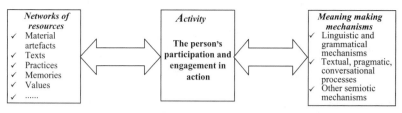

FIGURE 5.5. Resources, actions and meaning-making mechanisms.

concluded by linking her preference for the English magazine to issues outside the located event, namely her life and her children's education. Isaura's appropriation of the textual features, genres and broader contexts of production and reception of both magazines was selective and relevant only to her aims, in that she used these artefacts partially and sometimes dismissed them. There was thus an ambiguous dynamic between the construction of the reader by the magazine and the selection, construction and appropriation of those texts made by the reader herself in the process of engaging in activities with particular aims.

Three dimensions were involved in Isaura's participation in this event – *resources*, *actions* and *meaning-making mechanisms* (Figure 5.5). *Resources* include the material artefacts described previously and the ways these were handled and used in interaction. Those uses configured them as different texts, according to Isaura's aims and strategies of participation. However, resources also included other elements, such as Isaura's memories of past activities, subjective experiences, practices, values and discourses. They were part of Isaura's past or present membership and participation in a number of communities of practice, located in constellations and situated in social orders of very different natures. There were moments when Isaura drew from the material artefacts and used them as texts; elsewhere, Isaura dismissed the material texts and brought in narratives of personal experiences and evaluations of her social environment. Resources of different natures could be translated into linguistic forms and genres or just appropriated in other meaning-making processes. In this process, there emerged particular configurations of subjectivity.

Different sequences in the event describe Isaura's *actions* in broad ways. (Appendix 1 maps the relationship between resources, actions and meaning-making mechanisms in this event in detail.) These were steps in the interaction, where particular topics and aims were being negotiated. Topics and ways of handling them were partly configured by previous sequences, by the aims negotiated in those sequences and in the event as a whole, and by the ways they were negotiated between the participants in the event (i.e., Isaura and me). The dynamics between resources, participants and aims configured the outcomes of these *activities*. The analysis focusses on Isaura and the ways she used linguistic and non-linguistic strategies – from speech acts to ways of handling print, from decisions to hesitations, from gesturing and pointing to deictic verbal elements – to create relationships between resources at her reach. Isaura's participation was, however, moulded by a joint process of meaning making, related to the ways both participants understood each other's words and actions, also linked to personal histories of past participation. This process was, thus, unique for Isaura. It brought her own history and her own sign-making process (cf. Kress 1997), to the extent that the other participant could see it in interaction and discussed it with her in later meetings. To describe the other person's actions would mean analysing a different *activity*.

Meaning-making devices used by Isaura signalled, in one way or another, the textual and discursive dynamics of the sequences in the event. She confronted or associated, in textual ways, resources of different kinds and made sense of them this way. However, these textual devices were not a post-hoc "illustration" of the actions performed by Isaura or of the resources being drawn in interaction. In fact, it was the use of those particular language devices that brought the resources together, moulded and constituted Isaura's actions 'in *activity*'. They brought Isaura's involvement or detachment from the resources and from the actions in which she was engaging. There were explicit or implicit decisions that made her use those and not other language devices. Her decision making was intimately dependent on her own history of participation and her 'language history'. To look at the ways these language devices were distributed and associated as "styles" or "ways" in Isaura's practices would also help to understand her configuration of resources and, simultaneously, understand the ways she articulated them in new ways in future activities, in a dynamic process of *recombination*.

NEGOTIATING THE EXPERIENCE OF SELF: PARTICIPATING AND LEARNING AS SOCIAL ACTION

By engaging in the reading of two of her favourite magazines, Isaura went through a complex process of meaning making, where a dynamic flowed between participating in action and reifying this participation.

First, Isaura engaged in the act of negotiating the way in which the interview question made sense to her. As she chose to use these two magazines and favoured one, she *reified* her opinion. She then *participated* in the act of comparison. At each step, Isaura appropriated the artefacts described previously (firstly, magazines as a whole, then the problem pages and finally an evaluation of the representations of sex in both magazines) and brought them together with different experiences of her life, mostly encoded in narratives. Isaura then dismissed the texts and brought in other resources that could help her support her position: her experience of the market distribution of magazines in Britain, the *recognition* of different genres in popular magazines, experiences and memories of school, home and community and her children's sex education. In this last sequence, some aspects which had been reified as she participated in the act of comparing the two magazines were reappropriated and *reified* again (i.e., *recombined* or rearticulated) in more general terms, under broader issues of children's access to media representations of sex, sexual education and children's education. This last reification process anchored and generalised Isaura's evaluations in her identity as "a mother".

This dynamic is also found within each sequence of the event, within the language and meaning-making mechanisms that Isaura used to make sense of the texts in front of me. She appropriated items reified in the previous sequence, expanded them by associating them with others and further generalising them, thus engaging in a dynamic sign-making process. This can be further illustrated by looking at the analysis of a full transcription of one of the mentioned sequences (Appendix 2). In general, the use of simple present vs. past participle, mood and modality, generic nouns vs. personal or proper nouns illustrated Isaura's process of negotiating her own positions in relation to the resources that she was picking up. Through ideational and interpersonal functions of language, Isaura was "construing the

processes of 'the outside world', as well as those of inner consciousness" (Halliday 1993:107). As meaning making is also about forging
selves, Isaura negotiated, in the active dialogue between subjectivities, the way she made sense, not only of the world represented by the
magazines that she read, but also of the world that she experienced in
her everyday life, through the discursive mechanisms that supported
that moment of social practice. In this process, Isaura created her own
sense of self and her basis for understanding, deeply situated in the
contexts and in the materials that she had at her reach.

Behind all this was Isaura's motivation to learn. That was explicit
later in the conversation when she said. "I like to read it, and that's
it. Because one learns something with this magazine" (G2/A/632–
634). It was this reason that made it crucial to bring the ways in
which she brought together texts and other resources according to her
aims, situated in that particular moment of the interview. It brought a
focus to the ways learning was *done* in this interactive and discursive
process.

Two final things need to be said about this particular process of participation and learning. Firstly, that the choice of women's magazines
as Isaura's familiar literacy was not a 'free choice', but a situated one,
in terms of gender, economic, cultural or geographical "mappings
of the self" (Pile and Thrift 1995). Secondly, that in Britain, Isaura
used her familiar genre to deal with the institutional discourses that
she did not understand – such as the medical doctor's description
of her daughter's disease. This brought a number of issues to the
fore: women's magazines seem to be a "global" phenomenon, one
that crossed frontiers and languages, with the necessary adapting
processes to the local audiences. This meant that the configuration
of subject positions and the construction of the reader ran along the
same rough lines, thus bringing a certain "type of woman" and a certain type of "women's practices" to the fore. However, this "global
positioning" also meant that the genre could be appropriated as a
"way into" a number of more empowering local discourses, situated in particular configurations of time and space. Isaura seems to
have done that. By relocating her practice of magazine reading, she
learned English and used it as a way to understand the institutional
discourses otherwise opaque to her, because of language, register and
practice. By reading *Take a Break*, Isaura found a way of dealing with
the medical discourse in English. This global genre was thus used as

a point of departure for further learning and creativity at a local site. It is thus fully embedded in the social and the literacy practices that are part of the social dynamics of the global consumer society of late capitalism at the end of the twentieth century.

CONCLUSION

In this research, the Communities of Practice approach provided a useful mid-level framework when trying to locate people, practices and communities in a hybrid and informal context of migration but did not provide tools to understand the ways in which these are situated in broader social and discursive orders. When used to look at the person's lived experiences with literacy, it provided a focus on the personal process of changing participation in practice but did not acknowledge that the negotiations going on in this process, mainly described through the dynamics of participation and reification, are also discursive, semiotic and language-based.

This chapter makes an attempt to expand on these issues by looking at some language-based processes of making meanings as the person engages in activity. Activity implies the meeting of resources of various kinds, as well as the person's own participation in practice, each of these with its own "histories of being". Tension and conflicts that emerge from the meeting of these histories are thus resolved, silenced or resisted – in other words, enacted as the person engages in action and uses the meaning-making mechanisms at her reach. As activity implies the meeting of histories in mediated action, to look at the person in the doing has helped to understand that learning is not only about integrating events into communities of practice, but also about conflicting and problematic negotiation of meanings, situated in broader formations of practice and discourse. This view helps to account for agency and creativity. In this sense, dynamics of participation and reification can be further expanded to include the meaning-making mechanisms that individuals use in the course of their engagement in activities, in continuous, cyclic and dynamic acts of *repetition, recognition, reflection* upon and *recombination* of the resources as they emerge in activity and in the semiotic moment of practice. It thus helps to look at person's doings as mental, personal, social and discursive *acts of reinvention*, in a process of development that implies both personal and social change.

APPENDIX 1

Isaura Participating in Comparison between Maria *and* Take a Break

	Resources	Actions	Meaning-Making Mechanisms
Sequences/ activities	• *Material artifacts* • *Texts, layouts, formats* • *Practices and values* • *Memories and experiences*	• *Individual participation* • *Sequences of actions* • *Choices and negotiations*	• *Language strategies* • *Textual devices* • *Grammatical mechanisms*
Sequence/activity 1 [1–36]	*Negotiating topic* 1. Bringing personal experience when dialoguing with my interview question. 2. Positioning between "interview" (action included in academic research practice, me as researcher) and "personal experience" (real life of Isaura, Isaura as 'researched'). Isaura accepts role in the event. *Negotiating way into comparison* 1. *Take a Break* and *Maria* as two objects of analysis. Eventually drawing on one or other page, at random.	*Negotiating topic* 1. Bringing up the topic of *Maria* and *Take a Break.* 2. Going to room upstairs and fetching magazine. 3. Bringing up comparison by stating preference.	*Negotiating topic* 1. Use of attributes "the usual, *Take a Break,* the magazine"; use of definite article marked by smiling voice [16–18] 2. Comparative sentence, attributive and identifying clause "It's better than *Maria".*
Sequence/activity 2 [36–47]		*Negotiating way into comparison* 1. Negotiating who handles what materials. I handle *Take a Break,* Isaura handles *Maria.* Negotiation, flickering through random pages. 2. Bringing up attributes of both magazines. 3. Choosing *Take a Break* to start comparison and analysis; Isaura takes material out of my hands and states preference.	*Negotiating way into comparison* 1. Mental process "I like *Take a Break* better" in affirmative sentence followed by material attribute and negative sentence "*Maria* doesn't have anything of value in it". 2. "This magazine is good" – relational process of being, attributive use of 'be'.

Justifying preference

1. Using *Take a Break* as a whole object of focus.
2. The "problem page" section of *Take a Break* as "text" or object of analysis. "Stories of real life" bringing up individual's experiences of the social world.
3. Opening up the possibility of configuring personal experience to format of "real life story", as it appears in the magazine.
4. Exercising that possibility.
5. Bringing in personal experience of having to deal with medical discourse. "Função"/ function – echoing academic and medical discourses in Portuguese. Stating previous participation in one activity in which *Take a Break* was a tool to achieve the aim of dealing and understanding medical discourse and getting information.

Justifying preference

1. Negotiating way into justification, describing magazine, flickering through random pages of *Take a Break*. Bringing up "stories of real life".
2. Choice of way. Stops at 'problem page', comparison with *Maria's* problem page [54].
3. Evaluating textual resources of one vs. the other and bringing a personal attitude [76–78].
4. Bringing experience in the abstract [81–88].
5. And then narrative of personal life [93–123].
6. Concluding narrative and linking it to argument [123–127].

Justifying preference

1. Attributing and identifying "is good" "has stories" [51].
2. Use of 'deixis' to further identify 'stories'. Use of definite "these" to circumscribe reference. Use of "only has", "other things", textual and comparative terms.
3. Mood and modality "I could publish".
4. Use of generic third person "a gente" (one), link between material action and mental perceptive and cognition verbs. Use of present simple as form of habitual action.
5. Shift from present simple to past imperfect narrative mode. "Sabia qual era a 'função, mas'"/"I knew what the function was but . . .".
6. Tension between ways of bringing conclusion. Use of generic pronouns, interruption, decision for generic passive with mental cognitive verb "esclarece-se" (one gets instruction, lit. transl. one clarifies oneself).

(*continued*)

129

APPENDIX 1 (continued)

Resources	Actions	Meaning-Making Mechanisms
Bringing Maria as term of comparison	*Bringing Maria as term of comparison*	*Bringing Maria as term of comparison*
1. *Maria* as object of focus.	1. Shifting attention from *Take a Break* and picking up *Maria*, stating the restricted focus of *Maria's* problem page [131–136].	1. Cohesive device "agora" brings the new moment in the discourse.
2. Shifting focus to problem page. Problem page is text.	2. Opening to problem page and quoting from the text attitude towards it [137–141].	2. Direct quotations.
3. *Maria* as focus of analysis. Selecting particular pages as parts of the whole magazine. Attaching meaning to these in terms of Isaura's particular configuration of her own practice of reading this magazine.	3. Comparing the two [141–144].	3. Presenting sequence of actions in first person singular and present simple. 'I start reading', 'I see', 'I read jokes', 'TV does not interest me'. Subject is "I" with action and perception verbs, stating personal engagement with verbal processes.
4. Sexuality pages and explicit photograph as focuses of analysis. These pages are seen as the material instance of other eventually more explicit representations, experienced in previous activities. Sexuality page has its own history. Isaura also brings her own history of experiencing these pages in this magazine from previous activities.	4. Moving on to describe her usual way of handling *Maria*, opening magazine at particular pages, selecting the relevant ones and dismissing others [144–161].	4. More detachment from sexuality page: 'aparece aqui qualquer coisa as vezes da vida sexual'. Subject is not "I", but deleted and impersonal. Personal agency disappears. Shift to relational process, attributing 'explicit' to magazine.
	5. Stopping at 'sexuality' page and bringing a comment. Bringing her opinion about page as too explicit for young readers [162–168].	

Evaluating representations of sex in the two magazines

1. Magazines are dismissed; I am drawing from relevant topics in research 'aide memoire'; Isaura is drawing from her experience of the magazine market.

2. Isaura is drawing from her own home cultural practices and her daughter's social environment in London: bilingual use of language, parent–child relationships, frequent presence of relatives (linked to migrant family networks in London), available Portuguese medium magazines in the London context, stories about where children come from.

3. Recognition of different literacy genres as being related to different formats, types and amounts of photographs and written text.

4. Naming genres (sex vs. general access) and location of these in market distribution of these genres in the London context.

Evaluating representations of sex in the two magazines

1. I bring up 'explicit' and link it to comparison between *Take a Break* as 'English' vs. *Maria*. Isaura relates to this by backing opinion with distribution of types of magazines in England, and young readers as her criteria for 'good' or 'bad' literacies [177–186].

2. Engaging into personal narrative of her 4-year-old daughter's access to *Maria* and the influence on her sexual education [189–257].

3. Bringing up material modes of representation (photos vs. writing) as criteria for the distinction between types of magazines [260–266].

4. Bringing up the market distribution of general access vs. sex magazines in England. Photos and writing are important criteria for this distribution [267–286].

5. Responding to my question about forbidden literacies by handling *Maria*, and characterize it as a hybrid, with features of 'sex magazines' (explicit photos) and 'magazines of general access' (cooking recipes). Repeating children's access to literacies as criteria [287–309].

Evaluating representations of sex in the two magazines

1. Impersonal use of 'you'. Use of existential sentence with simple present, use of generic nouns "everybody", "children".

2. Shift to proper noun and to simple past. Use of 'past imperfect' for practices ("João was always getting angry, he spoke in Portuguese and she in English", and so on), simple past for actions within narrative. Direct quotations. Use of imperfect to bring the point of the story.

3. Bringing the word "positions" and association to 'photos' and 'writing'.

4. Use of simple present and impersonal agent, use of impersonal you.

5. Statement of mental judgment "I only condemn if …". Use of conditionals, use of plural they (the children).

6. a) Proper noun for her son, and use of conditional sentence (simple present – if he sees, he says); b) use of imperfect to bring in past experience.

7. Associating magazine and TV.

(continued)

131

Resources	Actions	Meaning-Making Mechanisms
5. *Maria* representing a 'hybrid' genre, out of place product, configured as different, other. Expecting 'article' with 'cooking recipe', not 'explicit photos'. The differentiation criteria based on values around children's access to literacies. Explicit representations equal bad literacies.	6. Expanding on children's access by bringing children's reactions to explicit representations of sex: a) stating in general; b) bringing in her son's eventual reaction to *Maria*; c) bringing in school experiences as factors of influence; d) generalizing about her own experience in past [320–351].	8. Use of conditional and simple present to state actions (generalised actions) – if he watches, I do; use of direct quotation to bring in instances of her son's reactions, use of simple present to state generalised ways of bringing sexuality in household vs. use of past tense to contrast with her own experience. Use of simple present to state usual tension between her ways and her mother's ways.
6. Expanding on values about what young children (different age groups) should or should not know. Tension home/school in children's learning, reference to past experiences of school; generation gap.	7. I bring in 'types of magazines' and Isaura expands to 'media', by associating magazines with TV. Stating opinion about the offer in the environment [352–357].	
7. Drawing on magazines as instances of 'media'; scope of action for adults in children's access to media and literacy in general, particularly representations of sex and violence. The whole comparison is linked to Isaura's position as a mother, her need to handle sexual education for children.	8. I bring in the personal scope of action in controlling children's access to literacies, Isaura brings up need of balance and negotiation and links access to literacies to children's socialization with sexuality in the household [358–409].	

APPENDIX 2

In this particular excerpt (sequence 3), Isaura was justifying the reasons for her preference towards *Take a Break*. Isaura was asserting that the magazine was good because she had an experience in which she had used this magazine as a way to complement and understand the information given by a medical doctor about her daughter's disease. Isaura learned from this magazine, because she had recognised herself and her daughter in the text of the magazine, whereas she did not recognise herself in the medical doctor's words.

The ideational component framed the whole excerpt. Isaura brought an attribute to the magazine (line 1) and ended up using a verb of cognition (line 66). She then used other language strategies that allowed her to slide from the former and arrive at the latter [1–20]. As she stopped at the *"Readers' reality"* page, she rearranged the nominal group "life stories" into nominal clauses "other things that happen in life" and "stories that people . . .". By using "I" and the modal "could", Isaura gave up distancing herself from what she was saying, and associated her own personal participation and experience to the real life stories of this magazine. "Stories that people . . ." turned into "I could publish my story" in line 21. This shift was followed by Isaura's engagement in a tension of proximity and distance. The use of the generic expression *a gente* (people) together with the present simple to the verbs *a gente lê* (people read), *a gente sente* (people feel), *a gente não sabe* (people don't know) hinted at the existence of a generalised practice of use around these magazines, semi-detached from Isaura. The direct quotation in the first person singular [line 29], where Isaura described the recognition that a reader experiences in the act of reading, was framed by the generic pronoun, as part of a general practice of recognition. In line 33, and through a cohesive device (*como quando*/just like when), Isaura then "told her story", the one she could publish in the magazine. In this story, Isaura linked her "I" to her daughter (thus bringing in her identity as a 'mother'), to the event with the medical doctor (thus bringing in her identity as 'a patient') and to the magazine (thus bringing in her identity as a *Take a Break* reader). By doing that, she was compensating "being a patient" with "being a reader" in order to understand an issue about which she felt responsible and worried "as a mother". To use

Wenger's words, she was "projecting her positions and herself onto the world" and "giving an independent meaning" to a personal experience of participation situated in time, place and social order. The excerpt thus ended with the use of a generic noun as subject, and a verb of cognition (one becomes enlightened/learns/*esclarece-se*).

1. **Isaura: Eh esta magazine é boa** [handling *Take a Break*]	1. **Isaura: Yes, this magazine is good** [handling *Take a Break*]
2. MCK: hmm	2. MCK: hmmm
3. Isaura: Ée. Tem mm. Tem várias histórias, coisas que que. se que acontecem que [turning the pages]	3. Isaura: Yeahh. It's got mm. It's got various stories that that happen [turning the pages]
4. MCK: hmmm [accompanying her as she turns the pages of the magazine]	4. MCK: hmmm [accompanying her as she turns the pages of the magazine]
5. Isaura: na vida. Tem estas huh [stops at a page]	5. Isaura: in life
6. MCK . . . estas vidas reais e tal.	6. MCK: real lives and such
7. Isaura . . . yeah	7. Isaura: yeah
8. MCK . . . e a Maria não tem essas coisas ou quê?	8. MCK: Does Maria not have those or what?
9. Isaura: Não, só tem problemas. ou	9. Isaura: No, it only has problems or
10. marido que a deixa	10. the husband that leaves her
11. Outras não sei quê @@@	11. I don't know what else @@@
12. MCK: e estas não é esse género de coisa?	12. MCK: are these not the same sort of thing?
13. Isaura: Não. Não	13. Isaura: No, no
14. MCK: Como é que é? Aqui é o quê?	14. MCK: How are they then? Here is what?
15. Isaura: é diferente.	15. Isaura: It's different
16. MCK: Como? Como é que é diferente?	16. MCK: How? How is it different?
17. Isaura: Sei lá. Não te sei explicar sei que é diferente	17. Isaura: Don't know. Don't know how to explain I know it's different
18. Também tem essa	18. It also has that
19. MCK: tenta explicar como é que é diferente	19. MCK: try to explain how it is different
20. Isaura: tem esses . . pro. <E>problem page you know<P> os problemas da vida também	20. Isaura: it's got those . . pro . . <E>problem page you know<P> life problems too

21. Mas. tem outras. coisas. que acontecem na vi. prontos histórias que as pessoas..

21. But. . it's got other. things. that happen in life. well. stories that people..

22. Tal como eu agora podia contar huh. publicar a minha história. a história daa. da Sónia

22. Just like I could tell huh. publish my story. the story ooof. Sonia

23. de doenças que acontecem

23. of diseases that happen

24. MCK: Ahh

24. MCK: Huhhuh

25. Isaura: e a gente às vezes lê aqui coisas

25. Isaura: and one sometimes reads things here

26. que a gente às vezes sente aquela. aquele sintoma e não sabe o que é

26. that one sometimes feels that. that symptom and doesn't know what it is

27. MCK: hmm pois

27. MCK: hmm right

28. Isaura: e lê..

28. Isaura: and reads

29. Noo. e huh "ahh! Mas isto é. Eu também tenho isto!"

29. In the. and huh "Oh! But this is. I've also got this!"

30. MCK: ahh

30. MCK: oh, right

31. Isaura: e ve. vem a realizar que a gente tem tem o mesmo problema que aquela pessoa teve

31. Isaura: and co. comes to realize that one has has the same problem that that person had

32. MCK: hmmm e tu achas que na *Maria* isso não acontece

32. MCK: hmm and you think that with *Maria* that doesn't happen

33. Isaura: como. Hmm não

33. Isaura: just like hmm no

34. Como. quando a Sónia tinha uns três anitos ela teve hmm

34. Just like when Sonia was about three years old she had hmm

35. huh um problema no sangue

35. Huh a problem in her blood

36. Tinha as

36. She had [

37. MCK: simsismsim [remembering previous conversations]

37. MCK: [yesyesyes [remembering previous conversations]

38. Isaura: plaklets <'checking up the right expression' intonation>

38. Isaura: plaklets [intonation – checking up right expression]

39. MCK: as plaquetas

39. MCK: plackets

40. Isaura: pois. ora. eu não sabia isso em inglês

40. Isaura: yes. well. I didn't know that in English

41. médico telefonou-me a dizer que ela tinha as <E>plaklets. low

41. the doctor called me to say she had her <E>plaklets. low

42. MCK: hmm uhuh uh

42. MCK: hmmm uhh uh

43. Isaura: <P>ora eu não sabia isso o que é que queria dizer

43. Isaura: <P> well I didn't know that what that meant

(continued)

44. Ele explicou-me não sei quê o que é ooo.	44. He explained me I don't know what what is theee
45. a função das. disso e não sei quê	45. function of the. those. and I don't know what
46. MCK: e esse médico era quê português ou inglês?	46. MCK: was this doctor Portuguese or English?
47. Isaura: e inglês yeah	47. Isaura: English, yeah
48. eeehh..	48. aanndd
49. MCK: Aqui na national health	49. MCK: Here from your <E>national health<E>
50. Isaura: sim	50. Isaura: yeah
51. mas muito bom	51. but very good he was
52. e então explicou-me e não sei quê	52. and so he explained and I don't know what
53. eehmmm e eu claro	53. aannndd I of course
54. pronto	54. well
55. Sabia qual era a função mas nnnum sabia bem..	55. I knew what the function was but I didn't know well..
56. MCK: hmm	56. MCK: hmm
57. Isaura: pronto porquê não sei que	57. Isaura: well, why that happened and I don't know what
58. Depois logo hmm dai uns dias comecei a ler esta magazine	58. Then hmm after a couple of days I read this magazine
59. Encontrei uma história tambem hmm a mesma coisa	59. I found a story also hmm the same thing
60. Com com o problema das plakletes e não sei quê	60. With. with the placklets problem and what have you
61. Ehhmm	61. aannnd
62. Pronto	62. Well [concluding remark]
63. Ehm . . .	63. Hmm
64. Pronto uma pessoa . . .	64. Well, one [impersonal pronoun]
65. MCK: pois tem a ver con[tigo nao é?	65. MCK: right it has to do [with you hasn't it?
66. Isaura: [esclarece-se	**66. Isaura: [gets informed**

Transcription conventions for this excerpt: [– overlaps;   [comments];   . short pause; . . long pause; . . . longer pause; @ laughs; <P> or <E>   switch to Portuguese or English.

References

Ang, I. and J. Hermes (1996) Gender and/in media consumption. In I. Ang, *Living Room Wars: Rethinking Media Audiences for a Post Modern World*. London: Routledge.

Barton, D. and M. Hamilton (1998) *Local Literacies: Reading and Writing in One Community*. London: Routledge.

Barton, D., M. Hamilton and R. Ivanič (eds) (2000) *Situated Literacies*. London: Routledge.

Billig, M. (1991) *Ideology and Opinions*. London: Sage.

Billig, M. (1996) *Arguing and Thinking: A Rhetorical Approach to Social Psychology*. Cambridge: Cambridge University Press.

Blackler, F. (1992) 'Formative contexts and activity systems: postmodern approaches to the management of change'. In Reed, M. and Hughes, M. (eds), *Rethinking Organization: New Directions in Organisation Theory and Analysis*. London: Sage, 273–294.

Blackler, F. (1993) *Changing Organisations*. Inaugural lecture, University of Lancaster.

Chaiklin, S. and J. Lave (eds) (1993) *Understanding Practice: Perspectives on Activity and Context*. New York: Cambridge University Press.

Chouliaraki, L. and N. Fairclough (2000) *Discourse in Late Modernity: Rethinking Critical Discourse Analysis*. Edinburgh: Edinburgh University Press.

Duranti, A. (1997) *Linguistic Anthropology*. Cambridge: Cambridge University Press.

Engeström, Y. (1999) Activity theory and individual and social transformation. In Y. Engeström, R. Miettinen and R. L. Punamäki (eds), *Perspectives on Activity Theory*. Cambridge: Cambridge University Press, 19–38.

Engeström, Y. and Miettinen, R. (1999) Introduction. In Y. Engeström, R. Miettinen and R.-L. Punamäki (eds), *Perspectives on Activity Theory*. Cambridge: Cambridge University Press.

Engeström, Y., R. Miettinen and R.-L. Punamäki (1999) *Perspectives on Activity Theory*. Cambridge: Cambridge University Press.

Fairclough, N. (1989) *Language and Power*. London: Longman.

Fairclough, N. (1992) *Discourse and Social Change*. London: Polity Press.

Fairclough, N. and R. Wodak (1997) Critical discourse analysis. In T. A. Van Dijk (ed), *Discourse as Social Interaction*. London: Sage, 258–284.

Goldstein, T. (1995) 'Nobody is talking bad'. Creating community and claiming power on the production lines. In K. Hall and M. Bucholtz (eds), *Gender Articulated: Language and the Socially Constructed Self*. London: Routledge.

Gray, A. (1992) *Video Playtime: The Gendering of a Leisure Technology*. London: Routledge.

Halliday, M. A. K. (1993) Towards a language-based theory of learning. *Linguistics and Education* 5 93–116.

Hermes, J. (1995) *Reading Women's Magazines: An Analysis of Everyday Media Use*. Cambridge: Polity Press.

Keating, M. C. (2001) *Routes Through Literacy: The Lived Experiences with Literacy of Portuguese Women in London*. Unpublished Manuscript, Ph.D. Thesis, Department of Linguistics and Modern English Language, Lancaster University, Lancaster, UK.

Kress, G. (1997) *Before Writing: Rethinking the Paths to Literacy*. London: Routledge.

Lave, J. and E. Wenger (1991) *Situated Learning: Legitimate Peripheral Participation*. Cambridge: Cambridge University Press.

Pile, S. and N. Thrift (1995) *Mapping the Subject: Geographies of Cultural Transformation*. London: Routledge.

Rogoff, B. (1990) *Apprenticeship in Thinking: Cognitive Development in Social Context*. Oxford: Oxford University Press.

Santos, B. (ed) (1993) *Portugal: Um Retrato Singular*. Portugal: Edições Afrontamento.

Santos, B. (ed) (2001) Globalização: Fatalidade ou Utopia? *A Sociedade Portuguesa Perante os Desafios da Globalização*, vol. 1. Portugal: Edições Afrontamento.

Santos, B. S. (1995) *Toward a New Common Sense: Law, Science and Politics in the Paradigmatic Transition. After The Law Series*. London: Routledge.

Swales, J. (1998) *Other Floors, Other Voices: A Textography of a Small University Building*. Mahwah, NJ and London: Lawrence Erlbaum Associates.

Wenger, E. (1998) *Communities of Practice: Learning, Meaning and Identity*. Cambridge: Cambridge University Press.

6

Communities of Practice and Learning Communities

Do Bilingual Co-workers Learn in Community?

Deirdre Martin

In the UK, about 8% of the population use languages other than English, and some of this group may speak only a minority language. Within these families, like other families in the UK, there will be children, young people and adults with speech, language and communication difficulties/disorders. When these families seek advice and support from health professionals who do not speak the same language, then both are at a severe disadvantage. These circumstances have led a group of health professionals, speech and language therapists (SLTs), to develop the paraprofessional role of bilingual co-worker.

This chapter explores, through a case study, the communities of learning and practice for a bilingual co-worker in a speech and language therapy department. The question: *Who is the bilingual co-worker's community of learning and practice?* drives a critical reflection on 'Communities of Practice' theory (Lave and Wenger 1991, Wenger 1998) and the contributions of an Activity Theory approach (e.g., Engeström 1999) in analysing the learning practices of bilingual co-workers and their colleagues in speech and language therapy. The chapter aims to add to responses to theoretical questions about understanding "communities of practice" and "learning communities" (Eraut 2002).

I start with the work expectations and learning demands of becoming a bilingual co-worker and the professional communities where co-workers develop their professional socialisation and identity. Data are drawn from interviews with key players in these communities. The central argument is that the complexity of situated teaching and learning in multilingual multiprofessional contexts cannot be fully explained by the theory of communities of practice. Activity theory is helpful in explaining these learning communities.

CONTEXT OF THE STUDY

Speech and language therapy services in the UK function within two overarching organisations. Professionally, the Royal College of Speech and Language Therapists (RCSLT) has a pervasive influence on professional identity. For bilingual co-workers in particular, they provide guidelines and structures, such as the Special Interest Group (SIG) in Bilingualism, to support professional development. The National Health Service, operating through local Primary Care Trusts, is the main employer of SLTs, assistants and co-workers and sets financial and accountability targets for services. Attendance and take-up of SLT services increases among linguistic minority clients when bilingual co-workers are employed (Winter 1999).

SLTs in the UK work with children and adults whose speech and language are substantially different from their peers, resulting in difficulties in communicating and learning. Causes may be medical, cognitive, social or unknown. For over twenty years, many speech and language therapy services have become multiprofessional by recruiting speech and language therapy assistants/aids (SLTAs) to support them in aspects of their work. Assistants support and run intervention programmes devised by therapists for individuals and groups of children in schools and clinics. They also assist in case history taking from parents/care-givers and in client assessment and carry out these tasks under the supervision and professional responsibility of therapists. They carry out clerical and administrative tasks, such as client contact, form filling and case note recording. They do not require a qualification or specialist formal training and usually receive in-service training from therapists and other SLTAs in the department. Training covers knowledge and skills about a range of speech and language difficulties/disorders that occur in children and adults, such as developmental or acquired, and occurring with other disabilities such as deafness, dyslexia, autism, learning and physical difficulties.

SLT BILINGUAL CO-WORKERS

The majority of therapists in England have one or more bilingual children on their caseloads (Winter 1999). Many SLT services have recruited bilingual speakers as co-workers[1] to support therapists in working with bilingual clients and their families, and the scenario in this case study is common to monolingual SLT departments in the UK.

Bilingual co-workers are expected to use linguistic and cultural knowledge of their minority community by interpreting and translating for their language community and to share this knowledge with therapists. In addition, they are expected to learn technical knowledge and skills about speech and language difficulties to allow them to support the work of therapists who do not share their language and culture. Expectations of their role usually go beyond those of monolingual SLTAs. Bilingual co-workers are expected to assess clients' home language and support the therapist to identify areas of difficulty, to interpret during case history taking and to offer cultural information about child care and communication practices to support therapists in identifying language delay or difficulty/disorder. They also support clerical and administrative tasks usually involved with the bilingual caseload, such as maintaining contact with bilingual clients and their families through telephone calls and letters. They are expected to progress to working independently in some areas both in English and in their other language(s). Speech and language services to diverse ethnic and linguistic populations may need to recruit several bilingual co-workers to meet the linguistic needs of the client population.

THE TEACHING AND LEARNING CHALLENGE

While the role of the bilingual co-worker is similar to that of their monolingual SLTA counterpart, working and learning that is mediated through different languages and cultural knowledges from those of the professional community repositions co-workers, transforming the teaching and learning endeavour of those involved. Bilingual

---

[1] The term co-worker here refers to bilingual personnel, and monolingual assistants are referred to as assistants.

co-workers are recruited into the communities of practice of SLT departments because monolingual therapists and assistants recognise that they do not have sufficient skills and knowledges to meet bilingual clients' needs. Co-workers bring additional knowledges about languages and cultures other than English to SLT professional practice. The intention is that they will 'expand' the knowledge and skills of the local SLT community of practice. Their new knowledges bring a disruptive energy to the monolingual SLT community of practice. How do SLT communities of learning and practice respond to this challenge?

In monolingual SLT departments with bilingual co-workers, therapists need to develop practices that make explicit the tacit linguistic and cultural knowledge of bilingual newcomers in the SLT community of practice. As such, the site affords the study of the relationship between tacit knowledge and technical knowledge through implicit and explicit learning. At an *implicit* level of learning the co-worker is expected to apply his/her *tacit* knowledge of community culture and language to English culture and language. At the same time, co-workers are *explicitly* learning SLT knowledge, professional capabilities and expertise in English only, while being expected to *implicitly* transform this technical knowledge into community language and culture in a way which can be useful to clients/families and therapists. The production of new knowledge by bilingual co-workers can be managed only partially by the monolingual professional practitioners. Two theories are drawn on to interpret this social teaching and learning context: communities of practice and sociocultural activity theory. They are discussed in relation to a third paradigm, learning communities.

COMMUNITIES OF PRACTICE

Eraut (2002) distinguishes between the theoretical notions of 'communities of practice' and 'learning communities', which I will extend in this case study. 'Communities of practice' is a term now appropriated by Lave and Wenger to mean situated learning through engagement in the activities of the community, which include specialist language, skills and cultural knowledge. Eraut notes that learning in communities of practice is understood as reproductive in nature, through induction of newcomers by 'old timers' who "acquire competence and status" (p. 3). Within these communities, newcomers can learn their identity and role as they move from peripheral participation in the community towards core participation. Eraut claims that this approach, with its focus on commonalities rather than diversity and agency, offers no explanation for how communities transform themselves.

Wenger (1998) describes communities of practice as characterised by three dimensions: mutual engagement, a joint enterprise and a shared repertoire, which are "a source of coherence of a community". In this study, Lave and Wenger's theoretical explanation accounts for how monolingual assistants are inducted into their 'community of practice' with training offered by therapists and experienced assistants. In contrast, it can only partially account for learning done by bilingual co-workers with monolingual professional practitioners. Co-workers may be able to learn some practices within the community of monolingual SLTAs, such as client contact procedures, form filling, activity and material preparation, yet there are other bilingual practices which they must create in working with therapists and bilingual clients.

SOCIOCULTURAL ACTIVITY THEORY

Where innovative learning takes place, a more complex theory of learning is needed than Wenger's, such as sociocultural activity theory (Engeström 1999 in Daniels 2001). Sociocultural activity theory derives from Vygotsky's ideas of learning through mediation. It interprets learning as both a social and individual process where two or more individuals work together on a common focus of learning to achieve a shared goal. This theory of social learning, like communities of practice, draws on ideas of mutual engagement and joint enterprise for learning. Sociocultural theory places mediation at the centre of the learning relationship, and one of the most important tools of mediating learning is language. Developments of sociocultural activity theory represent macro-levels of community learning, including social elements: community of learners, rules of engagement in interaction and division of work. Activity theory offers a means of analysing learning which is both collective and individual, which shows agency and which is not reproductive but innovative and transforming.

A bilingual co-worker in a monolingual SLT department is involved in at least three learning activity systems. The bilingual client with speech and language difficulties/disorders is the primary focus (object) of learning for the co-worker and the therapist. A second object of teaching and learning is the set of technical skills of SLT practices with therapists and assistants for the bilingual co-worker. A third focus of learning is the new bicultural and bilingual knowledge of the co-worker for the monolingual staff, SLTs and SLTAs, in order to apply their skills and capabilities in innovative ways. Eraut might call this third scenario a 'learning community'.

LEARNING COMMUNITIES

Eraut (2002:2) posits that learning communities, ideologically, "maximise participation through a culture imbued with inclusive, interdependent views of human relationships and democratic values". Learning is construed "as an integral part of reciprocal interaction, constrained and facilitated by skills, structures, networks and cultural factors, and raises questions about opportunities for mutual learning across professions and between professionals and their clients." In this sense, Eraut's description of learning communities is similar to the third activity system described previously. He suggests that this ideological construct is jeopardised in contexts of lower levels of mutual respect between professionals and other health workers, especially when learning is about their clients. Feasibility of introducing and sustaining equity in small groups is questionable when it is absent from the parent organisation.

There are issues of equity in multiprofessional departments between therapists and assistants, and co-workers included professionally as assistants, which have implications for developing learning communities for bilingual and multicultural knowledge. In the case of bilingual co-workers in departments with SLTs and SLTAs, it may be possible for the first and second activity systems, described previously, to achieve mutual learning since they usually concern only two or three people in the department (i.e., co-workers and the

SLT managing them) and are primarily client-focused. The 'learning community' (the third activity system) involves collective learning of the department about bilingualism and multiculturalism. Where collective participation is not maximised, there are implications for the bilingual co-worker. One outcome could be that the bilingual co-worker learns to become a monolingual assistant.

The remainder of the paper looks at reported evidence about how bilingual co-workers learn their practices. The discussion addresses the ways in which co-workers learn in 'communities of practice' and in 'learning communities', and the extent to which the three approaches to situated learning in organisations explain – or fail to explain – professional learning in multilingual and multiprofessional work contexts. Firstly, the case study approach is reported.

METHODOLOGY AND PROCEDURES

The study is a case study of a monolingual speech and language therapy service in a health trust in a unitary metropolitan borough in the West Midlands, UK. The study focuses on a bilingual co-worker, Harvinder[2], a Panjabi/English bilingual woman, recruited by the department. She has been a bilingual co-worker in the speech and language therapy department for two years. Three other people are featured in the study: Camilla, a specialist SLT, who organised and managed Harvinder's professional formal and non-formal learning; Jane, a monolingual English-speaking SLTA, who was Harvinder's mentor; and Heleama, a bilingual specialist SLT in a large speech and language therapy department in an adjacent health trust, who was an important teaching/learning influence on Harvinder and Camilla. Data are from the reported construction of learning about becoming a bilingual co-worker, drawing mainly from Harvinder's interviews and to a lesser extent on Camilla's, Jane's and Heleama's inteviews. I interviewed Harvinder and the other three women and asked them to recall and reflect on their experiences of working as a co-worker with Harvinder in the first two years of her being a co-worker. Over a period of five weeks, Harvinder was interviewed for an hour four times,

---

[2] Harvinder, Camilla, Jane, Heleama and Sarah are, for confidentiality reasons, not their real names.

and Camilla, Jane and Heleama were interviewed individually for an hour each. The interviews were held in the clinics where they worked and were tape recorded and transcribed. Harvinder volunteered to be in the study, and her colleagues – Jane, Camilla and Heleama – were subsequently invited.

As Chair of the SIG Bilingualism (RCSLT), I have been professionally involved in the establishment of the role, and development of training, for bilingual co-workers in speech and language therapy in the UK over many years. The SIG has drawn up professional policy guidelines as well as training and employment guidelines. I knew two of the informants, Heleama through the SIG Bilingualism Committee and Camilla through professional study days on bilingualism. I did not know Harvinder or Jane before the study.

Critiques on the Methodology

There are possible epistemological difficulties with a methodology which explores learning through reportage (Eraut 2000). Eraut argues that it is easier to report – that is, recall and reflect on – formal learning which is explicit and deliberative while it seems to be considerably more difficult to report on non-formal learning such as reactive and tacit learning. He argues that the learning process and range of learning can be investigated only with data capturing the actions and language of the learning events. Nevertheless, this case study of reported learning through interview data offers insights into the complexity of the communities of learning and practice for a bilingual co-worker in a monolingual SLT department, which have previously not been investigated.

ANALYSIS AND DISCUSSION

Wenger (1998) describes communities of practice as characterised by three dimensions: mutual engagement, a joint enterprise and a shared repertoire, which are "a source of coherence of a community". I assess the characteristics of Lave and Wenger's communities of practice in relation to the case study community.

Mutual engagement: Members of a community of practice are "people [who] are engaged in actions whose meanings they negotiate with one another" (Wenger 1998:73). In the SLT department, this was evidenced in negotiated relationships between therapists and assistants, as Jane says:

"like getting together with the therapist to do a joint session or a joint visit or waiting around maybe to get the groups running." (Jane, p. 27)

Yet there was no mutual engagement among the assistants around bilingual matters. As Jane notes, there was a "split" in the communities of practice, where the assistants dealt with learning around assistant matters and bilingual matters were dealt with by Camilla. (See data example 7.)

Joint enterprise: This is defined by the collective process of negotiation among those in the community, creating mutual accountability. In the SLT department, the joint enterprise was the management of a client's speech and language difficulty through assessment and intervention programmes and counselling teachers and family. There is a considerable amount of overlap of skills between therapists and assistants in managing the care pathways of children with speech and language needs. It is not evident that there is joint enterprise, overlapping and mutual accountability for bilingual clients. These clients are the responsibility of Harvinder and the therapists, particularly Camilla. Monolingual assistants are usually not involved.

Shared repertoire: When colleagues work together, they develop shared histories, ways of doing things and shared communication (words, phrases) which constitute a shared repertoire of practice. There are two critical aspects for Harvinder and her colleagues in developing a shared language of practice. First is the extent to which Harvinder learns the technical language of SLT to allow her to work with colleagues and clients. Harvinder is brought through a staged programme of apprenticeship to learn the technicalities of speech and language difficulties/disorders. Second is the extent to which her colleagues develop a shared repertoire of her language and culture in order to work with bilingual clients. The only evidence seems to be that Camilla is learning Urdu, the national language of Pakistan, and which some of the client group, who have Pakistani heritage, may speak. This is evidence of agency by Camilla towards establishing shared repertoires which she uses in her work with Harvinder (e.g., assessing bilingual children).

Furthermore, sharing language and cultural repertoires is more complex in this case study. Harvinder does not share the same language variety of the client group; she speaks Indian Panjabi and they speak Mirpuri Panjabi. Heleama is aware of this and addresses the professional issues involved (see data example 2) by raising Harvinder's awareness, making explicit her implicit language knowledge.

The fundamental contradiction which prevents a theory of 'communities of practice' from sitting comfortably in this context is the fact that Camilla and Jane induct Harvinder, through English, to work as a SLT bilingual co-worker in Panjabi and English. This contradiction of language use at the centre of learning drives us theoretically to look for theories of learning which deal with innovative expanded learning, such as activity theory (e.g., Engeström 1999).

Bilingual Communities of Practice

There were opportunities for Harvinder, arranged by Camilla and Jane, to access communities of practice of bilingual therapists and assistants. Heleama, her team of bilingual co-workers and the co-workers at the national SIG Bilingualism study days afforded opportunities for Harvinder "to connect to broader constellations" and negotiate further meanings for her identity, role and practices as a bilingual co-worker. Wenger describes this as the local-global interplay (1998:162), and Harvinder describes it as the "link".

Data example 1: Harvinder interview 2
Harvinder: But I think when they started they did a study day for co-workers. . . . I thought that was great because all the co-workers got together and we were able to swop ideas and any worries we had, which was really great. And they're planning on doing another one which will be good. I think we do need to – need that link really.

The 'global community of practice' refers to the other communities of practice that network to maintain the reproduction of knowledge of their work practices (Wenger 1998:162). An opportunity to develop the 'link' was through contact with Heleama and her bilingual SLT community of practice, who offer professional socialisation specifically focussed on practice in Panjabi. Heleama works with eight bilingual co-workers in her department, but Harvinder did not manage to meet with them because of her timetable arrangements.

Data example 2: Heleama interview pp. 3–4

Heleama: I actually trained her up as well because she spent the morning with me looking at multicultural issues . . . she's Asian but she's aware that she doesn't know too much about the other communities, like Muslims and the majority of the clients case load she works with in her patch are actually a Batwali group of speakers, or Mirpuri as we call them now . . . so we've had to sit down and look at the fact that her vocabulary is different from theirs. We went through . . . tests and said well look you've got to adapt that . . . and this is the type of vocabulary you need to look out for, the verb ending so we looked at how she could write down using the roman script exactly what the child said and then analyse it so she'd be able to work out what was going wrong but always refer to the therapist as well to get more linguistic and phonetic advice. I've shown her how to do a phonology test in Panjabi and given her stuff that we have here, so we've been quite good at sharing.

Heleama is making explicit Harvinder's implicit knowledges of her language and culture, which is not possible for Camilla and Jane. Harvinder has had less opportunity to learn in a bilingual community of practice with other bilingual co-workers because of structural constraints, such as time and place. A consequence is that her professional identity and role will be more influenced by her immediate monolingual community of practice of assistants.

Monolingual Communities of Practice

There were different types of learning opportunities offered to Harvinder in the SLT department to include her in the communities of practice: 'shadowing' (apprenticeship) and semi-formal teaching. Jane describes the non-formal learning offered to Harvinder.

Data example 3: Jane's interview p. 17

Jane: The only thing that I think that you have to get across in the first few months is that there should be no pressure put on them [newcomers] to do an activity on their own, it should always be together and they are watching to learn, they are not watching to take it easy. . . . I don't think I want to put any pressure on them so it's not a teaching – learning sort of environment really.

Similar opportunities are offered in Heleama's department for bilingual co-workers.

Data example 4: Heleama interview p. 20
Heleama: Part of the induction when they come in is they are not just inducted in the clinical specialisms and go to the specialist have a chat to them but I will get them to shadow one of the more experienced co-workers so that they can look at the work relationship and look very carefully at how the person writes down the information.

Harvinder is being guided through a formal syllabus of professional (technical) knowledge by the therapist, Camilla. She reports "pedagogical structuring", where Camilla, or Helaema, sets up sessions for 'teaching' knowledge about clinical specialisms (e.g., autism, feeding, assessment) or about administrative practices (e.g., form filling).

Data example 5: Harvinder interview 1 p. 10
Deirdre: Did you have to do any reading or listen to any –
Harvinder: I watched videos . . . on therapies being done with children. Camilla did give me some books to read, basically it was on stammering and dyslexia, just covering what are the problems children do have. But mainly a lot of the training was with Camilla and she explained a lot of things. She's always been there from day one, if there was anything I didn't understand or I felt I couldn't do.

Camilla recalls a clear programme of technical SLT knowledge, beginning with language development, difficulties and assessment and proceeding through a staged apprenticeship to independent practice.

Data example 6: Camilla interview p. 5
Camilla: Yes we looked at language development which was a little difficult because my knowledge of Panjabi development is, was, is small, although I had got some information about the early stages. We looked at taking language samples, looking at language stimulation tasks, helping her with that and she's gradually built up her skills in that area. Then we looked at difficulties with language development and we linked that with formal assessments. . . . I tried to stage it so that we did work one to one and then she went out and did the assessment with somebody and then she did it on her own.

The mutuality of sharing information and practices around bilingualism is limited within the assistants' community of practice where there seems to be a dominant discourse of monolingual practice.

Issues of bilingualism are dealt with in another community of practice, with Camilla.

Data example 7: Jane interview p. 27
(Discussing the SLTAs meetings every four months)
Deirdre: and the issues around bilingual assistants, . . . are [they] quite different from the questions and queries . . . generated by the others or are they in fact the same?
Jane: not really, a lot of it is very, very samey. Harvinder's problems, if you want to call them problems, are what we would be experiencing anyway
Deirdre: Like?
Jane: like getting together with the therapist to do a joint session or a joint visit or waiting around maybe to get the groups running. Things like that, minor things. Nothing is ever raised by, from what you were saying now, realising that Harvinder is never directly asked in those meetings, 'do you have anything you want to raise on the bilingual side?' It is never put across like that at all.
Deirdre: Is it usually generated between assistants' and therapists' work together as a team?
Jane: yes exactly, nothing at all with her being a bilingual assistant so . . . I think it is probably split . . . because there is Camilla and Camilla is her manager. It's raised with Camilla. So it's not raised within the assistants' meeting. . . . It's almost divided really that she is an assistant with us in the assistants' meeting and there is another part of Harvinder which is the bilingual assistant which is dealt with differently.

The perception of a 'split' in Harvinder's work practices indicates that there is more than a single community of practice for Harvinder in the SLT department.

DISTRIBUTED COGNITIONS AND SKILLS

The learning challenge for bilingual co-workers in monolingual SLT departments is to weave their tacit knowledge of non-English language and culture with the explicit learning of technical knowledge and skills about the nature and practice of speech and language therapy in another language, English. Furthermore, this new learning is not modelled or practised in the monolingual communities of practice of Camilla and Jane. It is generated in working with Harvinder.

In monolingual contexts, one approach to managing the weave between bilingual co-workers' tacit and new technical knowledges is through activities involving distributed cognitions and skills. Drawing on distributed cognitions is another practice of social learning, "when knowledge and skills are 'stretched across' other things and people" (Cole and Engestrom 1993 cited in Daniels 2001:107). Embedded within the learning activity between Harvinder, Camilla and Jane are practices situated within distributed cognitions and skills. That is, there are activities which demand a single representation of information obtained from the integration of distributed skills and capabilities between Camilla, Jane and Harvinder. Camilla's capabilities derive from technical knowledge and Harvinder's from her tacit knowledge of Panjabi language and culture. This is innovative expanded learning and different from the way Wenger and Lave and Wenger describe distributed cognitions, as 'the mechanics of group performance' (Wenger 1998:286; Lave and Wenger 1991:75).

One example of innovative learning drawing on distributed cognitions is in a phonological assessment in Panjabi; Harvinder elicits spoken words from a child while Camilla phonetically transcribes what the child says. A more frequent example occurs when Harvinder and the therapist discuss the information obtained from a variety of sources, such as a parent interview, case history, observations of a child, and they arrive at a "mutual understanding" of the child's problem. In these examples, the therapist is drawing on her own technical skills and trying to draw out the bilingual co-worker's tacit knowledge of the minority language and culture that she does not share. Camilla could be said to be 'creating a pedagogic context' (Daniels 2001:107) for both her and Harvinder's learning in which their combined effort results in a successful outcome, that of identifying salient information in case history taking for Panjabi-speaking children who may have language difficulties.

In the quote below, we see how Harvinder and Jane demonstrate agency focussed on an object, intervention for a speech difficulty in Panjabi, using distributed cognitions and skills.

Data example 8: Jane interview pp. 18–19
The only thing that I learnt and found interesting is that I was working on a child with the speech sound 'ch' and she [Harvinder] wanted to come and see because she was being asked to go and see a child and work on 'ch' in mother tongue first and she was saying 'I don't know how to go about this Jane because 'ch' is not a sound that is used very often in mother tongue'.

And we had this discussion which I wasn't aware that it is very minimal and you can't get the vocab [vocabulary], . . . it's going to be a really difficult sound for them to hold on to even if you did VC [vowel consonant] or CV or words it's something that they're not used to . . . we had to sit and try to work out pictures. . . . And it didn't work doing 'ch' in mother tongue because the vocab was so minimal so we went into English.

The theory of 'communities of practice' does not account for individual agency and object-directed learning. This example of learning is better explained by activity theory and theoretically points to an emerging 'learning community'. Empirically, more evidence is needed to support the notion of 'learning communities' as a framework for understanding Harvinder's learning with the assistants. Guidance and support for Harvinder and Jane to engage further in this type of learning would be likely to generate more new knowledge about bilingual work. This in turn would transform, rather than reproduce, the monolingual learning and practice of the assistants and include Harvinder. It would 'expand' their concept of their role and identity to include bilingualism rather than maintain it embodied in Harvinder.

SOCIAL FORMATION OF IDENTITY

Legitimate Peripheral Participation

This section looks at how Harvinder and her colleagues negotiate her identity and her role as a bilingual co-worker. Lave and Wenger (1991) and Wenger (1998) propose that members of a community of practice learn knowledge, skills and capabilities within that community which enable them to be competent members of it. They propose that newcomers to the community may not participate much because they are learning, or they may participate in a prescribed way, 'legitimate peripheral participation'. As competence is learnt, they move towards full participation, at the 'core' of the community. The negotiation of competence and non-competence along the lines of technical knowledge and linguistic and cultural knowledges is an important identity marker for Harvinder and her colleagues in identifying each other in the community of practice. Harvinder's bilingual practices are peripheral to the assistants' community of practice, and we need to look at theories of learning which emphasise agency and individuality to explain both the learning that is occurring and its trajectory.

Peripherality may be a mix of participation and non-participation, where non-participation is characterised by observing or being told what to do, or as we have seen for co-workers 'shadowing' others. Harvinder shared the assistants' office and became a peripheral member of their community of practice. As she learnt more, she has become a core member – contributing to and later running independently assessment and therapy sessions for monolingual English children with speech difficulties. Her comment that in the session "it all just flowed" indicates a degree of 'routinised' learning, which is one of the characteristics identified by Wenger's situated learning and apprenticeship.

Harvinder's work as a bilingual co-worker involves her translating into Panjabi a test originally designed for assessing developmental English grammar features. She is required to identify and use appropriate regional variations of vocabulary working with families. She advises parents on how to implement intervention programmes in Panjabi. She interprets for therapists and parents – "word for word" – so that she is as literal as possible, and in this way she believes that she is doing as she has been instructed by the therapists. More important, she feels that she will not make herself vulnerable to claims of misrepresenting the client, parent or therapist.

These practices are not in the repertoire of practice of the monolingual assistants. In fact, Harvinder does not share them with any other colleague in her department. She could only share them with bilingual colleagues in Heleama's department, which she has not yet managed to do, and the SIG Bilingualism study days. Harvinder works with therapists on case histories and assessments offering information about the home language and culture in a co-construction of new knowledge about the clients' difficulties. Harvinder and therapists work in 'learning dyads' rather than 'communities', since there are few opportunities to share these ways of working across the department.

Members of a community who feel that they are positioned on the margins, where full participation in the community is problematic, are on an outbound trajectory of the community of practice (Wenger

1998:166). It is possible to interpret Harvinder's position in the mono-lingual SLT department in this way. She is perceived by the assistants as "split". She learns practices to be an SLTA in a monolingual discourse and learns practices concerning bilingualism with the therapists, with Camilla and Heleama. Possibly as a way to resolve the "split", Harvinder considers that one trajectory of participation which would bring her towards fuller participation in the SLTAs' community of practice would be to take up a 'specialism' such as autism, and leave her bilingualism practices.

Data example 9: Harvinder interview 2 p. 46
Harvinder: Would I go into a specialist field? Well, really, being the only one [bilingual co-worker] I can't really think oh yes, I'd like to go into that and stay there because I have to cover everything and everyone really. Yes, with the bilingual children unless they get another bilingual co-worker and then I could maybe think oh, I'd like to go into say autism and work with children in that field. Then I might be able to but at the moment I can't really think that way. because I've got to work with all the therapists.
Deirdre: Yes. Do you ever talk about this with Camilla or –
Harvinder: Well, yes, I've said to Camilla and I've said to Sarah – the manageress as well, that yes, I'd like to acquire more skills in speech and language. I mean it covers a lot and I won't be able to do it all but it's nice to know what else is around.

It seems that Harvinder and the assistants did not construe participation in bilingualism practices as an 'inbound trajectory' towards full participation. By contrast, Heleama reported that bilingual and monolingual assistants fully participated in their community of practice in her bilingual SLT department. One explanation for the different perceptions of 'bilingualism as a specialism' is that specialisms are usually constructed around specific types of difficulty/disorder – autism, stammering, dyspraxia. Bilingualism is a social descriptor of a client group, like 'early years' or geriatrics. The recognition of bilingualism as a specialism in Heleama's department is a result of years of Heleama promoting the case and drawing on research and clinical need to persuade (mainly) monolingual colleagues and managers. Camilla is aware that to transform the monolingual community of practice to working with bilingual practices will require more expansive learning with assistants and therapists.

CONCLUSION

The chapter has addressed the question: do bilingual co-workers learn in community? The theory of situated learning and communities of practice (Lave and Wenger 1991, Wenger 1998) explains some of the ways in which bilingual co-workers learn to become participants in a monolingual speech and language therapy department, specifically where learning concerns the reproduction of knowledge. The theory cannot explain the expansive learning and creation of new knowledge which is at the heart of being a bilingual co-worker in a monolingual SLT service, evidenced in two important features of bilingual co-workers learning. Firstly, Harvinder brings with her tacit knowledge and capabilities of Panjabi language and culture that are essential to her work which are not shared by the so-called 'old timers'. Secondly, she and her monolingual colleagues engage in bilingual client-focused problem-solving which draws on distributed cognitions and creates new knowledge for all the participants. The implications for Harvinder's participation, identity and career trajectory as a bilingual co-worker are that she may not value her bilingual knowledge and skills as much as the new professional knowledge and skills that she is learning. To change this requires that the monolingual SLT department engage in new learning with Harvinder and become a 'learning community'. The expansive and innovative learning practiced by the bilingual co-worker and monolingual colleagues in the SLT department cannot be interpreted by Lave and Wenger's and Wenger's unidimensional theory of communities of practice. We need to draw on more complex theories of social learning, such as activity theory.

NOTE ON TRANSCRIPTION

Data have been edited to remove instances of 'washback' (*right, yes, mmm*) and hedging (*sort of, like, erhmm*).

ACKNOWLEDGEMENTS

I am very grateful for the co-operation of my colleagues in two Speech and Language Therapy Departments in the West Midlands in this research project and for the critical friendship of colleagues Stewart Ranson, Carol Miller and Karin Tusting.

References

Daniels, H. (2001) *Vygotsky and Pedagogy*. London: Routledge Falmer.

Engeström, Y. (1999) Innovative learning in work teams: analysing cycles of knowledge creation in practice. In Y. Engeström, R. Miettinen and R. L. Punamäki (eds), *Perspectives on Activity Theory*. Cambridge: Cambridge University Press.

Eraut, M. (2000) Non-formal learning, implicit learning and tacit knowledge in professional work. *British Journal of Educational Psychology 70* 113–136.

Eraut, M. (2002) Conceptual analysis and research questions: do the concepts of 'learning community' and 'community of practice' provide added value? Paper presented at AERA, New Orleans, LA, April 2002. Obtainable from author.

Lave, J. and E. Wenger (1991) *Situated Learning: Legitimate Peripheral Participation*. Cambridge: Cambridge University Press.

Wenger, E. (1998) *Communities of Practice: Learning, Meaning and Identity*. Cambridge: Cambridge University Press.

Winter, K. (1999) Speech and language therapy for bilingual children: aspects of the current service. *International Journal of Language and Communication Disorders 34 (1)* 85–98.

7

Moving Beyond Communities of Practice in Adult Basic Education

Steven Robert Harris and Nicola Shelswell

This chapter draws on our experience as adult basic educators to reflect on learning in communities of practice. We discuss the issues of marginality, peripherality, legitimacy, boundaries and identity encountered in our attempts to foster communities of practice in a series of innovative adult literacy and numeracy courses using information and communication technologies (ICT). In order to frame the concerns that underpin this discussion, the chapter begins with a brief overview of the recent history of adult basic education (ABE) in Britain and introduces the setting within which the courses have been developed, an ABE Open Learning Centre in the valleys of post-industrial south Wales. We describe how, in 1997, the installation of a network of computers with Internet access at the centre highlighted problems with existing procedures, training and resources, necessitating a search for new ways to integrate ICT into teaching and learning practice. In collaboration with staff, learners and volunteers, we gradually developed an approach based on fostering communities of technology-based practice through pair and group work on digital media projects. While this approach has brought many positive outcomes, and is now integral to most technology-based provision at the centre, we have also discovered contradictions between the way participation and learning are played out in communities of practice and the fundamental aims and concerns of ABE. The closing sections of the chapter reflect on those contradictions, which are now encouraging us to seek ways of moving beyond the communities of practice approach in ABE.

ADULT BASIC EDUCATION IN THE UK

In Britain, ABE refers to that part of the national education system concerned with literacy, numeracy and language development in adults. The lead organisation for ABE in England and Wales defines basic skills as:

The ability to read, write and speak in English (and in Welsh in Wales) and use mathematics at a level necessary to function and progress at work and in society in general. (Basic Skills Agency 2003)

In May 1997, the election of a centre-left New Labour administration heralded a shift in UK education policy which was to bring a major expansion of ABE provision. In June 1998, Sir Claus Moser, chairman of the UK Basic Skills Agency, was commissioned to report on the extent of adult basic skills need in the UK. The resulting document, *A Fresh Start – Improving Literacy and Numeracy* (Moser 1999), stressed the personal, social and economic costs of low basic skills, explicitly linking this "shocking situation" to various indicators of deprivation and marginalisation. National strategies for basic skills were reformulated on the basis of Moser's finding that for a significant proportion of the population[1] to lack basic skills has:

... disastrous consequences for the individuals concerned, weakens the country's ability to compete in the global economy and places a huge burden on society. People with poor literacy, numeracy and language skills tend to be on lower incomes or unemployed, and they are more prone to ill health and social exclusion. (Department for Education and Skills 2001)

The report offered a raft of recommendations, based on a greatly increased financial investment in ABE. Among twenty-one action points, the majority of which have subsequently been implemented,

---

[1] It is estimated that around 7 million adults, in England, 1 million adults in Wales and a further 1.2 million adults in Scotland need to improve their literacy or numeracy skills (Basic Skills Agency 2001, Department for Education and Skills 2001; Welsh Assembly Government 2002, Basic Skills Agency 2003).

Moser advocated the use of information and communication technologies in ABE, asserting that they offer "a powerful tool in the process of raising levels of literacy and numeracy" that "needs to be a staple of basic skills programmes" (Moser 1999, Sections 1.40 and 1.41).

This focus on ICT reflected the tenor of the times. New Labour explicitly linked their commitment to education with a strategy of re-creating post-industrial Britain as a "knowledge economy". At around the same time, academics and commentators in Europe and the US were beginning to express concern about a growing "digital divide" in access to ICT (Castells 1998, Schön et al. 1999, Timmins 2000, Norris 2001), a concern which also began to influence policy-makers. Programs of computerisation were initiated across the public sector, and ICT began to be seen as a significant factor in the development of basic skills provision. However, in 1997 ABE institutions were mostly lagging behind the rest of the education sector in taking up the new technologies, and there was little reliable research or guidance available for those who wished to take up Moser's challenge. The high expectations that e-learning and interactive products would act as an effective means of addressing basic skills needs did not begin to be critically examined by academic research until almost three years later (Mellar et al. 2001).

THE OPEN LEARNING CENTRE

The Coleg Morgannwg School of Basic Skills, a network of ABE outreach centres, is one of the principal providers of ABE in south Wales. Its administrative and teaching headquarters, known as the Open Learning Centre (OLC), are housed in converted shop premises in a small market town at the heart of the Valleys region. From the 1970s onward, the Welsh Valleys, once famous for coal and steel production, became home to high unemployment and persistently low levels of educational attainment. By the turn of the twenty-first century, this was one of the poorest areas of the European Union and, as recently as 2002, it was estimated that almost 40% of the adult population had significant basic skills needs (Welsh Assembly Government 2002). Through the 1980s and 1990s, a slew of national and European initiatives focussed on reversing the region's decline, attracting inward investment from multinational corporations and fostering the growth of small and medium enterprises in precision manufacturing, high technology and new media. The resulting upturn in the regional economy brought a growing recognition of the need for new skills development among the local workforce and emphasised the pivotal role of education in the region's recovery; the OLC and its allied outreach centres have been significant contributors to local economic and social regeneration strategies.

In early 1997, in a pioneering move for Welsh ABE, the OLC was equipped with broadband Internet access and a network of personal computers, printers and scanners. The impact on practice at the centre was profound, with a variety of effects becoming evident over the following months. In traditional literacy and numeracy classes, where the main teaching resources were texts and worksheets, computer-based activities were mainly limited to some word processing and occasional Internet browsing. Learners' ICT use depended on the support and supervision of tutors or volunteers with computer know-how, who at this time were in short supply. Consequently, learners wishing to gain or improve ICT skills often ended up somewhat isolated from the main learning group, working alone at the computers and not always fully participating in the literacy and numeracy activities going on around them. Overall, the effect was that these groups began to lose their cohesion, with ICT and basic skills activities running in parallel. Tutors were overstretched and learners unhappy with the level of support available.

Meanwhile, the centre had also begun to offer new courses in computer literacy. Mainly working individually, learners followed worksheet-based exercises using a variety of software packages. These classes were under the supervision of tutors who had been recruited for their ICT skills but were not necessarily ABE specialists; they were provided with further training in basic skills teaching once in post. These courses recruited well and quickly built up large waiting lists, but problems soon became evident. Firstly, it emerged that existing entry screening procedures were proving inadequate for ICT courses; a substantial proportion of enrolees already had some educational qualifications, formally putting them outside the remit of ABE. Secondly, although their initial assessments had made it clear that many of the students on these new courses had significant basic

skills needs (including many of those with qualifications), the structure of the courses offered little opportunity for seriously engaging
with those needs. And, among those learners with recognisable basic
skills needs, most proved unwilling to engage in traditional activities
explicitly focussing on numeracy or language use when invited to do
so. Their main reason for attending was to gain ICT skills; with home
PC ownership still uncommon at this time, many were simply loath
to spend time away from the computer.

THE IMPACT OF NEW TECHNOLOGIES

By late 1997, it was clear that while recruitment had greatly
increased – a significant measure of success in funding terms – many
of the new learners were not drawn from among those with acute
basic skills needs that it had been hoped ICT access would attract.
Meanwhile, both through the shared networks and in terms of teaching provision, previously autonomous OLC activities had begun to
overlap with those of other branches of the host college[2], bringing
new frictions and rivalries. Occasional unacceptable usage of the Internet by staff and students, and ongoing battles over technical support, brought other new problems to be dealt with. There was a feeling
among staff that teaching and learning provision had begun to frag-
ment and a fear that this fragmentation could undermine the strong
sense of a shared mission that had always made working and learning at the OLC so worthwhile. Nevertheless, there was also a growing
sense that exciting new possibilities were being opened up; not only
through the capabilities of the technologies themselves, but also because of the new social and skills mix that ICT had brought to the
centre. Against this background, OLC tutors and managers were becoming acutely aware that new strategies were required for ICT use
to be more closely and successfully integrated into centre activities.

The first step toward forming those strategies was made in September 1997, with the launching of *The Internet Club*, an experimental
course on the use of email and the World Wide Web. Influenced by

---

[2] In the UK, state-sponsored ABE is part of the Further Education sector and is mainly
administered through large regional Further Education colleges delivering a broad
spectrum of post-sixteen education and training.

the lead tutor's contact with the participatory design movement in computer science, learners and volunteers were encouraged to play a major part in developing learning activities (Harris 2002). Through participatory design, a connection was established with Lave and Wenger, and *Situated Learning* (Lave and Wenger 1991) became an essential reference point for these first deliberate, if tentative, attempts to foster communities of practice around the new technologies. Peer mentoring was encouraged, and legitimate peripheral participation was allowed – learners were able to "hang-out" around the technology, jointly learning and interpreting interfaces, sharing developing expertise or simply watching. Toward the close of the course, building Web sites and publishing them on the Internet began to address the requirement that "educational design must engage learning communities in activities that have consequences beyond their boundaries" (Wenger 1998:274). After a year, outcomes – in terms of retention, student feedback and accreditation success – were encouraging, and valuable experience had been gained.

FOSTERING AND DEVELOPING COMMUNITIES OF ICT-BASED PRACTICE

During the 1998–2000 teaching period, *The Internet Club* continued. In this year, under the guidance of a new ICT-literate centre manager with a background in project-based and contextualised learning, much of the traditional literacy and numeracy provision was reorganised to include the planned use of computers. In these *Combined Studies* courses, literacy and numeracy tutors collaborated with ICT-trained colleagues to deliver a mix of technology-based and traditional ABE activities. Although learners in these groups often still carried out ICT activities individually, and collaborative work and group discussions tended to take place away from the ICT tools, a much greater degree of integration was achieved. With a growing emphasis on group work around shared artifacts, *Combined Studies* began to develop into provision oriented toward developing communities of practice.

The 2000–2001 academic year brought the launch of the first (near) full-time ABE course to explore the use of digital media as a basis for teaching and learning. Modelled on the Boston Computer Clubhouse initiative (Resnick et al. 1999), the year-long *Computer Creative* course involved learners in the conception, planning, execution and exhibition of a variety of new media projects. Pair, small-group and whole-group activities utilised a range of traditional and digital tools to produce diverse physical and virtual artifacts – texts, pictures, video, animations and interactive applications. The course was explicitly designed to incorporate as many elements of the emerging communities of practice approach as possible and was meticulously documented throughout in a longitudinal field study using participant observation, interviews, video recording and the collection of documents and artifacts (Harris 2004). Early data from this study were used as a basis for formulating some of the key lessons that had been learned to that point and for deriving principles to guide the design of subsequent courses (Harris and Shelswell 2001).

In the following year, experience gained through *Computer Creative* provided the basis for a further expansion of ICT-based provision at the OLC. Aspects of the course were split off into a number of discrete project-based courses focused on developing literacy and numeracy through desktop publishing, Internet technologies, digital video and animation and computer programming. At the same time, a series of new introductory ICT/ABE courses were launched. By 2004, the cycle of development which began with *The Internet Club* had resulted in the communities of practice approach becoming central to almost all teaching provision using ICT, also influencing many of the non-technological courses offered by the centre.

Over the period outlined, the community of practice approach has undoubtedly been central to managing the OLC's successful integration of ICT into almost every aspect of teaching practice. Much has been learned and many issues have arisen. Attendance, retention and learning outcomes suggest that a majority of learners have found the courses worthwhile. Many participants have become increasingly committed to learning, both within and beyond the classroom, coming together – without prompting from tutors – to do course-related work outside of session times. Groups of learners have arranged to progress together to other courses at the OLC, preserving the core of their community. At the time of writing, one group has arranged to take a course together at a community learning centre unconnected with the OLC; another is continuing their filmmaking work at the

OLC through the summer break, while a third meets, every week at a learner's home to continue their projects. While such events might perhaps be unremarkable in other educational contexts, they are to be celebrated in ABE.

Clearly, ABE teaching and learning based on fostering and developing communities of practice around shared work with digital tools differ significantly from traditional approaches. One aspect of this difference is the way in which it becomes possible to combine some of the most useful features of the two prevalent modes of instruction in traditional ABE, *individualised group instruction* and *teacher-led small group instruction* (Beder 2004). By putting peer mentoring at the centre of the education process, and facilitating varying configurations of pair, small-group, whole-group and individual work, learning activity becomes more ubiquitous and continuous than in situations dependent on frequent teacher intervention. The spectre of students or groups spending long periods waiting for assistance, or conversely dominating the attention of the tutor, is effectively banished. Similarly, there is much less opportunity for, or sanction of, activities at the computer not related to learning outcomes. Learner participation is predominantly either legitimately peripheral or central and much more rarely marginal than was seen in the early days of computers at the OLC. While this has been a welcome outcome, ascertaining what *type* and *quality* of learning has been taking place is more problematic. In order to address this question, we will begin by considering the situated learning approach to ABE from the point of view of the tutor.

THE ROLE OF THE TUTOR

Adult basic educators are professionally and legally committed to the promotion of equal opportunities and democratic values. In addition to subscribing to these aims, many tutors are also personally motivated by the belief that supporting adults to improve their basic reading, writing and number skills may also help them to alter their view of their own potential. The hope is that learners will use new-found skills and confidence to pursue a wider range of educational and employment opportunities in ways that benefit themselves, their local communities and society as a whole. The term *empowerment* is often used as shorthand for this "envisioned synthesis of individual and collective change" (Page and Czuba 1999). However, such commitments inevitably involve tutors in difficult value judgements.

With a communities of practice approach, the role of the tutor necessarily becomes much more biased toward the management and regulation of social interaction[3]. As the links between literacy and exclusion made by the quotations at the beginning of the chapter suggest, it is precisely those individuals who experience the most difficulty integrating into dominant cultures who are also most likely to be ABE learners. Many learners are under-confident and less articulate than those in other branches of adult education. Within the constraints of a community of practice of fixed duration and specifically oriented toward certain types of activity, the danger is that more confident members may thrive, while those less socially able may find their disadvantage continued – or even reinforced and extended. As work patterns vary, tutors must try to foster collaborations between participants with similar or complementary approaches and abilities, and to tactfully discourage collaborations between those for whom a particular working arrangement is likely to be unfruitful.

Potentially, marginalisation and disempowerment can arise in a number of ways. Although providing peer support generally benefits mentors, allowing them to develop interpersonal skills and deepen their own learning, time spent in this way can also be seen as a diversion from one's individual goals. Some learners may simply avoid acting as peer mentors, while others seek roles that allow them to yoke another's efforts to their own ends. This was evident in the case of Cassandra[4], a confident female learner in her mid-60s who evidenced strong motivation in individual work while being markedly less enthusiastic about collaborative activities. When interviewed about her experience of collaborative pair working, she explained:

I'm strong-minded so I'll say let's get cracking and he'll be pushed along. . . . I discuss how he needs to achieve what I'm wanting and discuss content in a

---

[3] This contrasts views expressed in our 2001 paper (Harris and Shelswell 2001), written halfway through the cycle of development outlined here, at which point we felt that the primary role of a tutor was that of *facilitator*, a role involving much less active management of the social aspects of the group.

[4] Fictitious names have been substituted when discussing individual cases.

few seconds and ask him for objections, but what is there to discuss if he has no imagination or creative ability . . . ? He's happy with that.

Although Cassandra apparently found the collaboration satisfactory, the male student to whom she referred was one of the very few to leave the course before completion. Supporting others' activities may not always be effective in scaffolding their learning activity and may even impede their progress. Brian, an ICT-skilled *Computer Creative* participant, would frequently intervene in other learners' activities, only to carry out all the necessary actions himself, without offering explanation or giving those he "assisted" the opportunity to practice the skills demonstrated. Issues such as these may also arise at the small-group and whole-group level, when members who are committed to the successful outcome of a particular project find their goals conflict with others who are less committed or productive.

There is also the danger that ways of thinking and acting that materially contribute to marginalisation and disempowerment (e.g., the inappropriate use of profanity or the expression of racist or sexist views) may be reproduced and transmitted within the community to an unacceptable degree. Contentious issues such as asylum seekers – dealt with extensively and provocatively in Britain's popular press – have on several occasions provided the context for the expression of xenophobia in discussions among OLC group members. Adult educators have evolved many techniques to turn such incidents to positive use, for example by using the offending views as the starting point of a discussion or further research into the actual facts and opposing viewpoints. However, in a community of practice, the current status of the participants involved – central, peripheral or marginal to the practice – will be highly relevant to the outcome of such attempted solutions.

These are critical issues for adult basic educators. Communities of practice are in some senses self-regulating systems, with members putting checks and balances on each other's behaviour according to their shared understandings of the collective goals to be achieved. In order to function, communities of practice require the promotion of mutual respect and support between participants. ABE tutors must be prepared to actively intervene in order to ensure that the overall quality and direction of the community that emerges through

self-regulation is one that accords with principles of equity and empowerment. However, it is clear that this management role will always preserve power inequalities between teacher and learners; these
must also be made explicit and become accepted in order for the community to function. There may come times when a tutor must un-
equivocally declare a learner's participation as illegitimate in order
to preserve the integrity of the community. ABE tutors deeply committed to inclusivity may thus, paradoxically, become implicated in
processes of deliberate exclusion.

LEGITIMATION CONFLICTS

Despite Lave and Wenger's (1991:35) suggestion that "there may very
well be no such thing as an 'illegitimate peripheral participant'",
experience at the OLC indicates that, at times, choosing to define some
form of participation as illegitimate can be a significant stage in the
development of a community of practice. Communities are defined
as much by whom and what they exclude as by what they contain; at
times, an act of exclusion may be essential to their continued cohesion.
Questions of exclusion are often raised by participants who themselves seek ways to become more centrally included. On several
occasions, learning groups at the OLC have engaged in such practices, which we will refer to as *legitimation conflicts*. In such conflicts,
the legitimacy of a participant – whether central or peripheral – is
brought into question by other community members. If the person
in question is sufficiently peripheral to the practice, he may be ren-
dered increasingly marginal by other group members or make himself so by consciously withdrawing from contact with the group. In
many such cases, increasingly frequent absences are followed by the
learner "dropping out" permanently, with the legitimation conflict
being resolved by her departure. When the person involved is a more
central participant – such as a tutor – other types of resolution are
required.

Legitimation conflicts can develop around the phenomenon that
Wenger (1998:138) refers to as "experience driving competence". This
occurs when members with experiences and skills that have been significant in the formation of their identity, but which fall outside the
community's current regime of competence, attempt to change the

community so that it comes to recognise their experience as valid. For example, a long-term course participant, Harold, had been a successful building contractor. Despite his evident basic skills needs, Harold often tried to dominate group discourse with narratives revolving around episodes which demonstrated his superior skill and knowledge, compared with other members. Over the three years of his attendance, this behaviour led to frequent clashes and disruption and eventually resulted in his departure after a confrontation with a tutor. Members of his community openly expressed their relief. Similarly, a *Computer Creative* learner, William, who had once been employed in the broadcasting industry, continually criticised the conduct of video-based activities. From his point of view as an "expert", he attempted to disrupt power relations by challenging the tutors on the extent of their expertise. William refused to accept that the goals of the course were not directly linked to the technical skills over which he claimed ownership. Like Harold, he too left of his own accord but not before other learners in the group had requested his removal.

Although these negative examples are clearly problematic within the concerns of an inclusive ABE practice, legitimation conflicts around competence may also have much more positive outcomes. When such attempts succeed, they assert legitimacy of membership and can mark an individual's transition from peripheral toward more central participation. This was vividly brought home in the case of Christina, a female learner in her early thirties. A tutor, one of two involved in the course, had entered some students' work for an external accreditation early in the year, in the knowledge that there would be a further opportunity later in the year for the remaining students. On finding that her work had not been included on this occasion, Christina complained of unequal treatment, eventually convoking a meeting of the learning group at a time when the tutor in question was unable to be present. During this meeting, she argued passionately for the illegitimacy and marginality of the tutor's participation. For her, it became necessary to portray another's participation as illegitimate in order to preserve the validity of her own competence and assert the legitimacy of her membership. When legitimation conflicts involve the tutor, in order to preserve their regulating role, they must seek to avoid "two opposite tendencies: being pulled in to become full members or being rejected as intruders" (Wenger 1998:110). The tutors and learners involved successfully managed this, and the outcome was that as Christina became a more central participant, her assertiveness became a valued asset of the whole community.

BOUNDARIES OR BARRIERS?

As legitimation conflicts show, the spatial metaphors of centrality, peripherality and boundaries capture something essential about the nature of communities of practice; we are all acutely attuned to sensing where we stand with regard to such social groupings. Experience at the OLC has confirmed that sustained engagement always gives rise to positions and boundaries, sometimes very quickly. By observing the activities and developing social relationships within and around an initially disparate group of learners, we can detect those signs (high levels of attendance, early arrival at sessions, shared specialist vocabularies, evidence of collaborative work on course activities outside of session hours, and so on) which indicate that a community has begun to come into existence. Among several factors involved, the prospective duration of the course appears to be especially relevant to this process. When learners and staff are mutually committed for a lengthy period – say a whole academic year – the forms of activity we have come to associate with the emergence of a community of practice may become evident within as little as three weeks after course commencement. Courses over shorter periods gel at a slower rate and require proportionately more activities explicitly directed toward community formation. Though also implicated, frequency of contact and how long each contact lasts appear to be much less significant.

Another condition highly relevant to community formation, as Wenger points out (1998:253–254), is the depth of learning that is taking place. The sooner participants begin to feel they are really engaged in learning together, the sooner community formation ensues. For us, this observation has emphasised the need to plunge into learning activities right at the very start of the course, and to engage in activities involving the whole group until boundaries between that group and other practices begin to appear. Another essential condition is some stability in the physical and resource environment.

A learning group should be consistently linked to a specific setting (i.e., the same room and equipment). Our field study data show that participants establish "their" seats and use the same computers whenever possible, and that subgroups will tend to make a particular part of a room a habitual locale for certain activities. Where this is not possible, the formation of a community of practice proceeds much more slowly.

As we have already noted, communities of practice come to be defined, at least in part, by who is considered to be *outside* their boundaries. This presents special difficulties with regard to the policies of continuous enrolment adopted by ABE organizations seeking to accommodate the artificiality of the academic calendar to the realities of adult learners' lives. For later newcomers, their initially marginal place at the boundaries of a community of practice can as easily give rise to illegitimacy as to peripherality and centripetal movement – a difficult position for both newcomer and established members. Establishing the point at which it is no longer acceptable to attempt to induct new learners into an established learning group rests with tutors, who may then find that fostering a community of practice conflicts not only with their commitment to widening access, but also with organizational requirements to maintain enrolment levels. The quicker community formation takes place, the sooner such difficult decisions inevitably arise.

A reciprocal concern with boundaries is that community members "on the inside" may resist the need to move beyond them. As we have seen, one of the distinctive features of a communities of practice approach is the way in which participants become increasingly committed to learning and working together. Once formed, communities of practice are enduring, and learners frequently demand to remain on a course, even after their learning objectives and specific accreditation outcomes have been achieved. Perhaps ironically, a successful engagement in learning together can become an obstacle to further progress, as members begin to concentrate on finding ways of remaining within the familiar boundaries of their community of practice. Consider Sarah, a woman in her late thirties who has been repeatedly assessed as having severe literacy difficulties. On first attending the OLC in 1996, Sarah was withdrawn and lacking in confidence, and over six years of participation in courses using the communities of practice approach, she has always required a greater degree of support from tutors and peers than other learners. Yet, as her participation in learning activities has gradually moved from peripheral to central, her increasing ability with ICT has been matched by growing interpersonal skills and the blossoming of her problem-solving ability, particularly evident in numeracy activities. Sarah eventually adopted a 'supervisory' role in her classes, managing the distribution of session record sheets and assisting the tutor. And, building on her increasingly central role in the learning groups she has been part of, she began to be a legitimately peripheral participant in the wider organization of the OLC, carrying out small administrative tasks and helping staff with the production of learning materials.

For Sarah, school was a painful and damaging experience. Participation in the relatively "safe" environment of the communities of practice in OLC classes has been an important factor in her successful development as a learner. Yet, as she has now completed most of the courses available to her, remaining as a learner at the OLC grows increasingly untenable. She is clearly reluctant to leave, yet without an accreditation or funding route, the ABE system no longer has a place for her. Both she and her tutors are well aware that she is unlikely to find similarly supportive environments in other learning institutions, or in the workplaces her formal qualifications give her the opportunity to join. Much of her current learning involves finding ways to legitimate simply "staying put". Reflecting on cases such as Sarah's has both raised our awareness of some fundamental contradictions in the practice of ABE and led us to seek a deepened understanding of what *types* of learning take place in communities of practice.

LEARNING

Wenger's formulation of learning as *knowing in practice* has provided a powerful springboard for the developments at the OLC. Yet, while recognising the fundamental truth of his assertion that learning is a "living experience of negotiating meaning" which cannot be designed but "can only be designed *for*" (Wenger 1998:229), this definition does not sufficiently address the issues affecting the relationship between learning, empowerment and identity in ABE. In this regard, we have come to find ideas from the sociocultural tradition of cultural-historical psychology, activity theory and critical psychology – ideas which Lave and Wenger's work has been instrumental in introducing us to – becoming increasingly useful. This critical tradition in psychology has developed a multilevel framework that links individuals, their communities of practice and the wider organisational and societal contexts within which they are produced and reproduced. As well as influencing our understanding of the need for developing the institutional structures of ABE, these ideas are increasingly informing our classroom practice. In this section, we briefly set out how they connect with our experiences of learning in technology-based communities of practice at the OLC.

Individual motivation within collective activities can be seen as dependent upon individuals being able to realise their personal needs through participation in the satisfaction of collective needs (Leont'ev 1978, 1981a, 1981b). When individuals feel that by taking part in a collective activity they will gain improved control and a better quality of life, they are motivated to positively contribute to the creative expansion of that activity in new directions (Engeström 1987, Holzkamp 1991). Conversely, when collective activity seems to offer a person little possibility of improvement, they will tend to focus on coping with the contradictions between their own and collective needs, defensively seeking to avoid any lessening of their sense of control or any reduction in their possibilities for action. How individuals view the possibilities for fulfilling needs within a collective activity is often connected to their perception of where control is situated (Tolman 1991, 1994, 1999; Roth 2002). As a result of their socioeconomic and cultural backgrounds, and their own experiences at school and work, ABE learners are especially vulnerable to feeling that they have little or no control over their environment or personal circumstances. Often, the kind of learning to which they are most accustomed is directed toward what adult basic educators call "coping strategies", ways of being in the world that compensate for difficulties (with reading, say) rather than dealing with them.

The question, then, is whether learning in a community of practice can become *expansive*, in the sense that genuinely new ways of thinking and acting are opened up for participants, or whether it is more often *defensive*, in that what is being learned is mostly supporting or reinforcing existing attitudes and strategies. Clearly, these types of learning must be continually transforming into each other, in ways that differ among participants. The extent to which one or another type of learning comes to predominate in any community of practice will be dependent both on the specific circumstances within the community of practice itself and on conditions obtaining in the larger environment in which the community is situated.

The recent expansion of ABE in the UK has been accompanied by an increasing emphasis on the use of quantitative performance indicators in the quality monitoring process. The success of any program is judged primarily according to results in terms of accreditation, retention and progression rates. The level at which these outcomes are produced significantly affects the status of an organisation and those who work and learn there. Yet, such outcomes can often be of more significance to managers than tutors and to tutors than learners. Although many learners are pleased to gain qualifications, it is only rarely their primary motivation; many are indifferent to the process of accreditation itself. Tutors as often see outcomes as impediments to successful teaching and learning as measures of it. In our experience, the difficulty of sufficiently aligning these viewpoints can be exacerbated by the social dynamics inherent in communities of practice. For example, the need to demonstrate learning gains by each individual participant may make it difficult for tutors to fully support legitimate peripheral participation as, from the point of view of a tutor's need to support the production of outcomes, learners' participation must always be becoming increasingly more central in order to remain legitimate. Consequently, learners uninterested in outcomes must find strategies for maintaining their peripherality while at the same time avoiding marginality and risking exclusion. In enacting such defensive learning, members may use their social skills as a resource. Daniel, an extroverted male learner in his late fifties, contrived to spend an entire course based around digital filmmaking, moving between the various groups, chatting while work was carried out by others and never fully engaging with any task himself. The dilemma for tutors was that Daniel assumed a valuable role in building and maintaining the community of practice, within the boundaries of which the legitimacy of his peripherality was never questioned, while at the same time successfully resisting producing outcomes or engaging in learning that could be considered as expansive from the tutors' points of view.

IDENTITY AND TRAJECTORIES OF PARTICIPATION

From the point of view of situated learning theory, the task of ABE can be formulated as that of supporting trajectories of learners' identity development that encompass increasingly central participation in communities of literate and numerate practice. As we saw at the beginning of the chapter, ABE specifically aims to improve learners' opportunities for increased participation in society, an increased participation that is defined primarily in terms of economic productivity. What is sought is no less than the reconstruction of a learner's identity. Whether or not this is commensurate with empowerment, is, of course, open to challenge, pointing to the many contradictions inherent in the practice of ABE. What using Wenger's term does make clear is that such trajectories will always involve the alteration of learners' relationships to cultures within which their non-literate practices may have been an important component of their identity. The new prospects opened up by "the learning journey" also imply the leaving behind of familiar territory. Yet, as Wenger points out (1998:168), boundary crossing is especially difficult when membership in one community implies marginalisation in another. For many ABE learners, reconciling new aspects of identity and different forms of membership into a "nexus of multimembership" (Wenger 1998:159) may be the single greatest challenge they face.

Our experience at the OLC suggests the need to more specifically and transparently teach those integrative personal and practical skills which Wenger refers to as "reconciling aspects of competence" (Wenger 1998:160). Although such teaching is already partly present in ABE, especially in those classes (outside of the scope of the discussion here) that engage with the long-term unemployed on semi-compulsory, intensive full-time courses, it is currently far too easy for such work to become displaced by other concerns. Clearly, ABE learners who cannot integrate the new competences they gain through participation in communities of practice into their daily lives, so that they may use and further develop them in diverse social settings, risk continuing marginalisation and disempowerment. Happily, a number of our former participants have entered into more skilled and rewarding employment following membership in communities of ICT-based practice at the OLC. Yet, as successful as some individuals have been in the world of work, those communities have so far only rarely provided "paradigmatic trajectories" (Wenger 1998:156) which involve learners' onward progression into further or higher education. Despite significant progress toward widening access in further and higher education, the gap between ABE and other tiers of the UK education system remains wide and difficult to cross.

MOVING BEYOND COMMUNITIES OF PRACTICE

Our attempts to support the formation and development of communities of practice in technology-based courses at the OLC have brought us to boundaries from which practices new to ABE have begun. In the process, we have also found ourselves arriving at "the intersection of multiple regimes of competence yet not clearly within any of them" (Wenger 1998:255). There have been many beneficial outcomes for the OLC staff and learners, especially in comparison to the isolating and fragmented models of practice that first emerged under the impact of the new technologies. Yet, as our approach has evolved, we have become increasingly aware of the tensions and contradictions within it and of those inherent in the practice of ABE itself. The strength of the communities of practice model lies in its recognition of the legitimacy of peripheral participation, and the way in which it suggests that the success of a community of practice is measured by its *overall* productivity and sustainability, to which individual community members make diverse but equally valuable contributions. However, the practice of ABE must always prioritise the support and recognition of individual learning outcomes. Firstly, and most importantly, because empowerment hinges on individual development, which communities of practices may not always foster; secondly, because formal education systems predominantly measure, and reward, individual achievement. Based on this recognition, we are now beginning to accept that the further development of the approach we have described here may require us to move beyond our community of practice in formal ABE, into areas of informal learning and the public communication of science and technology which offer different opportunities and constraints. Above all, we have come to realise that while communities of practice "are a force to be reckoned with, for better or worse" (Wenger 1998:85), they offer no easy solutions for adult educators. While our early engagement with the idea was coloured by the positive values we associated with the notion of community[5], experiences at the OLC have made it clear that communities of practice are not, in themselves, "in any essential way an emancipatory force" (Wenger 1998:85). For us, moving beyond communities of practice continues to be a journey from innocence to experience.

References

Basic Skills Agency (2001) *Adult Numeracy Core Curriculum*. London: Basic Skills Agency.

Basic Skills Agency (2003) *The Basic Skills Agency Homepage*. Basic Skills Agency. [On-line] Available at: http://www.basic-skills.co.uk/. Accessed August 20, 2003.

Beder, H. (2004) *Learner Engagement in Adult Literacy Education Instruction: Contrasts Between Small Group and Individualized Instruction*. Paper presented at the National Research and Development Centre for Adult Literacy and Numeracy International Conference 2004, Loughborough, UK.

Castells, M. (1998) The informational city is a dual city: can it be reversed? In D. A. Schön, B. Sanyal and W. J. Mitchell (eds), *High Technology and Low Income Communities: Prospects for the Positive Use of Advanced Information Technology*. Cambridge, MA: MIT Press, 25–42.

Department for Education and Skills (2001) *Skills for Life: The National Strategy for Improving Adult Literacy and Numeracy Skills*. London: Department for Education and Skills.

Engeström, Y. (1987) *Learning by Expanding*. Helsinki: Orienta-Konsultit.

Harris, S. R. (2002) PD in Ponty: design-by-doing in adult basic education. In T. Binder, J. Gregory and I. Wagner (eds), *PDC 02 Proceedings of the Participatory Design Conference*. Malmö, Sweden: CPSR, 278–283.

Harris, S. R. (2004) *Design, Development, and Fluency: An Activity-Theoretical Approach to Human-Computer Interaction Research*. Unpublished Ph.D. thesis, University of Glamorgan, Wales, UK.

---

[5] See also Note 4 in Wenger 1998:288. It is striking how this work repeatedly emphasises the moral neutrality and potential negativity of communities of practice (e.g., Wenger 1998:132).

Harris, S. R. and N. Shelswell (2001) Building bridges across the digital divide: supporting the development of technological fluency in Adult Basic Education learners. In A. Mason (ed), *Proceedings of the FACE Annual Conference 2001*. Southampton: FACE, 42–51.

Holzkamp, K. (1991) Societal and individual life processes. In C. W. Tolman and W. Maiers (eds), *Critical Psychology: Contributions to an Historical Science of the Subject*. Cambridge: Cambridge University Press, 50–64.

Lave, J. and E. Wenger (1991) *Situated Learning: Legitimate Peripheral Participation*. Cambridge: Cambridge University Press.

Leont'ev, A. N. (1978) *Activity, Consciousness and Personality* (M. J. Hall, Trans.). Englewood Cliffs, NJ: Prentice-Hall.

Leont'ev, A. N. (1981a) The problem of activity in psychology. In J. V. Wertsch (ed), *The Concept of Activity in Soviet Psychology*. Armonk, NY: M. E. Sharpe.

Leont'ev, A. N. (1981b) *Problems of the Development of the Mind*. Moscow: Progress.

Mellar, H., M. Kambouri, A. Wolf, T. Goodwin, A. Hayton, P. Koulouris and V. Windsor (2001) *Research into the Effectiveness of Learning through ICT for People with Basic Skills Needs* (research report). London: Institute of Education.

Moser, C. (1999, 30/3/1999) *Improving Literacy and Numeracy: A Fresh Start – Report of the Working Group Chaired by Sir Claus Moser*. [On-line] Available at: http://www.lifelonglearning.co.uk/mosergroup/rep.htm. Accessed December 13, 2001.

Norris, P. (2001) *Digital Divide: Civic Engagement, Information Poverty and the Internet Worldwide*. Cambridge: Cambridge University Press.

Page, N. and C. E. Czuba (1999) Empowerment: what is it? *Journal of Extension, 37(5)*. www.joe.org.

Resnick, M., N. Rusk and S. Cooke (1999) The computer clubhouse: technological fluency in the inner city. In D. Schön, B. Sanyal and W. J. Mitchell (eds), *High Technology and Low Income Communities: Prospects for the Positive Use of Advanced Information Technology*. Cambridge, MA: MIT Press.

Roth, W.-M. (2002) Learning in Moussac. In L. M. Richter and R. Engelhart (eds), *Life of Science: Whitebook on Educational Initiatives in Natural Sciences and Technology*. Copenhagen: Learning Lab Denmark, 33–43.

Schön, D. A., B. Sanyal and W. J. Mitchell (eds) (1999) *High Technology and Low Income Communities: Prospects for the Positive Use of Advanced Information Technology*. Cambridge, MA: The MIT Press.

Timmins, N. (2000, 20th December) Digital divide grows in UK. *Financial Times*.

Tolman, C. W. (1991) Critical psychology: an overview. In C. W. Tolman and W. Maiers (eds), *Critical Psychology: Contributions to an Historical Science of the Subject*. Cambridge: Cambridge University Press, 1–22.

Tolman, C. W. (1994). *Psychology, Society, and Subjectivity: An Introduction to German Critical Psychology*. London: Routledge.

Tolman, C. W. (1999) Society versus context in individual development: Does theory make a difference? In Y. Engeström, R. Miettinen and R.-L. Punamäki (eds), *Perspectives on Activity Theory*. Cambridge: Cambridge University Press, 70–86.

Welsh Assembly Government. (2002) *The National Basic Skills Strategy for Wales*. The National Assembly for Wales.

Wenger, E. (1998) *Communities of Practice: Learning, Meaning and Identity*. Cambridge: Cambridge University Press.

8

'Communities of Practice' in Higher Education

Useful Heuristic or Educational Model?

Mary R. Lea

BACKGROUND

Global higher education is in a state of change. Its expansion at the end of the twentieth century has led to a burgeoning of new programmes, modules and courses. These include not just the development of interdisciplinary and new subject areas in mainstream academic departments but also those based less on traditional knowledge bases within academic disciplines and more upon vocational and professional bodies of knowledge and their practice-based concerns. At the same time, the concept of lifelong learning means that the learner is no longer regarded as the eighteen-year-old fresh from school, but now includes those entering and re-entering the university – conceived in its broadest terms – at many different points throughout the life-course. The university is no longer confined within its own buildings; courses are delivered in outreach colleges, in the workplace and online. With these profound changes have come new words associated with learning: 'distributed', 'flexible' and 'blended'. In short, the university is no longer the traditional bastion of knowledge, defined by either its disciplinary boundaries or its physical campus, colleges and buildings. It is against this backdrop that researchers in the field of teaching and learning in higher education are drawing upon the concept of communities of practice in order to inform practitioners, both university lecturers and staff developers, about new ways of understanding their students' learning.

The primary concern of this chapter is an attempt to recapture the relevance of the 1991 work by Lave and Wenger – in which they develop their concept of communities of practice – to teaching and learning in today's higher education. It pays particular, although not exclusive, attention to on-line environments, where the concept of communities of practice has been taken up most enthusiastically. The chapter argues that, in order to make the best use of this concept in terms of its implications not just for research but for practice in higher education, it is important to reclaim the early work on communities of practice for its heuristic qualities – a way of understanding learning as practice. This is in contrast to a top-down educational model, when practitioners aim to foster communities of practice artificially in their own particular context. The chapter also presents a case for taking account of recent work on academic literacies and the ways in which language works in discourse communities in higher education. In conclusion, the chapter argues that the concept can be a useful heuristic which enables a better understanding of the ways in which meanings are contested in today's higher education.

SOCIAL APPROACHES TO STUDENT LEARNING

Accompanying broader institutional change in higher education has been a shift towards new ways of thinking about learning, which reject both the behaviourist approaches, common in the 1960s, and those of cognitive psychology, which followed in the 1970s and 1980s. By the 1990s, new ways of approaching learning were being brought into play, influenced by a broader 'social turn' in the social sciences and a focus upon context (cf. Gee 2000). The main thrust of these approaches is the challenge that they make to a transmission model of learning, preferring to concentrate on the social and cultural nature of learning in any particular context. Such approaches appear regularly under different guises in the literature on student learning: distributed cognition, constructivism and situated learning. For example, the notion of constructivism dominates approaches to learning using information and communication technologies. In an influential article concerned with constructivism and computer-mediated communication in distance education (Jonassen et al. 1995), the authors argue for the use of constructivist principles for underpinning learning at a distance. The article concentrates on the benefits of constructivist approaches to learning: repositioning the tutor as a 'facilitator', the focus on personal meaning making and moves from the transfer of knowledge from teacher to student in favour of shared meaning making. The authors position this focus on constructivism within the paradigm of situated learning and suggest that learning is a 'socially negotiated process in which communities of practitioners socially negotiate the meaning of phenomena' (Jonassen et al. 1995:9). The article adopts an orientation which is common in this field more generally (cf. Kahn 1997), in that, despite claiming to take account of context, it excludes any theorisation of the broader institutional context of learning and the possible implications of this for the construction of meaning making.

Similarly, research into student learning in the phenomenographic tradition (Marton et al. 1997), which dominated understandings of student learning during the 1980s and 1990s in the UK and identified students as adopting deep, surface and strategic approaches to learning, also fails to take account of the broader institutional context in shaping teaching and learning. Thorpe (2002) links the use of these approaches to the concept of the independent and autonomous learner. She illustrates the move in thinking about student learning from this framework towards a focus on collaborative learning, which has been a dominant paradigm both in the literature on on-line learning and also in group work with students in face-to-face institutions. The focus then is upon learning as a social activity, an activity in which the autonomous student learner is seen to take responsibility for his/her own learning.

However, it could be argued that the predominance of these socially situated perspectives to student learning go hand in hand with broader institutional changes, where processes and procedures allow less time for contact between teachers and learners and rely increasingly upon learners charting their own voyages through the learning process. That is, rather than simply providing possibilities for alternative voices which could bring new ways of understanding learning, or a lens to help us make sense of these ever-changing environments, these approaches to learning are more closely aligned with the changing context of higher education. As Creme (2000) illustrates in her work on new forms of reflective writing in anthropology, the driver for any 'innovation' in student learning may well be more a need for faculty members to attend to increasing student numbers with dwindling resources, rather than any explicit philosophical commitment to more appropriate methods of teaching and learning based on social and cultural understandings of how people learn. Whatever the underlying drivers for this shift in thinking, it is within this arena of teaching and learning in higher education, with its focus on the autonomous and collaborative learner, operating in an increasingly diverse higher education context, that Lave and Wenger's early work on learning as participation in practice, and situated learning, has fast become common currency.

A RETURN TO LAVE AND WENGER

In their early work on situated learning, Lave and Wenger (1991) draw upon Vygotsky in order to develop an understanding of learning which challenges the basic premise that learning is a process by which learners internalise knowledge through transmission from teacher to learner in formal educational contexts. They focus on learning as participation in practice in informal settings, rather than in formal educational settings such as schools or universities. Their particular focus is upon learning as experienced in interaction with others. In looking at learning outside formal educational institutions, Lave and Wenger are concerned with the whole person acting in the world. In this context, they suggest that a theory of learning based on social practice is concerned with the socially negotiated character of meaning. The authors focus upon the way in which knowledge is socially constituted and see meaning as both contested and negotiated through participation in communities of practice. They stress that what they call *legitimate peripheral participation* is 'not an educational form, much less a pedagogical strategy or technique' (Lave and Wenger 1991:40). Instead, they develop the twin concepts of 'communities of practice' and 'legitimate peripheral participation' as useful heuristics – ways of helping us understand a social model of learning as participation in practice.

It is this perspective, that of a heuristic, which I argue here does not seem to have been taken forward in the recent literature concerned with teaching and learning in higher education. Instead, the focus has been on the benign nature of communities of practice, where there is a simple and smooth transition from peripheral participation as a novice to full membership at the core of the community's endeavour. This perspective does not take account of the more contested nature of participation in communities of practice, that is when participants are excluded from full participation in the practices of a community; for example, where students struggle to engage in the unfamiliar discourses or literacy practices of the academy, always feeling excluded and on the margins (Ivanič 1998, Lea 1998, Lillis 2001). It is in this nuanced examination of how participants are excluded at the boundaries that the work has most value for those concerned with teaching and learning in higher education. In addition, Lave and Wenger's contention that meaning does not exist outside the communities of practice in which it is being constituted forces us to ask questions about the very nature or existence of 'transferable skills', which still form the basis for many teaching practices in today's higher education.

Lave and Wenger argue for an alternative understanding of learning and a need to move away from some of the fundamental positions which they believe have tended to dominate debates around teaching and learning. In so doing they make a clear distinction between formal and informal learning and focus their perspective specifically upon informal learning. In terms of higher education (which is not addressed by Lave or Wenger), this seems a rather unnecessary distinction, since formal educational institutions such as higher education can still be sites of informal learning; notions of collaborative learning are premised upon this. Indeed, it is the appropriacy of the communities of practice paradigm to the complexity of formal learning contexts, which has resulted in the work being taken up so enthusiastically by those concerned with teaching and learning in higher education. Unfortunately, in the process of its being more widely interpreted, some of the most essential qualities of Lave and Wenger's original exploration of the concept of communities of practice have been lost.

The focus of this chapter, then, is on the use of this concept as heuristic. This particular orientation has not been followed through in Wenger's own later work. In Wenger (1998), he does develop the concept of communities of practice further and makes some direct reference to learning communities in educational settings, suggesting that educational design should be concerned with supporting the formation of learning communities. However, it appears that he is moving closer to the idea of an educational model and further from the heuristic qualities present in the original publication. His detailed discussion of education does not appear to offer much of value to the argument being explored in this chapter, since his primary concern is with ways of enabling formal schooling to take on more of the character of informal learning in communities of practice.

However, Wenger (1998) does move the notion of educational design away from the reification of knowledge and the teaching of skills and information towards the negotiation of meaning. He stresses that educational design is not concerned just with what he terms 'reification' but with forms of participation which provide entry into a community's practice. The practice itself, therefore, becomes the curriculum. This later analysis of Wenger's shares much with the constructivist models of learning and work on students' approaches and conceptions of learning, referred to previously. He argues that, even in formal settings, spaces are created for participation in the practices of the community; the inference being that the nature of these practices is primarily given by the core community. His shift of thinking to embrace formal school-based activity appears to be towards participation in practice as a reasonably benign activity with the central core community driving legitimate activity for participation. Wenger goes some way to acknowledging that this is a contested terrain but makes little attempt to theorise the more contested nature of the knowledge itself, or the ways in which this is negotiated by different participants specifically in relation to any broader institutional context. His main concern is with the relationship between what happens inside educational institutions and what happens outside, with a call for formal education to pay more attention to what goes on outside the institutional curriculum.

There has been, then, a subtle shift away from the rich ethnographic description of the 1991 publication, which provided an understanding of the ways in which organic communities of practice function, towards one of design and support for learning communities (cf. Wenger, McDermott and Snyder 2002). It is this subtle shift that, arguably, has erased attention to issues of power and authority, and how contestation over meaning is played out in institutional settings, towards a more benign approach, which provides little sense of agency for participants on the periphery. Although not explicit, Wenger's concern appears to be the development of learning communities as the core curriculum in educational settings, with educational design offering opportunities for engagement in these learning communities (Wenger 1998). His main thrust is to move away from a taught curriculum within a formal setting towards a learning community drawing its resources for participation from within and outside the formal institution.

COMMUNITIES OF PRACTICE AS AN EDUCATIONAL MODEL

The use of the term 'communities of practice' has now become ubiquitous in the literature of teaching and learning in higher education. A quick search of journal databases illustrates how often the work is cited. A similar search of the Web identifies many different contexts in which it is being used to generate on-line learning communities. What is evident, however, is that the concept is most frequently being used uncritically as a top-down educational model, in which practitioners are encouraged to follow some guidelines for developing their own communities of practice, in their own teaching context; this is in contrast to its use as a heuristic which enables a more complete understanding of the teaching and learning processes in different higher education contexts. In one area in particular, that of on-line teaching and learning, we see the use of the concept as a design aid for the formation of on-line learning communities. For example, Rogers (2000) outlines a framework based on Wenger's work which educators can use to design cohesive learning communities. This focus on designing communities seems to be related to some overlapping boundaries between work in this field and that of research into organizational learning, where the concept has been taken up extensively; Hildreth et al. (1998), for example, explore the concept of communities of practice in their examination of knowledge in organisations. In examining computer-mediated communication in communities of practice, and some contrasts between located and distributed communities of practice in a commercial company, they are concerned with 'not simply the transmission of fact and figures, or codified knowledge but.... with the interaction and communication between individuals in the group as people learn from one another, solve problems together and new knowledge is created' (Hildreth et al. 1998:276). Maybe because Wenger's later work and publications are particularly focussed on the applications of the concept to organisational learning (Wenger et al. 2002), it has now been adopted from its use in commercial contexts to an increasingly market-orientated higher education, where students are now positioned as customers and the university as a seller of different course combinations.

In one particular area of higher education, distance education, instructional designers have been concerned for many years with technologies for learning; in the last decade, they have moved their attention from print to the use of new technologies. This shift, also, has been accompanied by increased attention to situated learning and the implementation of constructivist principles in course design and delivery. For example, we have already seen how Jonassen et al. (1995) make explicit links between constructivism and Lave and Wenger's 1991 work in making their argument for the ways in which 'constructivist assumptions about learning imply a new approach to instruction' (Lave and Wenger 1991:12). The role of the designer is now to develop environments 'that engage learners and require them to construct the knowledge that is most meaningful to them' (Lave and Wenger 1991:13). According to the authors, 'Constructivist environments engage learners in knowledge construction through collaborative activities that embed learning in a meaningful context and through reflection on what has been learned through conversation with other learners' (Lave and Wenger 1991:13). Both 'constructivism' and 'communities of practice' are concepts drawn upon in this article without any critical exploration of their application in educational contexts.

A further example of the application of the term to an on-line learning environment can be found in Wegerif (1998), who suggests that the notion of communities of practice can be a useful aid to those developing online courses. He describes an example of an on-line course in which the tutor, an 'old-timer', put in deliberate spelling mistakes in his on-line messages in order to ensure that his students felt comfortable communicating on-line. According to Wegerif, the 'newcomers' felt relaxed about their on-line interactions. Wegerif argues that communities of practice can be used as a model resulting in effective practice in teaching on-line through the active building of on-line communities for collaborative learning. The online community is conceived as a learning community inducting students into 'good practice'. Similarly, in a face-to-face environment, Evenbeck and Kahn (2001) examine two projects which, they argue, demonstrate how inter-institutional communities of practice focussed on student learning can help universities create environments and develop practices to enhance learning. Putz and Arnold (2001) focus on the implications of the use of the concept of communities of practice in designing on-line seminars in the university.

The focus in the literature of this type is, then, generally upon design and implementation, rather than critique. Rather than using the concept to examine and understand learning in an organic context, attempts are made to build or foster what is designed as a community of practice, a learning community. In contrast, as a heuristic the concept enables exploration of the ways in which learning does or does not take place and foregrounds not just success but constraints on learning and on full participation in a community's practices. It provides a lens to examine how meanings are contested within a community, to explore the ways in which certain ways of making meaning are privileged to the exclusion of others within the academy, and how some members of a community might, therefore, always find themselves excluded and at the margins, never able to participate fully in the community's practices.

Since this chapter is primarily concerned with returning to the heuristic value of the concept, it does not draw in any substantive way upon the later work by Wenger but attempts to stay true to the heuristic qualities of Lave and Wenger's 1991 work, using this framework for understanding the different interpretations of a learning situation and the ways in which participants might be marginalised from the established communities of practice. One reason the 1991 work has not often explicitly been taken up in this way might be because one of its limitations is its inability to explicate how things work around the margins of a community of practice; in particular, how the discourses, genres and practices of what are termed newcomers are integrated into those of the established community. Change is presented as a fundamental property of communities of practice, but it is not particularly theorised. There is also little explanation of agency in terms of the newer members of the community and little acknowledgement of the ways in which their practices, not only those of the old-timers, also contribute to the community of practice.

Lave and Wenger point to a number of possible points of departure in exploring the contested nature of knowledge and participation and the ways in which communities of practice might operate to keep some participants permanently at the periphery:

We explore contradictions inherent in learning, and the relations of the resulting conflicts to the development of identity and the transformation of practice (Lave and Wenger 1991:91)

The social structure for this practice, its power relations, and its conditions for legitimacy define possibilities for learning. (i.e., for legitimate peripheral participation) (Lave and Wenger 1991:98)

Despite the fact that such perspectives are not elaborated on in any detail by the authors, it is still possible to use them as a starting point for examining the contradictions and conflicts which are part of everyday practice for learners. There is, then, a case for returning to elements of the early work which enable us to take a critical lens to the different communities of practice involved in higher education institutions and to examine issues of exclusion and the tensions around participation at the periphery. As Lave and Wenger indicate:

Different people give meaning to their activity in different ways.... Because the place of knowledge is within a community of practice, questions of learning must be addressed within the developmental cycles of that community.... The key to legitimate peripheral participation is access by newcomers to the community of practice and all that membership entails. But though this is essential to the reproduction of the community, it is also problematic at the same time. (Lave and Wenger 1991:100)

Control and selection as well as the need for access, are inherent in communities of practice. Thus access is liable to manipulation, giving legitimate peripheral peripherality and ambivalent status: depending on the organization of access legitimate peripherality can either promote or prevent legitimate participation. In other words, access can be denied by not giving productive access to activity in communities of practice. (Lave and Wenger 1991:103)

Focussing on issues of access and the contested nature of practice could help practitioners find out more about what is going on in any teaching and learning context and therefore understand more about its particular successes and failures. For example, little attention has been paid to peripheral participation in on-line learning contexts. However, it has been observed that some students make little or no contribution to on-line discussions. In an on-line Master's course in my own department, some students make explicit statements about their intention – for a number of different reasons – to stop partici-pating actively in the computer conferences, although continuing to read others' messages. This positions them on the periphery of their learning community, but non-participation in this instance is an active decision on their part. Similar analogies could be drawn with face-to-face contexts. Peripheral participation can, therefore, be enacted in different ways by different members of a community of practice, and choosing to remain on the periphery may be one way in which students retain power, and maintain their own sense of identity, in the learning process.

STUDENTS AS MEMBERS OF COMMUNITIES OF PRACTICE

What then of the different communities of practice being negotiated by students? It is likely that the focus on the distinction between old-timer academics and novice undergraduate students belies the fact that, on campus, the student is more frequently likely to come into contact with the departmental secretary – as an established old-timer – than members of academic staff. Similarly, the on-line stu-dent may have more to do with the learning technologists who are responsible for maintaining the technical helpdesk than with her tutor. Students in on-line courses often appear to spend more time discussing the requirements and procedures for assessment than any in-depth discussion of course content (Putz and Arnold 2001). Simi-larly, much of the time of a campus-based student is spent in activities such as accessing limited library resources or negotiating the univer-sity's procedures for assignment submission. All these activities bring students to the boundaries of very different communities of practice than that of the romanticised academic campus-based community or the collaborative on-line community invoked by the teaching and learning literature. Indeed, these often seem far removed from the reality of the actual lived – physical and virtual – student experience.

LANGUAGE AND MEANING

One way of understanding more about exclusion from full participation and the contested nature of meaning making is by paying attention to theories of language in use, as in Chapter 2 (this volume). Any theory of learning based on social practice must, inevitably, involve the ways in which meanings are invented and subtly transformed in interactions between participants in co-ordinated activities in a shared social and material world; and since language and meaning are fundamental to human activity, learning, thinking and knowing can occur only within a world which is socially and culturally structured through language. Although they paid little attention to theories of language, Lave and Wenger (1991) did recognise that discourse, and in particular ways of talking, is crucial to any full participation in a community of practice. However, this perspective appears to be rarely taken forward in the implementation of the concept to learning contexts. As a heuristic, it is possible to examine the ways in which different language practices might contribute to marginalisation and exclusion from a community of practice in, this instance, in higher education.

RESEARCH INTO ACADEMIC LITERACIES

Recent work in the field of work of academic literacies (Lea and Street 1998, Jones et al. 1999, Lea and Stierer 2000) has taken just such an approach and has much to offer in filling a gap in the situated learning paradigm, which has paid so little attention to any explicit account of language practices or the complex relationship between language and learning. Work in the field of academic literacies draws on linguistics and social anthropology in order to challenge the notion that writing is concerned with the acquisition of individual, cognitive skills, which can be transferred with ease from context to context. In contrast, it conceptualises writing as a contextualised social practice and examines the ways in which meanings are constructed through contrasting writing practices across the university. Academic literacies research has been carried out in different university settings with diverse groups of students, initially non-traditional entrants as reported by Lea (1994), Thesen (1994), Lillis (1997), Ivanič (1998) and Baynham (1995). Research has also included students studying at a distance (Stierer 1997; Lea 1998), non-native speakers of English (Pardoe 1994), post-graduate trainee teachers (Scott 2000) and students studying on-line (Lea 2000, 2001). Read, Francis and Robson (2001) focus on power relationships in essay writing, and Francis, Robson and Read (2001) add the dimension of gender and writing style to the field. Despite the variety of contexts being studied, the findings concerning students' struggles with writing and the gaps between tutor and students' expectations and understanding are remarkably constant.

Academic literacies research provides a methodology for understanding the ways in which meanings are contested in higher education. In particular, it is concerned with the broader social, cultural and institutional frameworks within which meaning is negotiated through particular texts, genres and discourses. It also moves away from a focus on the individual learner, paying more attention to the broader institutional context of learning and the ways in which meanings are contested within this framing (cf. Ivanič 1998; Lea 1998; Lillis 2001). It provides ways of theorising power and authority as they are played out in different communities of practice within the academy, in particular through the assessment process. Evidence from recent research in the field, with its attention to writing in the academy, illustrates profound gaps between students' and tutors' understandings of the requisites for written assessment. The research has highlighted the difficulties students have engaging in the dominant literacy practices of the academy; it documents the contrasting ways in which these are played out not just within particular disciplinary contexts – e.g., how to write in history – but through the requirements (both explicit and implicit) of particular departments or even individual tutors. Students, then, find themselves having to engage in what Lea and Street (1998) refer to as 'course switching', as they move between different writing tasks. As a result of such findings, academic literacies research suggests that writing at university is not about acquiring decontextualised, transferable skills but is concerned more deeply with issues of epistemology and what counts as knowledge in any particular context. With its focus on the ways in which students feel marginalised from full participation in the writing practices of the academy, this research offers a critique to the benign view of the novice student gradually moving towards full participation in a community of practice and engaging in writing practices similar to those of the established academic members of that community. With its ability to provide evidence for the contested nature of meaning making in the academy, there is then a strong argument for bringing research into academic literacies into closer alignment with the theoretical framing offered by the concept of communities of practice.

Academic literacies research has been valuable because it has foregrounded the relationship between language and learning in higher education, in particular the ways in which issues of student writing are integrally related to learning, raising questions about the nature of knowledge and the construction of meaning through texts in the university. On one hand, it is possible to conceptualise students and tutors as engaging in mutual engagement in the joint endeavour of teaching and learning. However, academic literacies research has laid bare the ways in which meanings are contested within the academy, and therefore participants are not engaged in a comfortable process of acculturation into the academy's communities (cf. Ivanič 1998, Lea and Street 1998, Lea and Stierer 2000, Lillis 2001). These authors provide compelling evidence for the gatekeeping role of university writing. That is, that the purpose of student writing is not merely to provide full participation to a community of practice with academics at the centre. In fact, it could be argued that most university teaching and learning practices are not about inclusion but tend to position undergraduate students as permanent novices, never attaining full membership of an academic community of practice. We need to have a better understanding of how different environments might afford different forms of participation and, in the case of on-line learning, ask questions about the ways in which such spaces are institutionally constructed rather than rely on the benign interpretation offered by collaborative learning paradigms and the repositioning of the tutor as facilitator. Bringing work on language, learning and literacies more clearly into the frame might help us to examine how far students and tutors really do belong to the same communities of practice in higher education; that is, how far an undergraduate student really is a novice member of the same community as the lecturers whose lectures she attends or the tutor she meets on-line.

CONCLUSION

The work on communities of practice has moved a long way since Lave and Wenger first illustrated this concept through examples from midwives, tailors, quartermasters, butchers and non-drinking alcoholics and foregrounded learning as participation in practice. During the last decade, situated learning has become increasingly popular as a paradigm for understanding teaching and learning in higher education. I have argued in this chapter that we need to revisit the early work by Lave and Wenger in order to explore the value of understanding learning through this lens. Unfortunately, too often the original qualities of the concept have been lost; it is infrequently being invoked in order to understand more about present-day practices in higher education but is more commonly used to underpin directives as to how to create effective learning environments. This has resulted in a lack of critique, in particular from an institutional perspective. There is little recognition of the complex nature of communities of practice in higher education contexts, with too much emphasis upon the student as novice being acculturated into the established academic community. I argue that the concept still has much to offer to those who want to understand more about their own students' learning, whether on campus or on-line, face to face or at a distance. It can help us to understand the ways in which institutional practices, including textual practices, are integral to some students' marginalisation and exclusion from the more central communities of practice in higher education. It can lay bare some of the differential ways in which meanings are both contested and constituted for participants in the processes of teaching and learning, both students and tutors. Both on-line and face-to-face study involve negotiating membership of many different communities of practice, engaging in their contrasting discourses and genres and negotiating some level of participation and membership, which are not dependent only upon access to the academic community. We need to understand much more about the lived experiences of today's students and the importance of different communities of practice in the learning process, which challenge the simple notion of the novice student on the periphery of the central academic community. Reinventing communities of practice as a heuristic is an important part of exploring and understanding learning contexts and their contrasting and often conflicting practices within the broad arena of today's higher education.

References

Baynham, M. (1995) *Literacy Practices*. London: Longman.

Creme, P. (2000) *Report on New Forms of Writing in Social Anthropology*. Department of Social Anthropology, University of Sussex, unpublished.

Evenbeck, S. and S. Kahn (2001) Enhancing learning assessment and accountability through communities of practice. *Change 25–26 (May/June)* 43–49.

Francis, B., J. Robson and B. Read (2001) An analysis of undergraduate writing styles in the context of gender and achievement. *Studies in Higher Education 26 (3)* 313–326.

Gee, J. (2000) The new literacy studies: from 'socially situated' to the work of the social. In D. Barton, M. Hamilton and R. Ivanič (eds), *Situated Literacies: Reading and Writing in Context*. London: Routledge.

Hildreth, P., C. Kimble and P. Wright (1998) Computer mediated communication and international communities of practice. In *Proceedings of Ethicomp '98*, March 1998, Erasmus University, The Netherlands, 275–268.

Ivanič, R. (1998) *Writing and Identity: The Discoursal Construction of Identity in Academic Writing*. Amsterdam: John Benjamins.

Jonassen, D., M. Davidson, M. Collins, J. Campbell and B. B. Haag (1995) Constructivism and computer-mediated communication in distance education. *American Journal of Distance Education 9 (2)* 7–26.

Jones, C., J. Turner and B. Street (eds) (1999) *Students Writing in the University: Cultural and Epistemological Issues*. Amsterdam: John Benjamins.

Kahn, B. H. (1997) *Web-Based Instruction*. Englewood Cliffs, NJ: Educational Technology Publications.

Lave, J. and E. Wenger (1991) *Situated Learning: Legitimate Peripheral Participation*. Cambridge: Cambridge University Press.

Lea, M. (1994) "I thought I could write until I came here": student writing in higher education. In G. Gibbs (ed), *Improving Student Learning: Theory and Practice*. Oxford: Oxford Centre for Staff Development, 216–226.

Lea, M. (1998) Academic literacies and learning in higher education: constructing knowledge through texts and experience. *Studies in the Education of Adults 30 (2)*, 156–171.

Lea, M. (2001) Computer conferencing and assessment: new ways of writing in higher education. *Studies in Higher Education 26 (2)* 163–182.

Lea, M. (2004) New literacy studies, ICTs and learning in higher education. In I. Snyder and C. Beavis (eds), *Doing Literacy Online: Teaching, Learning and Playing in an Electronic World*. Cresskill, NJ: Hampton Press.

Lea, M. and B. Street (1998) Student writing in higher education: an academic literacies approach. *Studies in Higher Education 23 (2)* 157–172.

Lea, M. R. (2000). Computer conferencing: New possibilities for writing and learning in Higher Education. In M. R. Lea and B. Stierer (eds), *Student Writing in Higher Education: New Contexts*. Buckingham: Society for Research into Higher Education/Open University Press, 69–85.

Lea, M. R. and B. Stierer (2000) *Student Writing in Higher Education: New Contexts*. Buckingham: Society for Research into Higher Education/Open University Press

Lillis, T. (1997) New voices in academia? The regulative nature of academic writing conventions. *Language and Education 11 (3)* 182–199.

Lillis, T. (2001) *Student Writing: Access, Regulation and Desire*. London: Routledge.

Marton, F., D. Hounsell and N. Entwhistle (eds) (1997) *The Experience of Learning* (2nd ed). Edinburgh: Scottish Academic Press.

Pardoe, S. (1994) Writing in another culture: The value of students' KAL in writing pedagogy. In D. Graddol and J. Swann (eds), *Evaluating Language*. Clevedon: British Association for Applied Linguistics/Multilingual Matters.

Putz, P. and P. Arnold (2001) Communities of practice guidelines for the design of online seminars in higher education. *Education, Communication and Information 1 (2)* 181–194.

Read, B., B. Francis and J. Robson (2001) 'Playing safe': undergraduate essay writing and the presentation of the student 'voice'. *British Journal of Sociology of Education 22 (3)* 387–399.

Rogers, J. (2000) Communities of practice: A framework for fostering coherence in virtual learning communities. *Educational Technology and Society 3 (3)* 384–392.

Scott, M. (2000) Writing in postgraduate teacher training: a question of identity. In M. R. Lea and B. Stierer (eds), *Student Writing in Higher Education: New Contexts*. Buckingham: Society for Research into Higher Education/Open University Press, 112–124.

Stierer, B. (1997) *Mastering Education: A Preliminary Analysis of Academic Literacy Practices Within Master-Level Courses*. Milton Keynes: Centre for Language and Communications, School of Education, Open University.

Thesen, L. (1994) *Voices in Discourse: Re-thinking Shared Meaning in Academic Writing*. Unpublished Masters Dissertation, University of Cape Town.

Thesen L. (2001) Modes, literacies and power: A university case study. *Language and Education 5 (2&3)* 132–145.

Thorpe, M. (2002) From independent to collaborative learning: new communities of practice in open, distance and distributed learning. In M. Lea and K. Nicoll (eds), *Distributed Learning: Social and Cultural Approaches to Practice*. London: The Open University/Routledge Falmer, 131–151.

Wegerif, R. (1998) The social dimension of asynchronous learning networks. *Journal of Asynchronous Learning Networks* 2 (1) 34–49.

Wenger, E. (1998) *Communities of Practice: Learning, Meaning and Identity*. Cambridge: Cambridge University Press.

Wenger, E., R. A. McDermott and W. Snyder (eds) (2002) *Cultivating Communities of Practice: A Guide to Managing Knowledge*. Boston: Harvard Business School Press.

9

Communities of Practice, Risk and Sellafield

Greg Myers

Etienne Wenger's *Communities of Practice* (1998) deals with 'a kind of community created over time by the sustained pursuit of a shared enterprise' (1998:45). The shared enterprise to which he returns throughout the book is a case study of an insurance claims department, which may be new to most of us in its details but is familiar in its outlines to anyone who has ever had a routine job in an office: the forms, the questions, the boss, the coffee break. We can admire the skill, resourcefulness and collaboration of a team doing a complex and potentially boring task, dealing with the anomalies and changes of any such complex process involving many institutions. It is a useful insight to focus on the gradual process of learning through 'legitimate peripheral participation', informal consultation, community memory and trial and error. I thought of many parallel cases that Wenger's overview might illuminate: my work as admissions tutor in a university department, scientific research groups (Latour and Woolgar 1979, Knorr-Cetina 1981, Lynch 1985, Ochs and Jacoby 2000), Thomas Edison's workshop (Bazerman 1999), US political parties (Schudson 1998) or an advertising agency pitching for a new account (Rothenberg 1994). All these processes involve a community around a shared enterprise that goes beyond what one person could do and produces something that may be useful (even if it is just a particularly flashy ad for Subaru).

But what if the enterprise is producing not only wealth, but risks? It has been argued that one defining feature of our society is that it is concerned with the distribution of risks as much as with the distribution of wealth (Beck 1992), and people are becoming more aware that there are few enterprises that produce one without the other. There are many possible definitions of risk; for our purposes, let us consider them as dangers about which there is some uncertainty (Lupton 1999, Slovic 2001). Of course there are many such dangers; part of what defines a community is the way 'dangers are selected for public concern' (Douglas and Wildavsky 1982). Perceptions of risk are bound up with our social identities, knowledge and relations to institutions (Irwin and Wynne 1996). So a focus on risk throws several complicating factors into the model of a community of practice: the possibility of action at a distance, unintended consequences of shared goals, uncertainty about outcomes and ambivalent identities. Looking at these issues may bring out some of the strengths and some of the apparent blind spots of a model of communities of practice that focusses largely on management of businesses. Similar criticisms of the application of the concept of communities of practice have been made in critical management studies. Contu and Willmott (2003), for instance, have pointed out that issues of 'language, history, and contradiction' were underdeveloped in Lave and Wenger's original book and further marginalised in later popularisations.

To consider how risk might be produced in a shared enterprise, I have chosen a single episode that has been reported in some detail, the falsification of MOX (Mixed OXide fuel) pellet measurements at the Sellafield plant of British Nuclear Fuels Ltd. (BNFL) in 1999. Sellafield is not just a nuclear power generating plant; since it is involved in recycling and production of fuel, it has been both a showplace for British nuclear technologies (since the 1950s, when it was called Windscale) and a focus of protests from environmentalists in the UK and from other countries bordering the Irish Sea and for public inquiries at various stages of its expansion (Wynne 1982, Bolter 1996). I am drawing largely on the report on the incident by the Nuclear Installations Inspectorate (NII) of the Health and Safety Executive (HSE), follow-up documents by the HSE and BNFL, criticism of BNFL, and of the HSE report, by Greenpeace and other organisations and newspaper accounts in *The Independent* and *The Guardian* (the two newspapers that devoted the most coverage to the story) between September 1999 and April 2000. Here is an attempt at a neutral summary: it is hard to make any statement about these events without making some judgement of the various accounts of what happened, but I am not trying to locate blame.

The Sellafield site of British Nuclear Fuels Ltd (BNFL) is devoted to a variety of processes for reprocessing waste from nuclear power plants. One of these processes is a demonstration facility for production of Mixed Oxide Fuel from depleted uranium oxide and plutonium dioxide for pressurised water reactors in other countries. (It is a demonstration facility, and not a production plant, because the government had not yet given the go-ahead for industrial production of MOX fuel, largely because it was not clear whether such production would be economically viable.) In this facility, the two kinds of fuel are powdered, made into pellets, which are baked and measured carefully before they are inserted into the rods that will be sent to customers. The pellets are handled in glove boxes, using tweezers, to keep the operators from any direct exposure to radiation, so even simple manipulations can be tricky. It is important that the pellets be of an exactly specified size (different for each country's reactors) so that they will not swell or rattle in the rods, events that could lead to material strains, leaks and breakdowns. The Quality Assurance procedures are agreed with each client as part of the contract. In this case, a contract with Kansai Electric Company of Japan required that the pellets be measured twice, once by an Automatic Inspection System that uses lasers to measure the diameter of the pellet at three points and rejects any pellet failing on one of these measures, and a second time manually. In the manual process, a sample of 200 is taken from each lot of 4000 pellets, and the diameters are placed in a V-shaped holder and measured manually by micrometer, in what is called 'overinspection'. For each pellet, the top, middle and bottom diameters are read off an LED display by one worker and entered manually in a spreadsheet by another. The process requires two people, and takes the two people between 90 and 120 minutes for each set of sample pellets. It continues on five shifts throughout the day. In order to ensure that the dimensions are actually measured and are entered properly, a Quality Control officer uses a computer comparison of spreadsheets to check for entries that may have been made up or copied from earlier batches.

On 20 August, a Quality Control officer found some suspicious similarities between sets of entries, and on 25 August the officer told the BNFL management that some of the entries in the spreadsheets had been faked. On 10 September, after *The Independent* had prepared a report of the incident, BNFL informed the unions representing workers at the plant and the Nuclear Installations Inspectorate. On 14 September 1999, *The Independent* published its account of the irregularities in an extensive feature story. At that time, a large shipment of MOX fuel was arriving in Japan, in an armed convoy, after a number of protests along the way and demonstrations in Japan. BNFL notified its client, Kasai Electric, but said that the irregularities in their records did not affect the batch sent to Japan. On 30 September, examination of the records of the Japanese delivery by a representative of a protest group showed that some of them could have been faked. On 17 December, *The Guardian* reported that the Japanese firm had found irregularities and would send the fuel back, and Japan, Sellafield's largest customer, would end its contract. On 18 February, the Nuclear Installations Inspectorate published a highly critical report. German, Swiss, Swedish and US contracts with Sellafield were suspended. The license for a new £300 million MOX plant was held up, partly because it was no longer clear who the customers would be (MOX fuel is not used in UK plants). Partly because of these events plans to privatise BNFL were put on hold. Five production operators and the Chief Executive of BNFL, John Taylor, were fired over the incident.

On 18 April 2000, the Health and Safety Executive published a list of 28 recommendations that had to be acted on before the MOX Demonstration Facility could re-open, most of them concerning management, training of operators and safety systems. These were finally completed ('closed out') on 11 May 2003.

The NII report and the HSE recommendations on which I am relying are official documents, not rich ethnographic descriptions of what goes on in reprocessing plants (for such descriptions, see Zonabend 1993 on a similar French plant; Bolter 1996). They were criticised by

Greenpeace and other groups for not going far enough to challenge practices at Sellafield, and for accepting management assurances on some points. But they do, with the intense press coverage, provide a level of detail about the details of practices that those of us outside an industry rarely get. Even from this bare outline, one can see that communities of practice might play a role in helping us to understand the practices of shopfloor workers, the way they related to and learned from each other, the ways practices depended on specific locations and equipment and the ways those inside and outside the shopfloor community attached different meanings to events. A similar argument has been made in an influential study of workplace safety in the construction industry (Gherardi and Nicolini 2000). But Gherardi and Nicolini consider a rather different kind of risk; if a construction worker does not wear a hard hat, or a scaffold is improperly constructed, the dangers are to the workers and their colleagues. Workers at Sellafield face similar, if less visible, dangers. But work at a plant fabricating nuclear fuel may also present dangers for people far away, in this case, in power plants and cities in Japan.

What I offer here is not an assessment of the evidence, the causes or the risks in this event, but an exploration using the framework of Communities of Practice. I argue that this framework can help us to understand some issues that were obscured in the public records on the case, with their focus on management control and written procedures, because it focusses our attention on the nature of communities, practices, participation, reification and learning. But the case also shows the need for some rethinking of the Communities of Practice model, to deal with language ('economies of meaning'), identities and localities in the production of risks.

COMMUNITY AND CULTURE

When the irregular records of batch measurements were discovered at Sellafield, the press and BNFL treated it as a matter of finding and punishing a few aberrant workers. That is usually the first response to a train wreck, oil spill or disease outbreak, to try to find who deviated from the prescribed procedures and treat it as a problem with them – to be solved by discipline, training and new procedures and monitoring. In this case, the treatment of the events in terms of individual actions simply does not fit the facts; the records had to be the result of people working together. The HSE report notes that any erroneous entries had to be made with the collaboration of two people, and that the entries had been made on four out of five shifts. Beyond that, they were to be checked by a series of managers who must have either ignored the errors or colluded. Beyond that, senior BNFL managers denied categorically that the errors could have affected the batch sent to Japan, when it proved easy for Japanese protest groups and the press to find out that these were affected. The incident seems to have been a part of the way the organisation worked, not a deviation from it. Investigations of accidents often come to this conclusion and then point at something like a 'culture of complacency' (BBC, February 17, 2000) and point out the need for a 'safety culture' (HSE Recommendations, Section 3.5). These phrases seem to acknowledge that there needs to be some attention to the way a community works. But Gherardi and Nicolini (2000) point to some of the simplifications involved in invocations of a 'safety culture'; in treating the culture as a problem and seeking to replace it with something more rigid and predictable, safety analysts fail to understand how situated learning takes place.

PRACTICES

The Sellafield incident also illustrates the gap between a procedure, such as 'over-inspection' as described for instance in the present tense in the HSE report (or in my account above), and a practice situated in a particular place and time, 'doing in a historical and social context that gives structure and meaning to what we do' (Wenger 1998:47). The practice involves coming to work, sitting or moving around, slipping or fumbling, having a break and finishing a shift; it also involves talking to workmates and watching them work. The HSE report does mention 'ergonomic factors', acknowledging that the measurement is a boring, fiddly business that involves placing one pellet after another in a V-shaped holder using a glove box, and reading off the numbers to another person who just enters these numbers in the computer. The report mentions the awareness by managers that this was a manual check on an automatic process, with the implication that the workers or the managers could have thought that it did not matter much. It also says that there was no excessive workload to account for the falsification (they multiply out the time per procedure and the number of procedures to be performed per shift, and find that the total just fits within a shift). In fact, shopfloor supervisors felt that likely bottlenecks came earlier in the process, with fabrication, and devoted their attention to that stage and location. All these comments acknowledge practices, but try to reduce them to procedures, so that the errors can be traced to a single remediable cause.

Wenger's account of the claims processing office (or any ethnography of situated work, such as Orr's account of photocopy technicians (1990), or Gherardi and Nicolini (2000) on construction workers, or Traweek on physicists (1988)) would lead us to go beyond these procedural descriptions, to ask what it was like to work there, how this pair of people assigned to an apparently unnecessary task related to each other, how a new worker found out that these entries did not matter much, how often they found any significant variations with all this checking, whether they rotated the jobs of reading off numbers and entering them and what their status was in relation to workers at other stages of the process. This would seem to be an entry-level job, without much independent responsibility, much need for knowledge of the whole process, or special skills besides the admittedly difficult one of manipulating a tiny pellet with tweezers in a glove box. So what are they entering?

PARTICIPATION

BNFL insists that the rest of the MOX rod manufacturing process was done without falsification or errors. How did the inspection of pellet diameter get marginalised, and how did the workers – at least eight people on four shifts – come to participate in another project, that of falsifying records? The HSE report describes the checks made to guard against made-up or copied entries (see the next section), and it is clear that to falsify the entries successfully required some specialised knowledge and coordination. Workers must have passed on tips about the data entry and also shared a sense of the seriousness, or not, of such an action. Practices must have been passed between shifts and passed on to new members of the teams. This, too, fits Wenger's definition: 'What I take to characterize participation is the possibility of mutual recognition' (1998:56), and the shift members must have had moments of mutual recognition of shared attitudes towards the job at hand. But this is not the kind of legitimate peripheral participation imagined in communities of practice, sanctioned by those in control, but an illegitimate peripheral participation passed on by those subject to control, and passed on, perhaps, partly in resistance to that control. After all, though the event was referred to as 'fraud' and 'forgery', the workers did not gain from the falsification the way fraudsters and forgers do; they did not receive money or take time off. They just passed their shifts in a way they found less annoying or boring.

One Greenpeace report (February 2000) made an issue of BNFL's changes in the automatic inspection device so that it allowed more pellets through. But in a way, this kind of threat is less worrying than the pellet falsification, because it involves a deliberate and documented change to the device. Similarly, the sabotage reported in spring 2000, involving throwing debris into the rod material, could involve just one disaffected employee, and the damage was easily detected and was probably intended to be easily detected. The pellet measurement falsification involves practices that are both less formal and more systematic – practices that are not easily modified just by producing new rules.

REIFICATION AND BOUNDARY OBJECTS

At the centre of the incident are the computer spreadsheets, reified forms of the process of measurement. Since the numbers were produced by a laser measuring system, they could just as easily have been entered automatically into the computer; the point of having one person measure and read out and another enter the numbers is presumably to show that someone had really paid attention. Apparently, there are limits to reification; there has already been an automatic measurement, and to serve its purpose as a check, this measurement must involve human agency and decisions. But having people do what the machine could do (and does) makes for a rather boring job. The one concession to ease of entry is the use of a spreadsheet, and that was also what enabled the system to be subverted – for such a spreadsheet has a facility for copying a number of cells at once.

That there were automatic checks on copied or false entries suggests that the designers of the system anticipated such practices. But since the cells were not copied from row to row, or from the same place in one sheet to the same place in another, the automatic checks on the spreadsheets did not pick up the copying. The spreadsheets are rather like a lot of forms we fill out and, as with all forms, one has to figure in practice what is really needed. Wenger gives examples in which a worker will not check information when it does not seem to be necessary. Garfinkel (1967) has a classic study of "'Good' organizational reasons for 'bad' clinic records". The records reify the inspection process, but they do not provide information in the usual sense; as far as I can tell, no one checks them later to find out the diameter of a particular pellet. They just serve as proof that the required checks have been made, rather as a sign-up sheet on a toilet wall shows it has been cleaned, and my marking of the typos in a Ph.D. thesis shows I did read that far.

The spreadsheets are designed to move between different localities, linking those localities, and they change meanings as they move; they are *boundary objects* (Star and Greisemer 1988). They were developed as part of a process of quality assurance negotiated with the customers, just as the claims forms used in Wenger's case were developed in consultation with clients and health professionals. Star and Greisemer stress much more than Wenger the way boundary objects can have very different meanings in the different communities. The striking example in this case is the way an academic working for Japanese environmental protesters could analyse the spreadsheets that came with the controversial shipments and use them to show that they were falsified and that BNFL was therefore lying; that is, they could be used to challenge quality claims, without even comparing them to the pellets they claim to represent. The pellets are also boundary objects, whether they are seen as waste, fuel or potential bomb materials.

LEARNING

The great strength of Wenger's account is his focus on learning. Learning from an incident seems to be what the official response to the falsification incident is about: BNFL and the HSE devise detailed procedures that will somehow replace the messiness of day-to-day practices; they elaborate the rule books, lines of responsibility, organisational tree and explicit training schemes. They assure us that such explicit procedures and organisational structures will keep such falsification from happening again. But this is not learning, either for the workers or the organisation; it is trying to avoid the need to learn. Wenger sees such a response to organisational problems:

'Someone who assumes instability [of practice] would be concerned that things left to themselves will slip into disorder, and may be tempted to devise overly detailed measures to maintain order. From this perspective, practice is unreliable; it lacks structure and is therefore unproblematically malleable'. (Wenger 1998:98)

In the Sellafield case, the practice of measuring the pellets is indeed unreliable – that much everyone grants. But it does not lack structure; it is not just a forgetting or a departure from norms, and it is not likely to be easily malleable. A response that focuses on procedures and organisation plans assumes that practice is determined by the institution, that a new set of rules, or rules about the rules, will have the effect of plugging the apparent gap in the processes, in restoring stability.

To be fair, the HSE recommendations for BNFL emphasise the importance of organisational learning; for instance, the HSE is concerned that incidents are not reported if they do not have potentially dangerous consequences, so the organisation loses the chance to learn from these incidents. But this view of learning takes it as formal and cognitive, a set of information that can be gathered and disseminated in a planned, structured and generally applicable way. Wenger would have us ask how the learning is situated in this place and these practices, how new recruits learn what the real rules of this organisation are, how they are applied and what the consequences of breaking them are. They seem to have learned them pretty well, in that most of the people doing this job seem to have shared the idea that the figures could be falsified without causing problems. Further up the management line, there is presumably a shared history of how one can ride out such public relations disasters. (They rode out this particular disaster – though the wider future of reprocessing is now in doubt, as I note in the coda.)

ECONOMIES OF MEANING

So far, I have focussed on the strengths of this model, what Wenger might have to tell the HSE and BNFL about their organisations. Now I would like to look at some aspects of the MOX incident that show weaknesses or vagueness in Wenger's treatment. As Contu and Willmott (2003) note, one weakness of many communities of practice studies is their lack of attention to language; language brings in historical constraints and contradictions in a rather messy way. One could consider this in terms of the uses of the word 'safety'. A letter to *The Independent* from BNFL, complaining of the newspaper's coverage, brings out some of these issues.

> We never 'take shortcuts' or 'play fast and loose' with safety, nor would we ever allow a commercial or production imperative to encourage unsafe working. Safety is our number one priority and always will be. Representatives of our customers are visiting the plant to inspect our data and Quality Assurance (QA) procedures in order to satisfy themselves that our fuel and systems are of the quality they should expect. It is quite ridiculous to describe this as 'crisis talks'. It should be borne in mind that these irregularities came to light as a result of BNFL's own QA procedures. The falsification of data at the heart of the story is not a safety issue, but one of quality assurance.' (Alan Hughes, September 16, 1999).

There are several assumptions about the meaning of 'safety' here. Safety can mean control of the risks to workers, control of risks to the community around the plant, control of risks in transport, control of risks in plants using the fuel and control of risks to the environment in the long term. Here, 'safety' seems to refer to the formal procedures in place to prevent accidents in the plant. The use of the term 'safety', rather than its complement 'risk', implies that the dangers can be systematically controlled. In his letter, Hughes defines the incident as a matter of quality assurance, not safety; the Japanese company just wants to be sure it is getting what it ordered. Then he says the very discovery of the problem came through established company procedures. Hughes is making the same distinction apparently made by the workers, between actions that have potentially dangerous consequences (safety) and routine matters of customer satisfaction. The workers seem to have assumed (though we do not know, because there is no testimony from them in the official documentation) that if the pellets were already measured by machine, and if pellet size was just a matter of meeting the customer's picky criteria, then these measurements were not a matter of safety (certainly not of the workers' own safety), but a matter of complex contracts that were the management's business. But for the Japanese government, local citizens, environmental activists and journalists, the issue of 'safety' may not be tied to formal procedures for preventing accidents. The casual attitude towards these particular measurements, which can be documented and checked, is read as an attitude towards other procedures that cannot be checked.

The HSE recommendations for Sellafield contain a comment on wording that may seem rather picky, but that goes to the heart of different definitions of safety. They note with approval BNFL's health and safety policy statement that says 'The Company considers that none of its activities is more important than the health and safety of its employees, its contractors, the general public, and the protection of the environment'. But they note with disapproval the use of the phrase 'The Company'; apparently their guidance document says that a senior officer must be specified. They reject the fallacy that responsibility can be invested in an abstraction, 'The Company', but they replace it with another notion that seems odd in this case, the idea that safety can be guaranteed from the top down, and by one person. They do not deal with the possibility that risk and safety are given meaning by groups of people, and that people in different situations inside or outside the company could see them in different ways (Gherardi and Nicolini 2000).

MULTIPLE AND STIGMATISED IDENTITIES

Critical readers of Wenger (1998) are puzzled by the way he assumes an enterprise has one shared purpose and the lack of attention he gives to conflicts and internal contradictions. The HSE report and recommendations raise several issues of identity. 'NII has some concerns that there may be a conflict of loyalties for shift team leaders. The conflict arises from STLs [Shift Team Leaders] being members of management yet not wishing to be alienated from the process workers. NII found no evidence of this at MDF [MOX Demonstration Facility]'. This acknowledges that there are at least potentially several different communities at the plant; for instance, those of management, supervisors, regular workers, contract workers, workers in different parts of the process and any given person may participate in multiple identities.

One aspect missing from Wenger is some idea of stigma, what Goffman calls 'spoiled identity' (Goffman 1963). Every study of Sellafield says that stigma is a key aspect of working in the plant or even just living in the area. The *Guardian* quotes the town clerk of Egremont as saying, 'When people ask you where you are from and you say Sellafield, they bounce back about 10 paces as though you are contaminated' (March 25, 2000). Apprentices, getting a secure job and learning a high-tech skill in a complex process, are also subjecting themselves to potential risks and (according to campaigners) bringing risks to their children, their communities and places as far away as Norway, Ireland, Switzerland and Japan. The sense of stigma comes out repeatedly in focus groups in northwest England (Waterton and Wynne 1999). This is not just an unfortunate matter that makes working or living there harder. Sellafield develops a strong sense of us vs. them, felt even by BNFL managers down near Preston, according to former press officer Harold Bolter (1996). One account of the way these problems are covered up is that Sellafield would seem to be high grid/high group (Douglas and Wildavsky 1982); its employees know their place in their group structure, and the community has a very strong external boundary. They may be proud of doing an important and highly technical job well and at the same time be afraid or ashamed of the way this job, this company, this place and even this region are seen. One's own concepts of danger and safety may change when one is seen as being in danger, or as a danger, oneself. Wenger's clerks may feel alienated by their work in an insurance company, but presumably no one treats them as doomed or dangerous.

LOCALITY

Wenger is useful in insisting that we focus attention first on the local (not necessarily geographically local) community that actually shares practices. That approach would lead us to see how differentiated and divided the world of Sellafield is, that even within the MOX facility there are separate sections with different problems, routines and kinds of monitoring. But in this case, the methodological principle of focussing on the local does mean we miss a lot. The newspaper reports of the MOX incident point to the wider effects in other arenas: the contracts with customers, the UK balance of trade in yen, the approval for the new MOX facility, privatisation of BNFL, the possible use by terrorists of MOX material and the position of the MP for the district. The case makes no sense unless one also notes that Sellafield is the main employer in an area of high unemployment, that it is a government-owned enterprise with contracts in other countries, that it can only continue because controversial programmes in other countries expand and produce the waste or use the fuel and that one of its main assets is the availability of a place and facility in which such feared technologies are allowed. Assessments of risk make no sense unless one follows the fuel along the path from reactor to MOX facility to production and measurement of the pellets, into the fuel rods, on the ships, to the new reactors in Japan, Switzerland or Germany. And this is typical of risk issues; a routine and apparently harmless practice in part of a plant in the northwest of England sends out ripples around the world and across financial, political and electrical systems.

CONCLUSION

In this paper, I have read Wenger's formulation of Communities of Practice, a revised, management-oriented formulation of a theory of learning, alongside the Health and Safety Executive's recommendations based on the report of the NII. Wenger clearly has something to tell the HSE, about the role of small, informal communities in the work of enterprises (the workers on a shift), about the importance of practices (the way the inspection fits in work routines), the ways processes involve people (such as new apprentices) and are reified in things (such as the inspection equipment) and about the importance of social learning. But proponents of Communities of Practice might also reflect on some of the lessons of the falsification incident and the report on it. The incident foregrounds language, ambiguities of meaning and contested meanings in a way that a Communities of Practice approach does not really grasp. It shows the way negative as well as positive identities may play a role in shaping a community of practice, bringing participants together while also keeping them apart. And the risk issues highlight paradoxes of locality; the report focuses on safety, but the risks here are experienced far from the pair of workers alone in the back room reading out the numbers and typing them in.

CODA

A draft of this paper was first delivered in spring 2002. Since then, there have been two appropriately contradictory codas. On the one hand, as I noted earlier, BNFL implemented all the organisational and documentary changes required by the HSE and was officially cleared. 'I am delighted to hear that we have closed out this report' said Norman Askew, the new chief executive hired when John Taylor was fired after the falsification incident (*Independent*, May 11, 2003). In this ending, the ability of BNFL to meet formal safety requirements and follow procedures is confirmed. But the incident was also part of another chain of events: the loss of Japan as a customer contributed to making the MOX Demonstration Facility uneconomical and the move to full production unlikely. It was one of a number of events that made the privatisation of BNFL unlikely and that led the government to consider a radical break-up and change in its role. Reports in the summer of 2003 suggest that BNFL will close all reprocessing by 2010, and Sellafield will then be a site for waste disposal, not fuel production (*Guardian*, September 26, 2003). These two chains of events, official investigation and commercial collapse, correspond to the two approaches to the incident, in terms of codes or of practices. As a matter of organisational codes and procedures, the falsification was a breach that was remediable by specific institutional changes. As a matter of a set of practices adopted within a community, its effects have been broader, longer lasting and harder to resolve.

References

Bazerman, C. (1999) *The Languages of Edison's Light*. Cambridge, MA: MIT Press.

Beck, U. (1992) *Risk Society: Towards a New Modernity*. London: Sage.

Bolter, H. (1996) *Inside Sellafield*. London: Quartet.

Contu, A. and H. Willmott (2003) Re-embedding situatedness: the importance of power relations in learning theory. *Organization Science* 14 (3) 293–296.

Douglas, M. and A. Wildavsky (1982) *Risk and Culture: An Essay on the Selection of Technological and Environmental Dangers*. Berkeley: University of California Press.

Garfinkel, H. (1967) *Studies in Ethnomethodology*. Englewood Cliffs, NJ: Prentice-Hall.

Gherardi, S. and D. Nicolini (2000) The organizational learning of safety in communities of practice. *Journal of Management Inquiry 9* 7–18.

Goffman, E. (1963) *Stigma: Notes on the Mangement of Spoiled Identity*. New York: Simon and Schuster.

Irwin, A. and B. Wynne (eds) (1996) *Misunderstanding Science*. Cambridge: Cambridge University Press.

Knorr-Cetina, K. D. (1981) *The Manufacture of Knowledge: An Essay on the Constructivist and Contextual Nature of Science*. Oxford: Pergamon.

Latour, B. and S. Woolgar (1979) *Laboratory Life: The Social Construction of Scientific Facts*. London: Sage.

Lupton, D. (1999) *Risk*. London: Routledge.

Lynch, M. (1985) *Art and Artifact in Laboratory Science: A Study of Shop Work and Shop Talk in a Research Laboratory*. London: Routledge Kegan Paul.

Ochs, E. and S. Jacoby (2000) Down to the wire: the cultural clock of physicists and the discourse of consensus. *Language in Society 26 (4)* 479–506.

Orr, J. E. (1990) Sharing knowledge, celebrating identity: community memory in a service culture. In D. Middleton and D. Edwards (eds), *Collective Remembering*. Newbury Park, CA: Sage.

Rothenberg, R. (1994) *Where the Suckers Moon: An Advertising Story*. New York: Knopf.

Schudson, M. (1998) *The Good Citizen: A History of American Civic Life*. Cambridge, MA: Harvard University Press.

Slovic, P. (2001) *The Perception of Risk*. London: Earthscan.

Star, S. L. and J. Greisemer (1988) Institutional ecology, 'translations', and boundary objects: amateurs and professionals in Berkeley's museum of vertebrate zoology. *Social Studies of Science 19* 387–420.

Traweek, S. (1988) *Beamtimes and Lifetimes: The World of High Energy Physicists*. Cambridge, MA: Harvard University Press.

Waterton, C. and B. Wynne (1999). Can focus groups access community views? In R. S. Barbour and J. Kitzinger (eds), *Developing Focus Group Research*. London: Sage, 127–143.

Wenger E. (1998) *Communities of Practice: Learning, Meaning and Identity*. Cambridge: Cambridge University Press.

Wynne, B. (1982) *Rationality and Ritual: The Windscale Inquiry and Nuclear Decision in Britain*. Chalfont St. Giles, Berkshire: British Society for the History of Science.

Zonabend, F. (1993) *The Nuclear Peninsula*. Cambridge: Cambridge University Press.

Semiotic Social Spaces and Affinity Spaces

From The Age of Mythology *to Today's Schools*

James Paul Gee

INTRODUCTION: FROM GROUPS TO SPACES

In this paper, I consider an alternative to the notion of a "community of practice" (Lave and Wenger 1991; Wenger 1998). This alternative focuses on the idea of a *space* in which people interact, rather than on *membership* in a community. I want to consider this alternative because I believe that the notion of what I will later call an "affinity space" is a particularly important contemporary social configuration with implications for the future of schools and schooling.

The notion of a "community of practice" has been a fruitful one. However, it has given rise to several problems, some of which are:

- The idea of "community" can carry connotations of "belonging-ness" and close-knit personal ties among people which do not necessarily always fit classrooms, workplaces or other sites where the notion of a community of practice has been used.
- The idea of "community" seems to bring with it the notion of people being "members". However, "membership" means such different things across different sorts of communities of practice, and there are so many different ways and degrees of being a member in some communities of practice that it is not clear that membership is a truly helpful notion.
- While Wenger (see Wenger, McDermott and Snyder 2002) has tried to be careful in delineating just what is and what is not a community of practice, distinguishing it from other sorts of affiliations,

the notion has been used by others to cover such a wide array of social forms that we may be missing the trees for the forest.

In my view, the key problem with notions like "community of practice", and related ones like "communities of learners", is that they make it look like we are attempting to label a group of people. Once this is done, we face vexatious issues over which people are in and which are out of the group, how far they are in or out and when they are in or out. The answers to these questions vary – even their very answerability varies – greatly across different social groupings. If we start with the notion of a "community" we cannot go any further until we have defined who is in and who is not, since otherwise we cannot identify the community. Yet it is often issues of participation, membership and boundaries that are problematic in the first place.

Take for example my own discipline of linguistics and try to construe it as a community of practice. Should we separate out applied linguistics, sociolinguistics, historical linguistics, theoretical linguistics and so forth as separate communities of practice? How long is the list? Or can we just treat linguistics as one big category? Is a person with a degree outside linguistics working on linguistic problems a linguist or not? Is a person with a Ph.D. in linguistics working on issues tangential to linguistics a linguist? Which of the many practices which linguists engage should we select to begin answering such questions? Is the matter of who is a linguist settled by negotiations within moment-to-moment social interactions, by larger institutional realities or by the opinions of certain "insiders"?

Or take a high-school science class. Johnny and Janie are both in the class. Janie is proactively attempting to engage with the science in the class, but Johnny is "playing the game" for a passing grade. Are they in the same community of practice or is Janie in a school-science community of practice and Johnny in a "doing school" community of practice. What sense does it make to say all the students in this class are in some (one?) community of practice just because they are all contained by the same four walls? Or if we think beyond those four walls, if some parents are helping their children in science, are they in the community of practice, too? What about the principal, the other science teachers, the reading specialist who comes into the class once a week, the author of the textbook or for that matter the curriculum specialists and policy-makers who help shape the classroom's practices in regard to science and schooling more generally?

I suggest that the problem here is trying to start with a label (like community of practice) which looks like a label for a group of people, a group which must then be identified in terms of its "members". What I want to suggest, instead, is that (at least, sometimes) we start with "spaces" and not groups. The spaces I want to start with are what I will call "semiotic social spaces" (I will use "SSS" singular, "SSSs" plural for short) because what I am concerned with about these spaces is the way in which people get and give meanings to signs within them.

Before I say what a SSS is, let me start with an analogy. It is hard to say who is and who is not an "American". (I mean by this not who is officially a "citizen" or not, but who is in "American culture", whatever that may mean. There are people who are not citizens who impress me as very "American" and there are citizens who impress me as not very "American".) For some purposes, it may be easier to draw the boundaries of the United States as a geographical space on a map and then look at how different sorts of people use that space – i.e., what they do there and what they get from that space (e.g., import or export from it).

Of course, I do not want to talk just about physical or geographical spaces. Just as people can enter a physical space like the United States, they can enter a virtual space like a website or a chat room. People interacting with each other about a specific disease on a patient empowerment website are in a virtual space together. There are spaces that are mixtures of the real and the virtual, such as a meeting in which some people are physically together in a room and others are interacting with the group via the Internet or over a video-conferencing system. People who play chess with each other by sending moves via email or letters are interacting, at a distance, in a space created by email or the postal service. Modern technologies allow the creation of more and more spaces where people can enter and interact with others (and with objects and tools) at a distance. So when I talk about "spaces" I don't mean just physical spaces.

My goal, however, is not just or primarily to introduce the idea of SSSs. Rather, it is to discuss a particular type of SSS that I will call an "affinity space". I will first define what I mean by SSSs generally and then define what I mean by an affinity space in particular. When I get to affinity spaces, I will argue that they capture one characteristically modern and important form of social affiliation, one that can fruitfully be compared and contrasted with other forms (Gee 2000–2001). I will define what I mean by a SSS through one concrete example, an example that also happens to be an affinity space. This will allow me to characterise what makes this example a SSS and then turn to what makes it an affinity space.

SEMIOTIC SOCIAL SPACES: AoM

To define what I mean by a SSS, I will use as my illustrative example the SSS of "real-time strategy" computer games, using the game *Age of Mythology* ("AoM" for short) as a paradigmatic instance of such a game (see http://www.microsoft.com/games/ ageofmythology/greek_home.asp). In a real-time strategy game, the player builds buildings, settlements, towns and/or cities for a given "civilisation", using workers to collect gold, farm land, cut wood and hunt animals to gain the necessary resources for building and sustaining his or her civilisation. As the player builds various types of buildings, he or she can use the buildings to construct or train different types of warriors and military apparatus (e.g., in AoM one can use a Temple to gain mythological figures, an Academy to train Hoplites, an Archery Range to train archers, a Stable to train cavalry, a Fortress to train heroes, a Dock to build various types of boats, a Town Center to get more villagers, etc., through many other choices).

Eventually, the player goes off with his or her "army" to fight one or more other players (real people or the computer) who have also been building up their civilisations during the same time. If the player waits too long, the opponent may be too strong, if the player does not take enough time to build up properly, he or she may be too weak to fight well. Timing is important and so are the decisions about what and where to build (and there are always a great many options).

In AoM, the "civilisations" one can play are ancient Greeks, Romans or Norse, building buildings from these ancient civilisations and eventually gaining, for example, various types of Greek soldiers, heroes, military apparatus and mythological figures to fight other civilisations. On the other hand, in *Galactic Battlegrounds* (a *Star*

Wars game), the "civilisations" one can play are the Trade Feder-
ation, Gungans, Royal Naboo, Rebel Alliance, Galactic Empire or
Wookies – all groups from the *Star Wars* universe. In *Galactic Battlegrounds*, the buildings, soldiers, heroes and apparatus are all specific
to one of these groups. For each "civilisation" in this game, there are
over 160 choices about what to build or train – each choice having
consequences for the other choices one makes. This is typical of the
level of complexity in real-time strategy games.

Now I will define a SSS step by step. To define any SSS, we need
first to start with some *content*, something for the space to be "about"
(remember, it's a *semiotic* social space). I will call this a *generator* for
the SSS. In the case of real-time strategy games, one of the generators
of the signs that make up the content of the space are actual games
like AoM. Such games offer up a characteristic set of multimodal
signs to which people can give specific sorts of meanings and with
which they can interact in various ways. We have seen some of these
above: "civilisations", warriors and heroes, buildings and real-time
competition.

Once we have one or more generators, we have a set of signs.
Now, we can look at these signs in two different ways, internally
and externally (Gee 2003). Another way to put this is to say that the
SSS has two aspects, an internal aspect and an external aspect. Any
SSS can be viewed internally as a set of signs (a type of content) or
externally in terms of the individual and social practices in which
people engage in respect to the set of signs.

We have already seen above some of the signs or content made
available for meaning making in AoM and other real-time strategy
games. If we point out that, in such games the player must in a real-
time competition collect resources to build buildings from which the
player can generate various types of virtual actors (e.g., warriors and
heroes), we are talking about the internal aspect of the SSS.

On the other hand, people actually play real-time strategy games in
the world, sometimes alone and sometimes with other people on the
Internet. They may also talk to other players about such games and
read magazines and Internet sites devoted to them. They are aware
that certain people are more adept at playing such games than are
others. They are also aware that people who are "into" such games
may take on a certain identity, at least when they are involved with

those games. For example, it is unlikely that people "into" such games are going to object to warfare in games, though, of course, they may object to war in the real world. When we talk about how people organise their own behaviours and their interactions with other people in regard to real-time strategy games (actually the signs these games make available for meaning making), we are viewing the SSS externally.

To take an internal view of the SSS of real-time strategy games is to ask about the design of such games. To take an external view of the SSS of real-time strategy games is to ask about the ways in which people organise their thoughts, beliefs, values, actions and social interactions in relation to the signs made available in such games.

Let us say, then, that every SSS has an "internal grammar" (namely, the design of its sign and their relationships) and an "external grammar" (namely, the organisation of people's thoughts, beliefs, values, actions and social interactions in regard to the signs and their relationships). I use "grammar" here for phenomena that are emergent (actually real grammars for languages are emergent too). The internal design of a game emerges from the work of designers as this work interacts with players' desires, skills, actions and interactions. The external organisation of people's thoughts, deeds and interactions with the signs that compose a game type (e.g., real-time strategy games) or a specific game (e.g., AoM) emerges from people's actions and interactions as these begin to take on some (however loose) regularity or patterning.

Thus, game designers and producers determine what counts as recognisable content (the internal grammar) for real-time strategy games by actually making such games. Over time, as they apply certain principles, patterns and procedures to the construction of such games, and pay attention to what players think about such games and do with them, the content of real-time strategy games comes to have a recognisable shape such that people not only say things like "Oh, yeah, that's a real-time strategy game" or "No, that's not one", but also "Oh, yeah, that's a typical real-time strategy game" or "Oh, no, that's a groundbreaking real-time strategy game."

On the other hand, people who play, review and discuss such games, as well as those who design and produce them, shape the external grammar of the SSS of real-time strategy games through their ongoing social interactions. It is their ongoing social interactions that determine the (changing) universe of possible (and emergently routine) ways in which people can think about, value, act and interact around real-time strategy games in general and AoM in particular.

And, of course, the acts of people helping to form the external grammar of the SSS as a set of social practices and typical identities can rebound on the acts of those helping to design the internal grammar of the SSS as content, since the internal designers must react to the pleasures and displeasures of the people interacting with the semiotic domain. At the same time, the acts of those designing the internal grammar of the SSS in terms of content rebound on the acts of those helping to organise the external grammar as a set of social practices and identities, since that content shapes and transforms (though by no means fully determines) those practices and identities.

So an SSS is composed of one or more generators (of signs and their possible relationships), an emergent internal grammar and an emergent external grammar. But one more thing is needed to define a SSS, namely one or more *portals* with which to enter the SSS (remember, it's a type of space, not a group of people). A portal is anything that gives access to the signs of the SSS and to ways of interacting with those signs, by oneself or with other people.

For AoM, there are a number of different portals. The disk on which the game comes, slipped into a computer so that one can play the game by oneself, is one such portal. An Internet site on which a player can play the game against other players in another portal. An Internet site in which players discuss the game or download content about the game is another portal. The strategy guide for AoM, which one can purchase (a book replete with information about the game, recommended strategies and a complete walkthrough of the single-player campaign), is also a portal. There are many others. Of course, the space one enters when entering an AoM portal is a subspace of the larger space of real-time strategy games (this is apparent on some Internet sites devoted to the game, which list links to the sites for other real-time strategy games).

Portals are places where people get access to interact with the signs generators have generated. But portals can also be or become generators themselves (though this is not always the case), if they allow people to add to the signs or change the relationships of the signs other generators have generated. So, for example, it is common on game sites on the Internet for fans to use software that comes with AoM, or other sorts of software, to build new maps (new environments within which to play the game) or to make up whole new episodes for the game. In this case, the portal is also a generator.

Likewise, a generator can also be a portal, though this need not always be the case. As we have said, the game disk is both a generator (it offers up the signs or content) and a portal, since one can use it to play the game and thereby interact with the signs.

Given that we can always ask whether a given generator is also a portal or a given portal is also a generator (and for whom), it is sometimes helpful to talk about a core or original generator for a SSS. In the case of AoM, the game is both a core and original generator. Some portals generate additions and supplements to the signs generated by this core and original generator. Furthermore, as the company patches or expands the game, the core generator is changed in response to feedback of many different types from the users of various portals.

Below I summarise in a diagram the definition of a SSS:

SEMIOTIC SOCIAL SPACE

Generator(s)
[gives us a set of signs and possible relations among them]
Internal Grammar   External Grammar
[design of content]   [patterns in thoughts, deeds and interactions]

Portal(s)
[offers access to signs and interactions with them]

Let us pause a moment to ask how these terms would apply to a science classroom and what sorts of questions they would lead us to ask. We first have to ask what is the generator that is the (or a) source of the sign system (content) that the classroom is interacting with. In the classroom, this might be the textbook, the teacher, lab materials and/or other things. For analytical purposes, we could restrict ourselves to one generator or consider several at a time. We also might (or might not) find that the textbook functions as the core or original generator.

We can then ask questions about how the signs generated by the generator are designed, in terms of both their internal relationships and who designed them. This is to ask about the internal grammar of the signs. In turn, we can ask questions about what sorts of thoughts, values, deeds, interactions and identities people take up in regard to these signs. This is to ask about the external grammar of the signs.

We can also ask questions about how the internal and external grammars reflexively shape each other, if indeed they do – i.e., how does internal design shape thought, deed and practice and how do thought, deed and practice shape and reshape internal design (e.g., does the teacher rethink the content based on student beliefs, actions and interactions? Do new editions of the textbook change, based on changing beliefs, values and practices? Do new generators or revisions of old ones change people's thoughts, deeds and interactions?).

We can also ask about portals, that is, what gives access to interactions with the signs, either by oneself or with others. The generator is often a portal (e.g., the textbook), but there are other portals, as well. For example, one portal may be small-group discussions, another might be typical question-and-answer sessions between the teacher and the class, another might be lab work. Of course, we would want to know who uses each portal and how, as well as the ways in which the portal shapes thought and interaction.

Finally, we can ask whether a generator is also a portal. Of course, if the students have a textbook and use it, this generator is also a portal. However, if the teacher is following a teacher's manual that the students never see, this is a generator that is not, in fact, a portal for the students (though it is for the teacher). And we can also ask if portals ever become themselves also generators. For example, can students through, say, their group work on a project change the sign system (content) with which the class is interacting in any serious way? Can they add new signs, subtract signs or change the relationship among the signs that the class is interacting with? If so, the portal of the group project is also a generator; otherwise it is not.

Let me hasten to add that it is degrees that are often of most importance here, not simply binary distinctions. We really want to know, for instance, how strong a generator a given portal is, not just whether it is one or not (perhaps it is a very weak one). We want to know whether internal (design) and external (behavior) grammars reflexively shape each other in strong or weak ways, not just whether they do or not.

My remarks have been, so far, pretty much just methodological. Instead of starting with, for example, the students as a "community", I am suggesting starting with, not the classroom as a physical space, but the classroom as a SSS defined by generators, an internal grammar, an external grammar and portals. This allows us to ask about what thoughts, values, actions and interactions go on in this space, by whom and with whom, without assuming any one group membership or, for that matter any membership at all. It also allows us to see whether the SSS extends beyond the four walls of the classroom. For example, email to scientists or field trips to science sites might be portals (and/or generators) in a given classroom that extends the SSS beyond those walls. A parent who is a scientist might be a portal for some students and not others.

AFFINITY SPACES

These methodological points are only a prelude to the main point I want to discuss in this paper. I want now to turn to a particular type of SSS that I will call an "affinity space". Affinity spaces are a particularly common and important form today in our high-tech new-capitalist world. It is instructive to compare affinity spaces to the sorts of SSSs that are typical in schools, which usually do not have the features of affinity spaces. This comparison is particularly important because many young people today have lots of experience with affinity spaces and, thus, have the opportunity to compare and contrast their experiences with these to their experiences in classrooms.

Let's return to *AoM*. The core generator for AoM as an SSS (remember this is a subspace of the larger real-time strategy game SSS) is, of course, the game itself. Its internal grammar is typical of real-time strategy games, a form that has been shaped quite strongly by the demands, pleasures and displeasures of players. This is true not only over time, as real-time strategy games change in response to player reactions, but also in the present. Games like AoM offer players (sometimes repeated) "patches" over the Internet to correct problems of many sorts players have discovered. Thus, this core generator is continually updated; the internal grammar is continually transformed by the external grammar of the SSS.

The portals to AoM as a SSS are, of course, the game (single-player and multiplayer), but also strategy guides, official websites and fan websites. These portals, as we will see, are also all fairly strong generators, too, adding to and changing the relationships among the signs generated by the AoM core generator (i.e., the game).

To define AoM as not just a SSS, but also an affinity space, I want to look at just one of its portals, namely the website AoM Heaven (http://aom.heavengames.com), a fan produced website. It would take several hundred pages to print this site out (not counting its many links to other sites), and it is updated every day. Some of the many things one can access from this site are:

The latest news about AoM, the company that made the game, what players are doing, and when and where they can play games against each other;
Polls that take votes on various questions and issues (e.g., "Have you played any custom scenarios for AoM?", "What do you think is the most useful classical age myth unit?", or "What aspect of the Norse culture impresses you most?");
Previews and reviews of AoM and other real-time strategy games;
Interviews with people about AoM and related matters;
Forums (discussion groups) to which one can contribute, each devoted to a different topic germane to AoM, including general discussions, strategy, the new expansion pack, technical issues, scenario design, mythology, clan discussions (a clan is a group that plays together), and other topics;
Links to other sites of interest to people interested in AoM or other real-time strategy games;
Ladder forums that give the rankings and scores of players who play against others on the Internet;
FAQs (frequently asked questions) that explain various aspects of the game and give players help with the game;
Strategy guides and walkthroughs for "newbies" (new players);
General information about and pictures of a new expansion of AoM that will appear soon (*Titans X-Pack*);
Game information which gives technical details and statistics about all aspects of the game (e.g., how long it takes to build each type of building);
Images from the game and artwork, including art by fans, inspired by the game;
Downloads of many different sorts, including new maps and scenarios made by players, recorded instances of multi-player games, and even

improvements players have made to different parts of the game's "AI" (artificial intelligence), for example, improvements to the "AI" used on maps with a lot of water or even programs players can use to adjust the AI in different ways each time they play the game.

This portal to the AoM SSS has a set of features that are definitive of what I will call an "affinity space". I describe each of these features below. Together they constitute a definition of an affinity space. We do not have to see an affinity space as an all-or-nothing thing. Rather, we can say that any SSS that has more of these features than another is more of an affinity space than the other or is closer to being a paradigmatic affinity space. The features defining an affinity space (eleven in all) – as these are exemplified by AoM – are as follows:

1. **Common endeavour, not race, class, gender or disability, is primary**

   In an affinity space, people relate to each other primarily in terms of common interests, endeavours, goals or practices, not primarily in terms of race, gender, age, disability or social class. These latter variables are backgrounded, though they can be used (or not) strategically by people if and when they choose to use them for their own purposes. This feature is particularly enabled and enhanced in AoM Heaven because people enter this and other AOM portals with an identity (and name) of their own choosing. They can make up any name they like and give any information (fictional or not) about themselves they wish to. This identity need not – and usually does not – foreground the person's race, gender, age, disability, or social class.

2. **Newbies and masters and everyone else share common space**

   This portal does not segregate newcomers ("newbies") from masters. The whole continua of people from new to experienced, from unskilled to highly skilled, from minorly interested to addicted, and everything in-between, is accommodated in the same space. They can each get different things out of the space – based on their own choices, purposes and identities – and still mingle with others as they wish, learning from them when and where they choose (even "lurking" on advanced forums where they may be too unskilled to do anything but listen in on the experts). Affinity spaces may have portals where people with more expertise are segregated from people with less (e.g., players usually choose who they will play against on multiplayer game sites in terms of their level of expertise), but they also have ones where such segregation does not occur.

3. **Some portals are strong generators**
   The portal allows people to generate new signs and relationships among signs for the AoM SSS. That is, the portal is also a major generator. Fans create new maps, new scenarios for the single-player and multiplayer games, adjust or redesign the technical aspects of the game, create new artwork and even give tutorials on mythology as it exists in the game or outside the game world.

4. **Internal grammar is transformed by external grammar**
   Based on what the players do and say on sites like AoM Heaven, the core original generator (the game) is changed via patches, new content and new expansions offered by the company that makes the game. That is, the internal grammar of AoM as a SSS is transformed by the actions and interactions (the external grammar) of players acting and interacting on sites like AoM Heaven.

5. **Encourages intensive and extensive knowledge**
   The portal encourages and enables people who use it to gain and spread both intensive knowledge and extensive knowledge. They can readily develop and display specialised knowledge in one or more areas (intensive knowledge), for example, learning how to tweak the game's AI and advising others in this area. At the same time, the portal encourages and enables people to gain a good deal of broader, less specialised, knowledge about many aspects of the SSS (extensive knowledge), which they share with a great many others who use the portal or otherwise use the AoM SSS. Intensive knowledge is specialised; extensive knowledge is less specialised, broader and more widely shared. This creates people who share lots of knowledge, but each has something special to offer.

6. **Encourages individual and distributed knowledge**
   The portal also encourages and enables people to gain both individual knowledge (stored in their heads) and to learn to use

and contribute to distributed knowledge. Distributed knowledge is knowledge that exists in other people, material on the site (or links to other sites) or in mediating devices (various tools, artifacts and technologies) and to which people can connect or "network" their own individual knowledge. Such knowledge allows people to know and do more than they could on their own. People are encouraged and enabled to act with others and with various mediating devices (e.g., level editors, routines for tweaking the AI of the game, strategy guides, etc.) in such a way that their partial knowledge and skills become part of a bigger and smarter network of people, information and mediating devices.

7. **Encourages dispersed knowledge**

   The portal also encourages and enables people to use dispersed knowledge, which is knowledge that is not actually at the site itself but at other sites or in other SSSs. For example, the portal enables and encourages people to learn about mythology in general, including mythological facts and systems that go well beyond AoM as a game. Much of this information is not directly in the AoM Heaven site, but on other sites it links to or in books or movies the site will mention or review. When an SSS utilises dispersed knowledge it means that its distributed knowledge exists in a quite wide and extensive network. When knowledge is dispersed in a SSS, the SSS does not set strict boundaries around the areas from which people will draw knowledge and skills.

8. **Uses and honors tacit knowledge**

   The portal encourages, enables and honors tacit knowledge – that is, knowledge players have built up in practice but may not be able to explicate fully in words. This knowledge may be about how to play the game, how to design new maps and scenarios for the game, how to form a forum party or a great many other things. Players (often tacitly, without verbal explanations) pass on this tacit knowledge when they interact with others via playing the game with them or interacting with them in other spaces. At the same time, the portal offers ample opportunities for people to try to articulate their tacit knowledge in words (e.g., when they contribute to a forum on technical matters like how to design good maps).

9. **Many different forms and routes to participation**

   People can participate in AoM Heaven or other portals to the AoM SSS in many different ways and at many different levels. People can participate peripherally in some respects, centrally in others; patterns can change from day to day or across larger stretches of time.

10. **Lots of different routes to status**

    A portal like AoM Heaven, and the AoM SSS as a whole, allows people to achieve status, if they want it (and they may not), in many different ways. They can be good at a number of different things or gain repute in a number of different ways. Of course, playing the game well can gain one status, but so can organising forum parties, putting out guides, working to stop hackers from cheating in the multiplayer game, posting to any of a number of different forums or a great many other things.

11. **Leadership is porous and leaders are resources**

    An SSS like AoM and a portal to it like AoM Heaven do not have "bosses". They do have various sorts of leaders – people who design the game or the website – though we have seen that the boundary between leader and follower is vague and porous, since players can generate content for the game or site. Leaders in an affinity space like AoM are designers, resourcers (i.e., they resource other people) and enablers (teachers). They do not and cannot order people around or create rigid, unchanging and impregnable hierarchies.

Affinity spaces are common today in our global high-tech new capitalist world (Gee 2000–2001, Rifkin 2000). Many businesses organise such spaces for their customers. For example, the company that makes the Saturn car creates websites and activities (e.g., social gatherings, newsletters, Internet chat rooms) around which its customers can identify as Saturn owners. Businesses in the new capitalist era (Gee, Hull and Lankshear 1996) of cross-functional, dispersed, networked teams and project-based work often seek to create affinity spaces to motivate, organise and resource their "partners" (they seek to avoid the term "worker" which implies a traditional boss–worker relationship in which one party "bosses" the other). Social activists, whether their cause be ecology, anti-globalisation or school vouchers, also often organise themselves and others in terms of affinity spaces (Beck 1999). In such spaces, people who may share little, and even differ dramatically on other issues, affiliate around their common cause and the practices associated with espousing it via affinity spaces that have most or all of the previously described eleven features. Fans of everything (e.g., movies, comic books, television shows, video games, various lifestyle choices, etc.) create and sustain affinity spaces of which AoM is, of course, just one of a great many. Scientists in many different disciplines network with colleagues, funders, policy-makers and the public across the globe via networks of activities, newsletters and other sorts of texts, websites, computer bulletin boards, email chains and conferences in ways that have progressively taken on more and more of the features of an affinity space.

There have, of course, been educators who have sought to create in classrooms something akin to an affinity space. The best-known efforts here, perhaps, are Ann Brown and Joseph Campione's classroom "learning communities" (see Brown 1994 for an overview). In my view, these "communities" – at least as they were described in idealised ways – could better be viewed as affinity spaces than as communities in any traditional sense. They involved the use of multiple sorts of mediating devices (computers and email to outside experts), distributed knowledge as students worked in teams with those mediating devices, dispersed knowledge as students drew on expertise outside the classroom and intensive knowledge as individual students chose to "major" in some aspect of the curriculum and help other students in that respect. At times, students taught each other, thereby taking over some of the teacher's traditional leadership role. These classrooms incorporated a number of the remaining eleven features, as well, and one could imagine this process (largely stopped today by our return to "the basics" and skill-and-drill under the new accountability and testing agenda) going much further (to the point where not all students would actually be in the classroom together face to face each day).

However, if we compare the eleven features of an affinity group to most classrooms today, we usually find that the classroom either does not have a given feature or has it much more weakly than a prototypical affinity space. In classrooms, the common endeavour is often unclear (e.g., "science", "doing school", "school-science", etc.) to the students and race, class, gender and disability are often much more foregrounded than they are in an affinity space. Furthermore, race, class, gender and disability are often much less flexible in classrooms and much less resources students can use strategically for their own purposes.

In classrooms, students are segregated by things like grade level, ability and skills more often than they are mixed together across the whole continuum of these. Even in heterogeneous grouping, the differences are small compared with the differences one can find and access in an affinity space. For example, I myself am light years away from being able to understand how to programme anything that would modify the AI of a computer game, yet I can access such information and the people connected to it at AoM Heaven (and did so and actually learned a lot).

In classrooms, portals are rarely strong generators where students both interact with the signs that constitute the content of the classroom instruction and are able to modify, transform and add to them, as well. Furthermore, rarely is the core generator (e.g., the textbook or the curriculum guide) modified ("patched") in an ongoing way based on student desires, pleasures, displeasures, actions and interactions.

In classrooms, students are encouraged to gain pretty much the same knowledge across the board, knowledge which is often extensive and not intensive, or some students are encouraged and enabled to gain intensive knowledge, but others are not. Furthermore, when some students do gain intensive knowledge, they are rarely allowed to teach the teacher and the other students. In an affinity space, no one is stopped from gaining intensive knowledge because someone else thinks they are "my low students" or "struggling". Classrooms are rarely spaces where everyone shares lots of interests and knowledge (extensive knowledge), while each person has his or her own intensive knowledge to add as a potential resource for others.

Classrooms tend to encourage and reward individual knowledge stored in the head, not distributed knowledge. They do not often allow students to network with each other and with various tools and technologies and be rewarded for doing so, rather than to be rewarded for individual achievement. Further, classrooms tend to narrowly constrain where students can gain knowledge, rather than utilise widely dispersed knowledge. Furthermore, they rarely honor, or even acknowledge, for that matter, tacit knowledge that cannot (at least for now) be verbally articulated. In turn, they usually do a poor job in giving students help and practice with learning how to articulate such tacit knowledge, when and where it can be articulated (and it cannot always be articulated).

Classrooms usually do not have multiple routes to participation, engaging their students in different ways, to different levels, in different contexts. They usually do not have multiple routes to status, rather, students get A's for narrow reasons, the same for all. Finally, in classrooms, leadership is not usually porous where it is, at times, hard to tell who is leading and who is following, where students sometimes lead and teachers follow, and where leadership is constituted by resourcing others and designing environments where they can learn on their own terms, rather than dictating what people "need" to do, believe, say and write.

But, one may ask: "So what? What does it matter that schools don't use affinity spaces? Why should they?" At this point I can only state a hypothesis in answer to these questions. Young people today are confronted with and enter more and more affinity spaces. They see a different and arguably powerful vision of learning, affiliation and identity when they do so. Learning becomes both a personal and unique trajectory through a complex space of opportunities (i.e., a person's own unique movement through various affinity spaces over time) and a social journey as one shares aspects of that trajectory with others (who may be very different from oneself and inhabit otherwise quite different spaces) for a shorter or longer time before moving on. What these young people see in school may pale by comparison. It may seem to lack the imagination that infuses the non-school aspects of their lives (Gee 2003). At the very least, they may demand an argument for "Why school?".

CONCLUSION

I have attempted here to offer a new analytic lens with which to look at classrooms and other learning sites. Affinity spaces are an important form of social affiliation today, places where effective learning occurs (Gee 2003). They are a form with which young people today are particularly familiar. These young people are in a position to compare and contrast how learning works in such spaces and how it works in schools, not always to the credit of schools. I believe that educators ought to do the same.

I also believe that each of the features that I offer as definitive of an affinity space can be present in a school curriculum or not. Thus, these features can be used as a sort of checklist of how much a given classroom verges on being an affinity space or not. While not every reader will accept my value system in terms of which affinity spaces are a good, effective and modern way to organise learning, nonetheless, the features of affinity spaces are similar to the core features that some educational reformers, on wholly other grounds, have argued are crucial for deep learning (e.g., Brown, Collins and Duguid 1989, Brown 1994, diSessa 2000).

Finally, I believe that the notion of affinity spaces can do lots of the sorts of work we have asked the notion of a "community of practice" to do, but without some of the baggage that "community" carries. The notion of affinity spaces can lead us to ask some new questions about classroom learning or ask some old ones in new ways.

References

Beck, U. (1999) *World Risk Society*. Oxford: Blackwell.

Brown, A. L. (1994) The advancement of learning. *Educational Researcher 23*: 4–12.

Brown, J., A. Collins and P. Duguid (1989) Situated cognition and the culture of learning. *Educational Researcher 18 (1)* 32–41.

diSessa, A. A. (2000) *Changing Minds: Computers, Learning, and Literacy*. Cambridge, MA: MIT Press.

Gee, J. P. (2000–2001) Identity as an analytic lens for research in education. *Review of Research in Education 25* 99–125.

Gee, J. P. (2003) *What Video Games Have to Teach Us About Learning and Literacy*. New York: Palgrave/Macmillan.

Gee, J. P., G. Hull and C. Lankshear (1996) *The New Work Order: Behind the Language of the New Capitalism*. Boulder: Westview.

Lave, J. and Wenger, E. (1991) *Situated Learning: Legitimate Peripheral Participation*. Cambridge: Cambridge University Press.

Rifkin, J. (2000) *The Age of Access: The New Culture of Hypercapitalism Where All of Life Is a Paid-for Experience*. New York: Jeremy Tarcher/Putnam.

Wenger, E. (1998) *Communities of Practice: Learning, Meaning, and Identity*. Cambridge: Cambridge University Press.

Wenger, E., R. McDermott and W. M. Snyder (2002) *Cultivating Communities of Practice*. Cambridge, MA: Harvard Business School Press.

Author Index

Subject Index

(*continued from page iii*)